TALKING WITH ANGELS

This book consists of protocols and notes describing actual events which took place in Hungary during the years 1943 and 1944.

TALKING
WITH
ANGELS

A document from Hungary
oral text by Hanna Dallos
transcription and commentary by Gitta Mallasz

English rendition
by Robert Hinshaw

assisted by Gitta Mallasz
and Lela Fischli

DAIMON VERLAG

With heartfelt thanks to all who have been so helpful along the way.

Talking with Angels,
a document from Hungary, transmitted by Hanna Dallos,
recorded and edited by Gitta Mallasz,
English rendition by Robert Hinshaw,
assisted by Gitta Mallasz and Lela Fischli.

For a list of other-language editions of *Talking with Angels*
please see the last pages of this book.

Cover: for an explanation of the front cover sketch, see the 85th Dialogue.

ISBN 978-3-85630-777-6

Newly revised and expanded fifth English-language edition, 2020

A TECHNICAL NOTE

The dialogues comprising this book have been transcribed from handwritten notes in the Hungarian language by Gitta and Lili during the actual events, as dated. Many of the original dialogue notes (including all of Joseph's and the personal notes of Lili) were subsequently lost, and some dialogues were incompletely recorded (as indicated). Many of the accompanying explanatory texts in italics were added immediately after a dialogue, while others were added during the preparation of this text.

It is hoped that the rather unusual mode of notation employed in this edition will help to convey at least an approximate impression of the *experiential* quality of these dialogues: certain words were pronounced with emphasis and subsequently underlined in the notes (indicated here by italics). Others had an almost palpable feeling, engraving themselves indelibly into the participants. They were designated in the notes by capitalization of the first letter, a practice retained in the present edition. The most powerful words and sentences of all are indicated by the use of all capital letters.

The word *Ö* is an all-encompassing Hungarian pronoun for the Divine. This simple word has neither masculine nor feminine connotations: it is both and all. Because there is no equivalent in the English language, we have elected to retain the original word *Ö* here. This may seem strange at first, but it is hoped that the reader will soon adjust to it. The advantage of being able to avoid using inappropriate pronouns seems to outweigh all other considerations.

The particular intonation of *Ö* enabled the participants to immediately know whether The Divine or Jesus was being referred to. As a means of differentiating in this edition, we refer to the Divine with *Ö*, and to Jesus with 'He,' 'Him,' or 'His.' The pronoun *Ö* was always pronounced with great veneration. Gitta Mallasz had the feeling that it referred to God or Jesus, but she could not always clearly perceive the difference. When Gitta believed it referred to the Divine, it was marked with capital letters, and when it referred to Jesus, with 'He', 'Him' or 'His.' This mode of differentiation has been maintained.

PREFACE TO THE REVISED AND EXPANDED FIFTH EDITION

In the many years since *Talking with Angels* was first published, considerable additional information has come to light and it has been made a part of this new edition of the dialogues. Much of this material was given to Lela Fischli and me directly by Gitta Mallasz in response to our questions regarding content and context. We had long and detailed conversations and correspondence with Gitta not only while working on our own respective translations into German and English, but also in connection with numerous other translations, which we have been coordinating and supporting since the early 1980's.

When the dialogues were originally published, Gitta withheld some textual passages for various reasons. This was often to avoid having the texts become too lengthy (in accordance with the wishes of the original French publisher). She also found some text passages too obscure, too personal, too fragmentary or likely to be misunderstood. In a few cases, she felt the texts were simply not translatable because of their unique poetic essence in Hungarian.

However, in working with translators and other interested readers over the years and decades, we found this previously excluded material to be so helpful for a better understanding of the dialogues that we have recently elected to include it – (first in the German, now in the new English-language edition and soon in the French as well) –, even if the translations cannot do justice to the beautiful flow of the often rhyming Hungarian prose. The most substantial addition in this new edition is the inclusion of the messages of *Morgen*. While agreeing that these messages could not be adequately translated in all of their original beauty, we nevertheless felt that their inclusion would contribute significantly to a better understanding of the dialogues.

This new material, also including some additional notes by Lili, has been carefully woven into the present edition, at times with explanatory notes. The result is a longer text, but hopefully one that is able to provide

6

a more clear picture for the reader of how the dialogues transpired and were understood.

The only survivor from the group of women deported from Katalin was Eva Dános, one of the jolly jokers who was first a close friend of Lili, and then of Hanna as well. She was present during some of the final dialogues (see the comment by Gitta on page 459). Immediately upon her release from the Dachau concentration camp in the summer of 1945, Eva Dános wrote down all that she could recall in a shocking diary-like report describing her deportation experience. This document was first privately circulated in English translation in her new homeland Australia by the author in 1989. Eleven years later it was published as a book in Europe, *Prison on Wheels* (Daimon, Einsiedeln). This was followed in 2001 by a German edition (*Zug ins Verderben*, Langley-Dános, Eva, Daimon, Einsiedeln) and a French version, including a biography of the author, in 2012 *(Le Dernier Convoi*, Editions Albin Michel, Paris). This detailed report by Eva Dános augments and clarifies the final commentary by Gitta Mallasz in *Talking with Angels.*

According to Eva Dános, sixteen women from the war factory were taken prisoner on December 1, 1944, including two nurses who had been responsible for care of the Katalin workers. Everyone in this group had feared that both Father Klinda and Gitta would face grim consequences because of the mass exodus by the others. On December 2, these women and about a thousand others were transported to Ravensbruck in the very last convoy of Hungarians to depart Budapest for Germany.

Eva Dános reported that it was impossible to volunteer for commandos in the concentration camp. Also, any indication or even proof of Aryan origins would not have resulted in release or any form of privilege. In Ravensbruck, there were many non-Jewish prisoners engaged in forced labor.

Hanna died during the night of February 28/March 1 near Bayreuth, and Lili during the night of March 2/3 near Augsburg, both while on a prisoner transport train between Ravensbruck and Burgau, where they were being taken to work on assembling engines for fighter bombers. Eva Dános' document provides an authentic first-hand account of the sufferings of prisoners during the final months of the war and is a moving testimonial of humanity and friendship under the worst of conditions.

A memorial plaque was placed in the Augsburg Cemetery 'Westfriedhof' in 1950, marking the final resting place of Lili Strausz and 234 other victims.

Hanna Dallos-Kreutzer is buried, together with other victims, in the municipal cemetery of Bayreuth, where a memorial marker was erected in 2015.

Gitta Mallasz died in France in 1992. She was posthumously honored in May of 2012 in Paris by *Yad Vashem* (Museum of Martyrs) as a *Chassid Umot ha-Olam*/Righteous Among the Nations, for the rescue of more than a hundred women and children who had lived in Katalin. This award is presented to non-Jews who risked their lives to save Jews during the Holocaust.

R.H., Willerzell, 2019

PREFACE TO THE FIRST EDITION

This English language publication of the 'angel dialogues' was a long time in coming: the remarkable events documented here took place in Hungary during the late stages of the Second World War, in 1943 and 1944.

As their life situations, and gradually their very chances for survival, grew ever darker, the four close-knit friends were suddenly met by a force which came to be known to them as angels. This extraordinary encounter continued for seventeen months; *Talking with Angels* was the first unabridged translation of their original Hungarian protocols to be published. Three of the friends eventually perished in Nazi concentration camps, and the sole survivor, Gitta Mallasz, was obliged to remain underground with her precious documents and to concentrate on supporting her family of seven (her parents, her brother, and his wife and children), who had gone from wealth to poverty during the war. This phenomenon of radical change from one station in life to the next always accompanied Gitta. Her struggle for survival in postwar Communist Hungary was to last more than fifteen years. When the opportunity finally came for a new beginning – her parents had died and her nephews and nieces reached adulthood –, Gitta was able to make her way through the iron curtain to France with the precious black notebooks wrapped tightly in bed sheets in her one small suitcase.

In Paris in 1960, life began anew at the age of 53. Gitta reestablished her considerable reputation as a stage-set and graphic designer and she met and married Laci, a dear man who had also emigrated from Hungary. With help from him and a few close friends, she began the difficult task of translating the protocols of the dialogues into French, her third language after Hungarian and German. Through one of these friends, the existence of the dialogues was brought to the attention of a prominent French radio journalist, Claude Mettra, who, after reading them, invited Gitta to be a guest on his weekly national program, "The Living and the Gods." That famous first 90-minute interview, broadcast live by *Radio France* on April 22, 1976, marked the beginning of the dialogues becoming publicly known.

Gitta had long been aware that making the dialogues accessible to all was part of her task: she understood them to be important for more than just the four original participants, but she had had no means of making them available to others. Now at last she had a forum.

Radio France was deluged with letters responding to her impressive message. Claude Mettra packed together a large bundle of them and marched to the modest but renowned Parisian publishing house, Aubier Montaigne. Gitta's manuscript was quickly accepted, trimmed and prepared for publication, appearing later in 1976 as *Dialogues avec l'ange* (Aubier, Paris, 1976). Though practically unadvertised, it became an immediate sensation and was reviewed and discussed on radio and in newspapers throughout the land.

It is interesting to note that the dialogues had their first and greatest public success, and were met with such a resounding echo, in *France*, of all places: a land of people known for sharp intellect and skeptical rationalism. Perhaps this is because of the document's straightforward, down-to-earth character, in contrast to so many other publications dealing with esoteric matters.

Gitta herself chose to remain in the background. After her radio appearance, she declined all of the inevitable public-speaking invitations and continued to live her normal daily life in relative anonymity. It was not only her natural modesty that kept Gitta out of the limelight: she had a strong aversion to the tendency people often had of attributing their hopes, fears and admiration to her personally, to their wanting to make her into a kind of 'guru.' She was convinced that the real message is for each reader to find an own personal relationship to the words of the document, *to experience it themselves.* This is also the reason why photographs of Gitta and the other participants are not published with the dialogues.

In 1973, Gitta and her husband retired from Paris to a small farmhouse which they themselves restored in the Dordogne region of the French countryside. Laci built all of the furniture by hand from local materials. Far from the city and close to nature again, as in her childhood, Gitta continued to live a simple life, to respond to the many letters concerning *Dialogues avec l'ange* over the years and, to her greatest joy, to devote her energies to working on foreign language editions of the dialogues.

In 1983, her quiet life in retirement ended when she received a speaking invitation she had never anticipated: the C.G. Jung Institute of Zürich asked her to talk with its students about her experience with the angels. Having been deeply impressed during the arduous years in Budapest after the war by Jung's writings, and later greatly comforted by his descriptions of dialogues with his inner guide, Philemon, in his biography*, Gitta felt that she could not say 'no' to this invitation. She made the long train journey to Zürich and spent two lively evenings, first describing and then discussing her experience of the dialogues with a full house of fascinated listeners.

The tremendous resonance in Zürich convinced Gitta that it might, after all, be appropriate for her to reveal more of her personal experiences in connection with the dialogues, along with the actual protocols, and in the ensueing years, she made extensive speaking tours and conducted workshops throughout France, Switzerland, Holland, Germany, Austria and Belgium.

Further, Gitta came to feel that it was appropriate to put her energies to work forming the often personal material of her correspondence with readers, and later, of her speaking encounters, into a book. The result was *Die Engel erlebt* (roughly: "the angels experienced"), originally published late in 1983 in German and French (translations have followed). A second book, *Weltenmorgen* (roughly: "dawning world"), followed by *Sprung ins Unbekannte* ("Leap into the Unknown") continued Gitta's ever more personal response to the many questions addressed to her in the time since the dialogues' first publication.

---

* *Memories, Dreams, Reflections by C.G. Jung*, recorded and edited by Aniela Jaffé. Pantheon, New York, 1961, pp. 182 ff.

Work on this English-language edition of the dialogues began in 1984. A shortened English edition had been published in 1979 in a limited printing. Then it was decided to go back to the beginning and carefully work with Gitta, word by word, on the basis of the original handwritten Hungarian texts to create a complete transcript of the dialogues in English. This was to prove a laborious and time-consuming process, but a very rewarding one. Hanna conveyed from her inner ear to the Hungarian language and now this translation takes the dialogues one step further into English.

In numerous sessions in Willerzell, Einsiedcln and Gitta's Girardel, and with almost daily communication between these meetings, the new English edition slowly took form over the course of the next four years. Along the way, several fragments came to light that had been neglected or edited out of previous editions of the dialogues, and, as questions arose during the English-language formulation, explanatory notes were added.

After Gitta's devoted husband Laci died in 1982, she continued to live alone in the little farmhouse in Girardel. Then in 1988, just as the final proofs of this book were on their way to the printer, she suffered a nearly fatal accident: her life was spared, but both arms were broken. She understood her survival to indicate that her earthly task had not yet been completed.

Gitta then went to live in a small cottage on a farm, close to young friends in the northeastern part of the country. Here she continued to have her all-important independent existence in her own little 'hermitage,' but without the at times almost total seclusion of her previous abode in the south. Her public speaking engagements became less frequent with increasing age, but she made the occasional trip by 'TGV' into Paris for ever larger audiences and continued to fulfil her task in a variety of angel-related projects and her far-reaching correspondence. She died in May of 1992.

***

What is it that makes *Talking with Angels* so gripping, so humanly appealing? For me, an important part of it is the *naturalness* with which these four ordinary young people – none of whom had experienced religious instruction – accepted the sudden appearance of 'angels' into their everyday existence. That this luminous and numinous event came just at the darkest hour of their lives is surely significant: it shows that possibilities for new ways and for transformation do come to us at times when there seems to be no solution – if only we are open to them!

The angels taught Gitta and her friends – and continue to teach us – that earthly existence is only a part of a whole: once we realize this, death is not something to be feared. As we become aware of the ever moving, the undogmatic – what the angels teach as *Light* –, we learn that not the eternally repetitive is eternal, but the *eternally new*. The angels tell us that the more light we are able to bear, the more aware we become and the closer we come to our 'peak,' the meeting point with our own angel. Our personal angel strives to descend from above and meet us at this same point. Thus, we are not alone in this endeavor, even if our way of going about it is very individual. Whatever *way* each of us goes through this experience is not of importance: only *that* we do so, each in his or her unique way. That is, for me, the essence and the inspiration of these dialogues.

Gitta never tired of reminding her listeners and readers that she was not the *author* of this text, but 'merely' the *scribe.* She considered it her task to make the dialogues available to others. When asked not long before her death, how she felt about the dialogues Gitta answered:

"You know, those words are like seeds that were sown by the angels. They lay dormant in the earth for 33 years. They finally broke through the hard crust of the surface for the first time in 1976 with the publication of the French *Dialogues* in Paris and from there, they spread like wildfire – no, like *Lightfire.* Now the new, the Springtime of humanity, is here – and these words represent a very real possibility for all."

The angels said:

> WHAT COULD BE MORE NATURAL
> THAN OUR TALKING WITH EACH OTHER?

May this book help many new dialogues to be born....

R.H., Willerzell, 1988, 2006

INTRODUCTION BY GITTA

As a point of departure for the events which follow, I would like first to give a brief introductory sketch:

It is important to note the ordinariness, the simple life led by my three friends and me up until the dialogues began. But it was a time of increasing political tension and ever more questions arose about the meaning of our lives, and our futures. Nevertheless, this life we had was a preparation for what was to come.

I was sixteen years old in 1923 when I first met Hanna. We were both students at the School of Applied Arts in Budapest, where we worked at neighboring tables. From the first moment, Hanna was open and very friendly towards me, but I was the product of a military family proud of its motto: 'Above all, be strong!' Thus I was surprised and puzzled by Hanna's affectionate nature. In my upbringing, any display of feelings had been considered a sign of weakness and even a simple kiss of departure was cause for embarrassment.

Hanna, whose father was an elementary school principal, grew up in the more natural atmosphere of a modern Jewish family and she was accustomed to showing her feelings spontaneously. Despite these differences in temperament and upbringing, we became close friends in the course of the next three years.

After final exams, however, our ways parted and we seldom had contact. Hanna continued her studies in Munich, while I threw myself totally and blindly into sports: swimming championships, national records and the adulation which Hungary showered upon its sports heroes fed my pride and kept me indulging in a superficial lifestyle for the next four years. It was during this period that I made the acquaintance of Lili, who was giving courses in movement therapy. Her warm and natural manner attracted great numbers of pupils and I soon realized that the reason for her overcrowded classes was that her students were experiencing something going far beyond physical relaxation: their inner essence was being nourished.

I heard little from Hanna during my sports idol days. She had married Joseph, a quiet man, who was a furniture designer by profession. His very presence had a soothing influence on his surroundings. I often observed this later when we lived together in Budaliget: in the village inn, where the townspeople had the habit of engaging in heated political quarrels, the atmosphere would inevitably calm and all would become peaceful within moments of Joseph's arrival. This was a typical effect of his silent way of being.

When I finally had had enough of sports, I decided to seek out Hanna once more. She and Joseph had settled into a work studio in the *Ilona-utca* on the hills of Buda, overlooking the Danube to a gorgeous view. With great patience and understanding, Hanna helped me find my way back to artistic activity, something I had completely neglected since completing my studies. Without her accompaniment, I would never have been able to regain my joy in creative work. As it turned out, the three of us eventually founded what soon became a very successful graphic arts studio.

In the years 1934 and 1935, anti-Semitism was already widespread in Hungary. Thus, as the only non-Jew in the group, it was my role to obtain government commissions, primarily for touristic events and advertising, whereby my sports reputation and status as the daughter of a high-ranking military officer were beneficial assets. Unfortunately, I always had to hide the fact that my colleagues were Jewish.

The 'soul' of our professional group was undeniably Hanna. She possessed tremendous powers of concentration and intuition which enabled her to immediately grasp the essence of an artistic conception, as well as its practical realization. She had the knack of being able to solve problems with a wonderful blend of common sense, clear psychological insight and, above all, humor.

By this time, Hanna had some graphic pupils of her own and, many years later, one of these young artists, Vera, told me: "The intensity of Hanna's teaching touched not only our professional development, but our entire being. It demanded so much of us that some students simply could not bear it and chose to leave. Hanna never critiqued a design without our feeling personally touched, even if it involved only the most trivial advertising graphics. She considered every line of a drawing to be the manifestation of an inner event. During the actual lessons, our contact with her was quite different: she would intuitively tune in to another wavelength and read our drawings like a doctor reads an X-ray, but with affection, firmness and cheerfulness.

Before beginning to speak, she sometimes had no idea of what she was going to say and was then astonished at her own words. As a young student, I was very attached to her and she became a model for me. But Hanna completely rejected this dependency on my part. She would say to us, 'After two or three years of my teaching, you must find *your own inner teacher.*' For her, the most important thing was to awaken the new being in us: *'the creative individual, freed from fear.'''*

Our studio prospered. And yet, ever more, we had the feeling that we were living on the edge of a cliff. Collective blindness was on the rise, along with a flood of organized political lies. If something were promised by the Nazis, for instance, one could be sure that just the opposite would occur. A strong desire was welling in us to find the truth – *our truth* – beneath so much deception. This led Joseph and Hanna to seek and ultimately find a small house not far from Budapest in the little village of Budaliget, for the purpose of starting a new and simple way of life. I soon joined them there and we worked just enough to support our daily needs. Lili joined us on the weekends.

The quiet village life was beneficial to our inner development. However, this period began for me with a growing feeling of emptiness. An inexplicable expectation of a coming *something* deeply disturbed me and I often went for daylong walks in the forest in search of peace. Again and again, even at mealtimes, I would catch myself looking toward the garden gate in expectation of this 'something' or 'someone' that should come and change my life. In the evenings, we would often discuss our experiences and try to discover the sources of our problems. Hanna's intuitive gifts were a great help, but still we all felt ourselves to be at a dead end.

We were interested in the great religious currents of humanity and our bookshelves held The Bible, the Bhagavad Gita, philosophical and literary texts, works of Eastern authors from the past (Lao Tse) and present, as well as writings of Meiser Eckhart were essential in our library. Yet none of us was practicing our religion of origin.

We felt ourselves to be standing before a world of lies, brutality and all-pervading evil. At the same time, we were convinced that the meaning of our lives must be buried somewhere, and that the cause of our not finding it must be in ourselves.

With this in mind, we decided at one point that each of us should write down as clearly as possible our individual problems, so as to better be able to discuss them together. One day over black coffee, I read aloud what I had written to Hanna, who dryly remarked that this was nothing but the familiar old stories, warmed over yet again. It was all too true, and I was painfully aware of my blatant superficiality. I was asking Hanna questions that I could just as easily have answered myself, but it was less strenuous to have the answer simply 'served' to me.

At this point, the dialogues begin. They were to take place nearly every Friday afternoon at three o'clock for the following seventeen months.

PART I

THE DIALOGUES IN BUDALIGET

"Go your *own* way!
Any other way is straying."

Friday, June 25, 1943

1. DIALOGUE WITH GITTA

*In the face of my superficial attitude, Hanna feels a tension arise
which grows into indignation. And then, fully awake and with
eyes open wide, she suddenly has the following vision: a strange
force seizes my pages of notes, rips them to shreds and dashes
them to the floor in complete disapproval of this inferior effort,
so short of my capabilities. Hanna is about to say something but
suddenly stops as she senses that it is no longer she herself who
is about to speak. She just has time to warn me:
"It is not I who will speak to you."
And then I hear the following words:*

— Enough of your shallow questions!
It is time for you to assume responsibility for yourself!

*It is Hanna's voice that I hear, but I am absolutely certain that
she is not herself speaking; her voice is serving as a kind of
instrument. I have the feeling that I know whoever is addressing
these stern words to me and so I am not totally overwhelmed;
I rather feel that something quite natural, which had to occur,
is finally taking place. I am filled with a bright light, but there
is nothing joyous about it. On the contrary, it illuminates my
darkest interior with merciless clarity and I am compelled to see
myself without deception.
I am shown what I might well have written about myself, had I
truly been self-searching and honest, and I feel deeply shaken –
and guilty. In the wake of my sincere shame, Hanna senses the
indignation ebbing in the one who is speaking through her.*

— It is better now: repentance is also forgiving.
It is time for you to transform yourself.

BE INDEPENDENT!
You have too much and too little.

G. I do not understand ...

— Too much inert matter – too little independence!

I feel that this refers to my lazy and dependent way of thinking.

— The seed is not sown on hard ground.
You will be tilled by endless searching.
What has been good will become bad.
What has been bad will become good.

> *A long silence ensues. It is finally broken by the following question:*

— Do you know me?

> *These words touch me to the core. I feel with an inexplicable certainty that I do know the questioner, that it is my inner teacher and guide; but I have no memory-image to accompany this feeling. I perceive only thick layers of mist, which obscure and prevent recognition. I am unable to break through it, despite my best efforts.*

— Do you know me?

> *This repetition penetrates me all the more. I am at the threshold of remembering and try with all my strength to illuminate the dark layers. But it is for naught. I cannot.*
> *Hanna feels that the one who speaks through her watches me with empathy during my struggle.*

— You are pagan, but that is *good.*

> *I sense that, by 'pagan,' my roots are meant.*

— You will be baptized with the Water of Life.
You will receive a new Name.

The Name exists, but I cannot yet reveal it.
Prepare yourself for it!
You may ask a question!

*I am incapable of asking even a single question. I am too filled
with the growing awareness of what is happening to me.*

— 'The one who speaks' is tired.
Give her strength!
We will meet again!

*Immediately after this remarkable encounter, Hanna and I write
down what we have heard. This is not difficult, for every word
has engraved itself permanently into our memories. Hanna
describes her experience of the event as follows: "During the
entire dialogue, my perceptions were heightened. I could see the
room, you, and all that was going on inside of you, with great
clarity. At the same time, I was fully aware of our visitor, whose
feelings were of an entirely different quality than ours. But I can
describe them only in inadequate terms such as 'indignation,'
'love' or 'tenderness.' It was difficult to find words to express
what was to be communicated through me. In one and the same
moment, I was experiencing both intense anticipation and great
joy."*
*A single question burns in me: "And the promise of return ...
when – if ever – will it be fulfilled?"*
Hanna answers: "Perhaps in seven days."
*In the evening, we tell Lili and Joseph about our extraordinary
experience. Joseph, who had been a materialist in his youth,
reacts skeptically and adopts a cautious attitude. Lili, however,
very much wants to be present the following week and offers to
take notes of any subsequent dialogues.*

23

Friday, July 2, 1943

2. DIALOGUE WITH GITTA

It is a difficult week: the uncertainty of my inner visitor's return makes me uneasy. In addition, the starkly accurate image of me which had been revealed is difficult to bear. At about three o'clock on Friday afternoon, we are sitting in waitful expectation and I am painfully aware of having made no progress during the week.

Suddenly, the silence is broken by these words:

— What have you achieved? Have you learned?

I think back on the past week and, at this moment, I would like nothing better than to sink beneath the floor. Nonetheless, I feel that I have changed in some small way, and I say timidly:

G. Yes.

— For the time being, or forever?

Now I feel so worthless that I burst into tears.

— No self-pity! Are you afraid of me?

G. No.

— I, too, serve.

These words console me, and I am filled with a joyous feeling of trust: my teacher serves and this is something we have in common.

— Ask!

As a birthday present, Hanna had recently painted a portrait of me in which I sit on a mountain top holding a crystal sphere, whose facets shine in a rainbow of rich colors. The symbol of this sphere of light has great meaning for me, and I long to hear my teacher say something about it.

G. How might it be possible for me not only to *understand,* but also to *live* the symbol of the sphere?
— I have the sphere of Light with me.

I DESCEND TO YOU – YOU ASCEND TO ME.

G. How?
— Believe it, and you shall grow with this belief.

In the word 'belief,' I feel a living force, in no way connected with the intellectual affirmation of a religious creed.

— When the time is ripe, it will happen.
Can you bear the sphere of Light?

I answer superficially, without really understanding the question:

G. Yes.
— Are you worthy? Are you *pure* enough?

I hesitate:

G. *You* know it.

Hanna feels that the one who speaks through her is observing me as though I were a foolish child, ignorant of what she is saying.

— Though the sphere is heavier than the earth,
the CHILD plays with it,
for it is formed of one and the same substance: LIGHT.

The word 'CHILD' is used in an entirely new way which I am unable to grasp. I listen as if through fog, and bluntly ask:

25

G. Can one play with it?

— The CHILD plays – the adult creates.

The fog thickens. I am completely confused.

G. Then am I too small for the sphere?

The piercing reply strikes me like lightning:

— Too *big* !

Hanna sees that my little 'I' is too big and dominating. But I do not understand, and ask stupidly:

G. Where am I too big?

Hanna feels indignation rise in my teacher at this lack of comprehension on my part. Although a powerful purifying gesture would have been called for, she fails to rally sufficient strength in herself to carry it out and is only able to transmit the following words:

— Be reborn!
What is big – collapses.
What is hard – disintegrates.

The gesture of burning force, which Hanna had been unable to make, would have set off this 'collapsing' and 'disintegration' inside of me, Hanna later tells me.
After a long silence, I hear the consoling words:

— You are never alone.

Friday, July 9, 1943

3. DIALOGUE WITH GITTA

> *This week has been less difficult than the previous one, but on Friday, the obscuring inner layers of fog return. It begins to dawn on me that I have been living carelessly in this fog for 36 years without even being aware of it. But now I do at last see it, and it is a real problem.*
>
> *As we chat together after coffee, Hanna suddenly hears a single word, sternly spoken:*

— Enough!

> *It is three o'clock and I had not been ready to receive my inner teacher.*

— Have you prepared yourself for the feast?

> *I feel so worthless that I begin to cry.*

— Do not cry in my presence. There is no time for that!

> *Hanna feels my visitor's indignance. Clearly it would have been more suitable to be joyful.*

— Ask.

G. How might I hear your voice *always* ... ?

— ... and be a *puppet* !

G. I do not understand.

— THEN YOU WOULD NOT BE INDEPENDENT.

> It is *your* task to approach *me.*

G. *(Timidly:)* May I ask a question?

— That is why I am here.

G. Should I fast on Friday?

I thought that fasting might be a means of spiritual purification.

— No. Let the proper measure of each day
be your fasting.

Pointing to Hanna:

— Give her something to drink!

Very surprised, I get Hanna a glass of water.

G. Why is it so difficult to really love my family?
— The family is flesh ...

*Hanna sees that my family strengthens just what is already too
strong in me: matter.*

— When you have rid yourself of the superfluous,
then you will be able to love.
G. Is that far off?

— THE FAR IS NEAR – THE NEAR IS FAR.

G. May I know your name?

*This question comes from a desire to be able to call my teacher
at any time, and thus feel secure.*

— The name is still matter. Seek what is *behind* it!

*The dark layers of fog torment me. My question is actually a
desperate cry for help:*

G. I am in the dark ... what should I do?

— GO YOUR OWN WAY! ANY OTHER WAY IS STRAYING.

After a long silence:

— Sing for me in the forest!

I cannot believe my ears: me ... sing? Having hidden my feelings behind a thick coat of armor since childhood, this strikes me as absolutely absurd.

G. I think I misheard ...

Each word is now uttered with emphasis:

— SING - FOR - ME - IN - THE - FOREST !

Without being aware of it, I lean forward, and I am immediately held back by a gentle but firm gesture:

— You are too near.

I ask myself if my density is unbearable ... ?
Or is the radiance of my teacher too strong for me?

G. I had a dream, but its meaning is not clear to me.
— You are a part of the way. I am a part of the way.
Ö* is the WAY.

The word Ö is pronounced with utter reverence. Hanna is now too tired to go on. Thus, the remainder of what she was to convey is related to me afterwards as a message:

— To *will* is not a step forward; it is a hindering wall.

I feel this is a reference to my overzealous, willful striving.

---

* See the Technical Note on p. 5 for an explanation of Ö.

Friday, July 9, 1943

3. DIALOGUE WITH LILI

> *Lili would also like to ask some questions. She takes the place opposite Hanna, who is resting, as I move over and prepare to take notes. After a brief silence, we feel a presence of warmth and gentleness.*

— I am here.
You called me – I called you.

> *The intonation of the voice has changed completely: now it is tender.*

— You may ask!
L. When will I open myself to what is above?
— You are deceiving yourself. Deception is fear.
But you have no cause to fear.
L. What is my first task?
— Do you know your sign?
Here it is:

> *Gesture outlining a triangle pointing downwards.*

L. Could you explain my task in another way?
— You are named: 'the one who helps.'
The helper should not fear.
I bring good news: you are dear to me.
Do you *want* to see me again?
L. Yes.
— Then you will not see me.
Do you *wish* to see me?
L. Yes.

— Then you will not see me.

In light of the previous dialogue, I now realize that neither will nor wish can bring our teachers closer to us. Lili, rather confused, bursts out:

L. I only want to see you better …

— WHEN THE TASK REQUIRES IT – YOU WILL SEE ME.

I obey.

L. I would also like to be able to obey.

Touching Lili's forehead:

— There is too much here …
In the body, you are the last-born.

(Lili was the youngest child of a large family.)

— In spirit, you are the first of the new-born.
I now take leave of you.

I am absolutely delighted that Lili has found her inner guide, whose tender, radiant presence allows even me to completely relax.
In the days that follow, I am totally occupied with "not wanting" and "not wishing."

Friday, July 16, 1943

4. DIALOGUE WITH GITTA

It is Friday. My life has gone through a fundamental change: possibilities hitherto undreamed of have appeared and I am aware of so much that is new. Joyfully, I prepare myself for today's dialogue. But then, after lunch, a cold fear suddenly seizes me, and I become haunted by the question: "What if my teacher does not come ... does not appear anymore?" I desperately try to cast this thought away, but it returns again and again, ever stronger, fed by a fear of falling into the void of my previous empty life. Then, all of a sudden, I realize that it is wrong for me to bind myself, even to the very thing which means the most to me. This fearful clinging to my inner teacher will have to be sacrificed. It is an unavoidable challenge, and I know it is my task.

Inner detachment is more difficult than anything I have ever before experienced. It is as though I cut myself off from my own life. At three o'clock, Hanna calls me. I soon sense the presence of my guide, who, however, remains silent and, after a while, I am nervously uncertain about whether the silence is going to be broken. With a sigh of surrender, I say to myself: "Thy Will be done." At this moment, I see [my eyes are open] a fire burning before me, its smoke rising straight up to heaven.

Then I hear the following words:

— The time has come. *Now* you may ask!

G. What is my path?

— Listen well:

AT ONE END, LOVE. AT THE OTHER END, LIGHT.
YOU ARE SUSPENDED BETWEEN THE TWO.
THAT IS YOUR PATH.

A hundred deaths are between the two.
Love is bearer of Light.
Love without Light is nothing.
Do you understand me?

> *I do understand, but it strikes me as very difficult to let my 'little
> I' die a hundred times. I sink my eyes, discouraged.*

— Look at me!

> *The familiar face of Hanna, neither beautiful nor ugly, takes on
> another expression and reflects an almost frightening dignity.*

— At one end ... I.

> *Gesture from above to below:*

— At the other end ... it.
Between the two ... you.
G. What is 'it'?
— Your 'little I.'

> *Disdainfully, I think: "What a self-centered creature, this 'little
> I.'"*

G. I know my 'little I' well, all too well, but you I do not know well
enough!
— Foolish child!

> *I later come to understand these two words as meaning: 'How
> could you possibly know your little I? You do not know even a
> single cell of your body! As little as you know me! How long will
> you continue to be so blind?'*

— *It* and *I* are united in the task.
Do not divide what is one!
Before the Divine, nothing is small!
Do not judge!

G. Teach me, for I know nothing!
— Have I not taught you?

With false modesty, I say:

G. Oh, yes, I know that I ask silly questions.

Hanna perceives my teacher's thoughts:
'What a childish game!' But she feels authorized only to say:

— You are foolish!… Ask!

I know that I have been seen through like glass,
and I stubbornly protest:

G. Why should I even ask, when you always know beforehand what I
want to say … you see my thoughts!
— From the heart to the mouth is a handspan.
Make this your way! Do you wish to know much?
G. Only as much as my task requires.

— THOSE WHO ASK ARE MORE DEAR TO THE DIVINE THAN THOSE
WHO KNOW.

Last night, I dreamed I saw a human figure in glowing colors,
radiating harmony, strength and peace.

G. What does my dream mean?
— The new Individual formed from your image.
G. Will I become this individual when I shed what is superfluous?

— YOU ARE THE ONE WHO FORMS –
NOT THE FORMED.

G. What must I do to become *the one who forms*?

Now Hanna's body seems to lose its usual qualities and trans-
form into an instrument serving totally, with nothing held back:
her movements are simple, meaningful and dignified. Even her

arm seems different to me. It radiates concentrated force, the muscles tense, and I am strongly reminded of Michelangelo's sculptures. An abrupt gesture strikes like lightning.

— BURN!

I am struck, jolted, filled with wonder. But all this vanishes instantly when I notice that Hanna is shivering. She bids me to bring her alcohol: just today, by 'coincidence,' I had bought a small bottle of pure alcohol. I drip some onto a sugar cube and give it to Hanna. Soon her strength returns and she reveals: "I had to concentrate all of my energy so that a burning force would ignite in you. Your detachment was the key. You had to sacrifice and to learn independence, even from your inner teacher."

Friday, July 16, 1943

4. DIALOGUE WITH LILI

After a short rest, Hanna feels ready for the dialogue with Lili, who is wearing a blue skirt and a red blouse.

— You have dressed yourself upside-down.
L. What do you mean?
— Blue belongs above – red, below!
  Red carries the blue.
  This is also relevant for your work.

Lili immediately understands that the bodily 'red' should support the spiritual, the 'blue.' Then she reflects on her teaching of the previous week and its results.

35

— Pay no attention to results!
What *'was'* … is no more.
What *'is now'* is already the *'it was.'*
There you can no longer help.
May 'the one who helps' direct her attention
to where the *'shall be'* is born.
It occupies little space, but from it,
everything can be formed.

> *Lili, who is physically fragile and often in poor health, has been ill.*

— Are you tired?
L. No, I just don't feel well.
— This we know.
If blue is above, it strengthens;
if red is below, it softens, it weakens.
In the same way,
the weak body is a burden when it dominates.
Red, Eros … is earthly love.
Blue is heavenly love.
Purple is *His* color.

> *The word 'His' vibrates with deep reverence. As a painter, I know that the combination of red and blue results in purple. I understand the word 'His' as referring to Jesus, who united earthly and heavenly love.*

— You may ask another question!
L. Will I receive *help* with my work …
or will I have to do everything by myself?

— IF YOU BEGIN BY YOURSELF,
THEN YOU WILL RECEIVE HELP.

In the ensuing silence, I begin to wonder just what sort of evolutionary possibilities are open to us as humans, and immediately I receive a response to my silent question:

— I am speaking to you:
This is the direction of human evolution:

> *These words are accompanied by*
> *an upward gesture at a 45° angle*
> *to the right.*
>
> *I am astonished to learn that human evolution is not only a matter of spiritual (vertical), nor only of material (horizontal) development, but of equal parts of both.*

Friday, July 23, 1943

5. DIALOGUE WITH GITTA

> *All week long, I have been thinking about 'burning.' On Friday morning, I decorate the little room that opens to the garden with flowers. As we sit waiting for the dialogue, Hanna feels luminous forces assembling in a semi-circle behind her.*

— Speak!
G. Last week, you spoke of the 'hundred deaths.'
   I would like to 'die' now, to *surpass* my 'little I' …
— It is not a matter of *surpassing,*
   but of becoming a bridge.

> *I am so overjoyed at the presence of my inner teacher that tears well up in my eyes.*

37

— Do not flood the seed with water!

I understand that all my emotions have to be transformed into burning.

— THE DIVINE SPARK SPRINGS BETWEEN ACT AND MATTER.

I am aware that something extremely important has been revealed to me, but I have no idea what it means. In the silence that follows, Hanna continues to feel the presence of luminous beings. All eyes are focused on me.

— We are many and we expect much of you.

A sense of responsibility arises in me, and I offer all of my strength joyfully.

G. I would so much like to know my *task* now!

— *Task* is just a word to you.

G. Can you reveal the task to me?

— The one who speaks finds no words.
These words have not yet been born.

G. What could bring them to birth?

— Your deepest desire.

G. My desire to serve?

— Mighty and wondrous is your task.

The vibration of these words conveys to me a foretaste of a completely new life-intensity.

G. You said, "we are many." Who are you all?

— THE CHORUS.

Behind the spoken words, I sense an infinite multitude in perfect harmony. I wonder: could my teacher be what we humans call an 'angel'?

With lowered eyes and upward turned hands, the following words are gently spoken:

— We sing praise, we praise the Divine.

For the first time in my life, I feel what genuine adoration is, and I softly ask:

G. Do you always see Ö?

A swift motion stops me, as though I had touched something forbidden.

— You know not what you say. Ask another question!
G. How could I always hear the voice of my heart
without having my head interfere?
— Do you not feel the difference?
G. Yes, but everything moves so slowly,
and I want to serve now!
— You often lose your way.

Hanna senses a hesitation: before me lies a long and difficult path which gradually leads to awareness, to more consciousness. My angel sees a storm approaching, and sees that the heavy weight of my family and my lack of self-confidence might overwhelm me before my goal is reached. Time is short. Hanna pleads in her heart: "Please show her the short way! I will vouch for her!"

— Listen well! Your path is not difficult!
Be cheerful! Be light!
The one who speaks cannot express it clearly!

A vertical flamelike motion of remarkable lightness, and then a heavy, downward motion like flowing water.

— FIRE IS LIGHT – WATER IS HEAVY.
IF YOU FEEL HEAVINESS,
THEN YOU HAVE STRAYED FROM THE PATH.

> *After the dialogue, Hanna explains in detail what she had not been able to verbalize at the moment: "It is important for you to find a happiness you have never known before, a new smile: Lightness! If you feel weighed down, you are off the path. If you carry your burden lightly, then you are on the path. It all depends on you. You will be able to find this new smile only by living life to the fullest!"*

— Ask!

G. Where are my limits?

— Limits are only here:

> *The hands form a cylinder, closed on the sides, open at the top. It seems to express that limits are necessary in matter, but that the way up is free.*

G. Then I am you?

— *(smile)* Not yet. Enough for today!

> *By this time, Hanna is so tired that she immediately falls asleep. Lili was unable to be here today.*

Friday, July 30, 1943

6. DIALOGUE WITH GITTA

*I have carefully prepared a long list of questions
for today's session:*

— I cannot stay for long today.

*This opening of course disappoints me,
and I say very hesitatingly:*

G. May I ask a question?

There is a silent nod.

G. Why were there so many of you last time?
— Because your task has grown.
G. What do you expect of me?
— When the seed sprouts, you will know.

*I have worked hard on myself all week
and am eager to hear some praise.*

G. Do I water the seed enough?
— You know that perfectly well yourself.

*This dry reply makes the falsity of my attempt
to draw praise all the more obvious.*

G. The dead of my family came to me in a dream.
   Can I do something for them?
   Am I neglecting them somehow?
— Many of the dead are weaklings ...
G. How could I help them?
— By harvesting.
G. How can I harvest?

— Ö CREATED YOU AFTER MY IMAGE.

These words touch me deeply: I exist in the image of my angel!

G. Why do you have so little time today?

— So as to teach you measure.
I will answer one last question.

I hurriedly search through my papers for the most important question.

— I have time ...

I relax, and now my question comes from the heart:

G. In what way do I least resemble your image?
Once I know, I will tear it out of myself!

— Uncertainty.

G. I do not understand.

— Do not waver.

I lower my eyes.

— Look at me!

Hanna's facial expression transforms, seeming to take on the austere solemnity of an other-worldly dimension.

— I depart ...

I continue to feel the silent presence of the angel for a few minutes more, and in this stillness, the deep longing awakens in me to become identical with my inner teacher's image.

Friday, July 30, 1943

6. DIALOGUE WITH LILI

L. Thank you for coming again!
— Thank Ö, who sent me!
L. Why is it so difficult for me to free myself
from my 'habitual I'?

— WHEN YOU TASTE THE BETTER –
YOU LEAVE WHAT IS LESS GOOD.

With unquenchable thirst,
you will search for the better.
L. Why am I so unsure of myself that I don't even know what I need?
— Freshen up your palate, for you have spoiled it
with so much worthless food.

*This appears to refer to Lili's having studied a wide variety of
educational methods of body movement in past years at foreign
schools.*

L. Why do I progress so pitifully slowly,
and why do I so often lose my head?
— They are directly related:
one is the consequence of the other. Do not rush!
I am protecting you.

Gentle, protective gesture around Lili.

L. I don't even know what to call my work,
what kind of a name to give it.
— A name is already a conclusion.
But at this point, you are still at the beginning!

The numbers of young students who participate in Lili's courses are swelling by the day. As political uncertainty and mistrust spread and decimate morale everywhere, the task of teaching relaxation becomes ever more vital – and more difficult!

L. My work seems to be lacking something basic ...
   What is it?

— BELIEF IN Ö ... IN ME ... AND IN YOURSELF.

   Listen carefully! In preparation for our next meeting, try to
   formulate the essence of your work.

L. Thank you!

Friday, August 6, 1943

7. DIALOGUE WITH GITTA

As a result of last week's lesson in 'measure,' I decide to ask very few questions today.

— Ask!

G. I don't see things clearly, my heart is weak and hesitant. How could
   I see you more clearly, how could I better feel your presence? I
   would like to form myself after your image.

— The creature perceives the lack;
   yet the Divine, the only Reality, can be but intuited.
   May your intuition guide you!

G. How could I carve your words into myself, so that they shine?
   I always fear that they will fade ...

— FEAR IS THE REFUGE OF THE WEAK.

44

There is no question of my wanting to belong to the weak! Thus,
I am quick to protest:

G. I am not *that* afraid!
— (with severity:) You are that afraid.
G. Then I will work to free myself from it.
— Do not work – believe!
    Believe, and then there is nothing to be afraid of.

> *I feel this belief to be not religious confession, but a living,*
> *transforming force.*

— Listen well!
    The measure of suffering is unknown to you.

> *Ever since childhood, I have avoided suffering whenever*
> *possible by lying. But when I do suffer, then I torture myself*
> *mercilessly with self-reproaches.*

— WELCOME SUFFERING AS A MESSENGER FROM HEAVEN.
    BUT LET IT DEPART WHEN IT IS READY TO LEAVE.

G. How can I welcome suffering and still be joyful?
— *(smiling)* By following the good path: your *own* path.

> *I have more questions, but, recalling the lesson of measure, I*
> *remain silent.*

— I speak: We are not disappointed in you.

> *In the word, 'we,' echoes once more the perfect harmony of*
> *a multitude: the Chorus. Hanna later tells me: "Your teacher*
> *was pleased that you exercised measure. And your unanswered*
> *questions will be answered: Imagine a white sheet of paper. The*
> *answers will appear on it. They will be ignited by the intensity*
> *of your questions."*

Friday, August 6, 1943

7. DIALOGUE WITH LILI

L. I thank God that you were allowed to come again...

   An atmosphere of deep reverence follows the word, 'God.'

   ... and I am grateful for all that I received this week in Budapest.

   Lili had felt unexpected help.

L. I have not thanked with prayer for all this ...

— YOUR WORK IS YOUR PRAYER.
   PRAYER IS WINGS FOR THE WINGLESS.

   Your wings are already growing.
L. Will you tell me what my weakest part is?
   I would like to improve it.
— No. For the time being, simply *rejoice!*

   *Lili has suffered from an extremely unhappy childhood and joy
   has been her greatest lack.*

L. I was happier this week than ever before in my life.
— I was happy, too, my little servant.

   Lili has been trying to define her professional work.

L. I was unable to complete my task ...
— It will never be *completed* ...
L. I wanted so much to bring something whole, something well-
   rounded.
— Roundness belongs to the infinite:

   Gesture forming a spiral.

L. I feel that I have so *much* to do!

— *Much* is illusion. If you feel it to be *much,*
then you are in error. There is not *much,*
but just *one* thing to be done.

    Gesture of offering upwards.

— May heaven bless you.

    There are moments during the dialogues when I am afraid that
    I will not be able to write down everything that is said. But then
    Lili's teacher waits until I have caught up before proceeding
    to the next topic. This occurs several times, which seems to
    indicate that our note-taking is desired.

Friday, August 13, 1943

8. DIALOGUE WITH GITTA

    Before the dialogues began, we all occasionally had impres-
    sive dreams, and to distinguish these from 'ordinary' ones,
    we referred to them as 'teaching dreams.' Each of them had
    a powerful effect on all of us. We would often discuss them
    at the breakfast table and try to unveil their hidden meaning
    together. Hanna's dreams, in particular, were often concerned
    with universal themes, as I became more and more aware with
    the passage of time.

— It is time to ask!
G. Last night, I know that I dreamed of a new Host,
    but I do not understand the meaning of the dream.
— The Host is an image of creation.
The New Host is an image of the New Creation.

47

G. Matter appeared to be very important in the dream,
but that, too, is unclear to me.

— Listen carefully! Human sin – Adam's sin –
caused matter to be cursed.
When the curse ends, matter will again be sacred.

MATTER IS THE CHILD OF GOD.

G. How might I strengthen my belief in such a way that it would lift
me above duality?

— It is not your belief that is weak, but your vision.

G. I do not understand.

— You look – but you do not *shine*.
Your eyes are not made for looking.

G. Do I look to the outside too much?

— No. Look in a completely different way: transform!

*There is lightning – fast flick of the hand, conveying a sense of
immediate and total change.*

G. My love often fails … and it is so difficult with my family.

Raising the left hand:

— THE CREATURE YEARNS FOR LOVE.

Raising the right hand:

THE CREATOR LOVES.

The two are not balanced in you.
And this will continue to be so for a long time to come.

G. Last week, I expected your answer to appear on a white sheet, as
you had said. But it came in another form.

— *(smiling)* Your mistake was that you paid attention only to the form.

G. That is true, but you answered me just the same.

— THE TRUE QUESTION
BRINGS FORTH ITS OWN ANSWER.

*Hanna later warns me: "Don't ever – even for a moment! –
depend on the strength of your angel! Only your fire calls forth
the answer."*
After a silence:

G. Even now, I have tears of emotion in my eyes,
though I am well aware that you do not like
sentimental feelings …
— Such feelings separate you from me.
I cannot descend to that level.
True feeling is different, as I will soon show you …
Let us pray …

We all remain in silent prayer.
My heart lifts, and I am filled with a deep peace.

— *This* is true feeling.
May you be blessed!

Friday, August 13, 1943

8. DIALOGUE WITH LILI

L. I thank God that you have come again!
— I am listening to you.
L. Is it all right to completely let myself go when I am alone?
— Only upward.
L. Why am I so often in despair, and torn in half?
— You are not always united with your other half.
But you are not far from being ONE.

49

You are making progress.

L. Would it be right for me to teach small children?

— You are a child yourself. What is the problem?

L. I do not have enough contact with children.

— The separating veil is: what is known.
Believe me,
there is *no difference* between adults and children.

L. Why is it that I am so seldom able to be a child?

— KNOW THE DIVINE
AND YOU WILL AGAIN BECOME A SMALL CHILD!

L. I still try too hard to find the Divine.

— IT IS Ö WHO SEEKS YOU.
LET YOURSELF BE FOUND!

L. That is very difficult.

— That is your task. Help others to learn it too!

L. I would like to always feel as happy and fulfilled as I do now, but often, I just feel 'flat.'
Why does this happen to me?

— Because the sprout is still small.
Speak!

L. I am afraid to go back into the city …

Lili spends only the weekends in Budaliget. The dark political atmosphere in Budapest creates an unsettling pall that affects all of its inhabitants.

— What are you afraid of?

L. That the city will drag me down, because I am not yet strong enough.

— Fear not – I am helping you. We will be together.
The city has become an empty sea-shell …
inside, it no longer exists.

It is a petrified curse.
Even its dust is cursed, for nothing grows in it.
But in you, the sprout grows.
Take good care of it!
Raise your heart!

For the first time in her life, Lili feels the force of true prayer. She bursts into tears.

— See how near Ö is! If you raise yourself up
into the infinite, we can always be together.

Friday, August 20, 1943

9. DIALOGUE WITH GITTA

Last night, I had a dream: I am standing on a seemingly end-less plain. Suddenly, a white horse of tremendous strength and beauty appears. At the same time, a spiral-shaped pathway winds up into the heights. I feel that the white horse would be able to carry me into these heights.

— I am ready.
G. What does the white horse mean?
— Become able to ride it!
G. How ?
— By becoming lighter than the horse.
G. What is it in me that is so heavy?

During the dialogues, Hanna's language is of exceptional beauty and simplicity, close to the very roots of Hungarian. However, in this case, she finds only a trivial slang expression for what is to be communicated, and my angel is reluctant to accept this:

— Don't let yourself '*be done in*' by the deceiver!

I recall that I was very judgmental the day before.

G. Oh, do you mean yesterday? Yes, I fell right into the trap. How could I avoid that in the future?

— Be more *aware!*
 Ask!

G. How might my pictures radiate the new Light and awaken desire for it in everyone who sees them?

— The Light shines through you.
 I will tell you something.
 LIGHT is the same as light.
 They sound the same, but the weight of the sound
 – the resonance – is different.

G. Should I take up painting?

— You will surely succeed at it.
 Each of your pictures is a step upward.
 Begin at the bottom. Don't fly!
 You have wings, but many others do not.
 Do you understand now?

G. Oh, yes – now I do!

I am happy, and Hanna feels my angel rejoice.

— We can already talk together. Ask!

G. How can everything I do become an offering?

— Every act that is not for yourself is an offering.

G. How might I free myself from my '*little I*'?
 I despise it!

— By *not* despising it!

G. I do not mean my body …

— I know perfectly well what you mean.
It is clear:
you despise it because you are afraid of it.
It teaches you in the same way as I do.

LEARN TO LOVE THE CURSED,
AND YOU WILL FIND YOUR RIGHTFUL PLACE.

G. What is the quickest way to find my place?

— BY NOT HURRYING ...

The one who hurries, hurries only towards death.

Pointing in the direction of the garden, where Joseph is reading.

— He tarries ...
G. Who?
— The *son.* I cannot name names.

I realize that our 'given' name is not the true one – that which expresses our deepest, inner nature.

— IN HASTE, YOU APPROACH DEATH FROM THE FORE.
IN LINGERING,
YOU APPROACH DEATH FROM THE REAR.
IN ACTING AT THE RIGHT INSTANT,
YOU KNOW NO DEATH.

Hanna sees an image of what has been said: life itself as a vertically vibrating line, fine as the finest edge of a sharpened sword blade.
By acting in the right instant, we are this line – in the 'here and now' – and alive.
If we rush, we are in the future: death from the fore. If we linger, we are in the past: death from the rear. Acting at the right instant is being in touch with eternity.

— Enough for today.
You will be able to create.

The hands hover over mine,
and I feel a force pass through them.

Friday, August 20, 1943

9. DIALOGUE WITH LILI

L. May I ask?

Affirmative gesture.

L. I don't understand the lesson I received last week in Budapest.

Lili had tried to sense in which of her students the new seed
might sprout.

— DO NOT JUDGE!
Ö is the driving force.
If a seed is there, it will sprout.
Do not try to find where it is ...
Your judgment is not necessary.

L. Thank you! And thank you for last night's dream.

— Being awake is more important
than dreaming dreams.

L. I would like so much to be awake ...

— YOU ARE DREAMED.

L. What does that mean?

— DREAMS ARE IMAGES – YOU, TOO, ARE AN IMAGE.
BUT SOON THE DIVINE WILL AWAKEN IN YOU.

L. How can I help the members of my family?
— You have a big family. Ö helps through you.
Have faith!
L. Why do I have pains in my back and neck every morning?

> *An undesired, youngest child, Lili has been oppressed by her family since birth. Now the angel makes her aware of her 'real' family: all of humanity.*

— You were obliged to bow before the *unworthy.*
If you bow before Ö – Who alone is *worthy* –
you will be made straight again.
L. Does every physical illness have a psychological cause?
— A tree bears fruit. A good tree bears good fruit.
Matter is neither good nor bad,
for it is essentially inert.

THE PAIN IN YOUR BACK
DOES NOT HAVE ITS ORIGIN IN YOUR BACK.

Now it is my turn to ask a question:
What have you been happy about lately?
L. My dream, my good day in the city and, most of all:
you.

— ONLY IN JOY AM I PRESENT.

May you be blessed by Heaven!

> *I notice that the word 'God' is seldom used. Perhaps because this word has been so overused and covered with speculative thinking and sentimental emotion, and has lost the sense of the sacred? But when 'HE' or 'HIM' are voiced, we feel touched to the depths of our beings, and we experience a sacred dimension.*

Friday, August 27, 1943

10. DIALOGUE WITH GITTA

At last, a week of joyful anticipation!

— Let us give thanks!

With a radiant smile:

— Today it is good to be here.

Hanna later tells me that, during the first dialogues, she had often felt how difficult it was for my teacher to descend and be in our dense atmosphere. Now my joy makes it much easier. Pointing to the glass of water:

— Water brings me closer to you.
What *water* does for me ... *fire* does for you.

I understand that the more I burn in joy, the nearer I come to my angel ... but the angel's fire must correspondingly be diminished with water, that I might support it.

— How can I help you?
G. When I touch someone I love, I often feel a force streaming through my hands, but not through my eyes. Why is that so?
— I will explain it to you:
You strive from below to above.

The hands form a cone:

This is how you are formed:
strong below ...
ever more slender toward the top.
Matter is inert.
It is your task to raise it up.

Indicating the eyes:

— Matter and spirit meet here.
Matter needs to be raised to this level,
for here it ignites and radiates out through the eyes.

Indicating the throat:

— But here you block the rising force with emotions,
it becomes water and flows back.
From the throat to the eyes,
matter becomes ever more subtle, but still it is matter.
Keep the way pure!

(Silence)

G. I am not yet able to act at the proper moment …
— What needs to be done has a voice,
and you have ears to hear it. Close your eyes!

I obey, and feel a force streaming into my ears.

— From now on, you will hear better. Ask!
G. I suffer from not being able to love enough …
— Do you know why?
G. It might be because I was unable to paint …
— You were unable to paint
because you were unable to *love.*

EVERY TRUE ACT SPRINGS FROM *LOVE.*

Take heed! 'The nameless one' led you astray.

*I am immediately aware of what this refers to: yesterday,
two young students had made the long way from Budapest to
Budaliget and unexpectedly appeared at our doorstep. I had
been on the verge of leaving – to 'sing for my angel in the
forest' – in preparation for the next dialogue. After hesitating*

57

briefly, I left it to Hanna to deal with the young visitors and went on my way. As might be expected, however, I was unable to sing. Everything seemed meaningless, and a feeling of utter emptiness made any contact with my angel impossible.

— 'The nameless one' can assume even *my* form in order to lead you astray.

It now becomes perfectly obvious to me that I behaved unfeelingly in this situation. I am gripped by a fear of not being able to feel the difference between my true, inner teacher and some false one.

— You can recognize 'the nameless one' in your heart, for its name is 'emptiness.'

G. I know that emptiness and meaninglessness are traps, but still I fall into them.

— In the moment that you *know* it, it is already too late.
You go too far: you fail to stop when you should.

I then realize that, because my attention is usually directed to the outside, I tend not to notice that 'the nameless one' has slipped into me until it becomes obvious in my outer behavior. Were I to direct my attention inward, however, I could then detect the danger in advance ... and thus become able to defend myself.

— Ask.

G. Why do I have such a burning sensation in my eyes?

— Because you weep. You are wasting water for tears.
Everything that lives needs water in order to shine.
You would already be able to shine, but instead you weep.
You are lacking this water.

G. What is the difference between true and false feelings?

— True feeling is inwardly 'immobile.'
But you love first *this* ... then *that* ...

58

Gesture indicating the motion of waves:

— Water moves, in waves.

TRUE FEELING IS MOTIONLESS,
LOVES EVERYTHING ... AND *SHINES.*

Your sign is the SUN.
The sun is motionless and shines everywhere.
This is not the sun you see with your eyes;
that, too, is but an image.
Speak!

G. For a moment, I felt my task very clearly,
but then everything became blurred again.

— THIS MOMENT LASTS AN ETERNITY;
IT NEVER BEGAN, AND IT CAN NEVER END.
ONLY *YOU* WAVER.

Give your best effort!
I always take your image with me
and present it to the chorus.

> *Hanna sees a transparent image of me, which my angel super-*
> *imposes upon earlier, transparent images. Thus, any changes*
> *I go through from week to week become clearly visible. The*
> *images of me are placed in the center of a large cone, formed*
> *by the chorus of angels. All eyes are now focused upon the*
> *images, with neither judgment nor criticism, but a SIGHT that is*
> *all-penetrating.*
> *From above – from the focal point of the cone – shines the Gaze*
> *of the Divine.*

— May Heaven bless you!

> *The next day, Hanna explains to me that my feelings themselves*
> *are, of course, vital; nevertheless, I know that I need to find a*

new or different attitude towards them. If rising feelings are repressed prematurely, they become stuck in the throat and are choked off. If they are allowed to rise freely, all the way to the eyes, their initial strength becomes diluted into tears. But if feelings are offered to the Divine just as they reach the level of the throat, then their force becomes transformed into Light, which rises up and shines out through the eyes.

Friday, September 3, 1943

11. DIALOGUE WITH GITTA

It has been a very difficult week and I am feeling quite discouraged. We sit waiting for a long, long time, and Hanna senses that my teacher is having a hard time trying to reach me today.

— Speak!

G. I thank God that you could come.
   Please teach me true prayer, so that my feelings might rise above the level of water.

— Its name is: *offering.* I will explain a great rule to you:

EACH TINY CELL PRAYS,
AND THE PRAYER OF ALL CELLS TOGETHER
IS TRUE FEELING.

Do you understand this?

G. Not completely …

— For you, raising yourself is difficult –
   For me, lowering myself is difficult.

60

G. *(in despair:)* It should not be difficult for you!
I want so *much* to do … to make it easier for you!
— Do not attempt *much!* Your task is the 'less.'
The *less* is difficult!
See the difference between *much* and *less!*
Much is watery, diluted.

    Gesture flowing downward:

— *Much* of the population is diluted.
Less is nearer to the Divine.
And the Divine is ONE.

    *This lesson seems to concern the opposition between dilution
in the 'much' and concentration in the 'less' – as with the cone,
which is broad at the base and narrow at the top.
Long silence.*

— Lift up your heart. Today it is not easy to be here.
G. This week I was able to love a bit more, but it is still far from what I
am longing for.
— The moon is bright only when the sun shines on it.
But you are not a moon.
Do not wait until it is required of you to shine!

YOUR MOONS ARE DARK.

    *With my inner eye, I see a sun that devours its own rays. The
utter horror of this image is unbearable.*

G. How terrible!

    *Hanna often suffers from stabbing heart-pains without apparent
organic cause. Her dreams are premonitions of catastrophic
events.*

G. What can I do about the pains of my friend …

A forbidding gesture interrupts me:

— Are you still without faith?!
The two of you are united in the *task.*
Individuals, fates, destinies, events ... are no more than froth on the
waves of the sea.

What I have heard leaves me stunned,
and I remain silent.

— You have two questions left.
G. The sun is my sign.
I understand this, but I do not yet live it.
— You also hear my words only with your ears.
G. Why was I unable 'to sing for you' yesterday?
— Because I was far away from you.
G. Was that my fault?
— It was a trial, not a punishment.
I was there, where we one day will be united.
The distance indicates the size of your task.
Nothing is concealed. We see everything!
Honor the Divine Law in even the smallest thing!

Realizing the enormity of my task,
I am discouraged.

— Rejoice! You have every reason!
It is all a trial.
Let me console you: you are beginning to take form.
I will always be with you.

Friday, September 3, 1943

11. DIALOGUE WITH LILI

Lili, who was unable to attend last week's dialogue, has been having a very problematic time, and she feels depressed.

— Lay down your burden!

L. I do not understand.

— Has this week been heavy?

L. Very heavy ...

— Anything that weighs heavily is a burden.

L. Why did I fall so terribly deep?

— The one who helps descends into the depths.

I GIVE YOU THE KEY TO THE DEPTHS.
ITS NAME IS: THE TASK.

You are chosen.
You can *descend* at any time;
you can *ascend* at any time.
This depends on you alone.
Are you aware of this?

L. Yes, I am, and I thank God for this grace.

An intense silence filled with prayer follows.
With amazement, I discover the power of the word.
Lili pronounced the word, 'God,' and immediately her angel was
filled with a deep adoration; Lili then quite naturally followed.

— It is I who transmit each of your thoughts,
each of your prayers, each of your acts.
Never forget this!
In each of your acts, I am always at hand.

IN EACH OF YOUR ACTS,
YOU ACT IN MY PLACE.
TAKE HEED! DO NOT DISFIGURE ME!

There is only one wall that can separate us:
I might call it the 'deceiving one,'
your 'false self.'
Do not forget the key!

I CAN BE PRESENT IN EACH OF YOUR ACTS
IF YOU ACT WITH ME.

Many trials await you.
I am always with you.

Friday, September 10, 1943

12. DIALOGUE WITH GITTA

> *Today we are all very happy: for the first time, Joseph is attend-ing our dialogues as a silent listener. He has read our notes and feels them to be true nourishment.*

— In the Name of the Divine; I wait.
G. Thank you for last night's dream.
   I have been able to learn from it,
   but I do not yet understand the 'timeless.'
— What is it that you wish to know?
G. By now, I should understand the timeless
   since you have already spoken to me about it.
— 'Yet' and 'already' are time.
   I teach you, and *yet* you do not understand.

That is what separates us.

G. How could I bridge this distance?

— WITH THE MIDDLE.
THE ACT AT THE RIGHT TIME
IS AN ACT OUTSIDE OF TIME.

Only there am I, and there you understand
with your heart, not with your head.
Is that clear?

G. (overjoyed:) Oh, yes!

— *Now* you listened with your heart.
The timeless is now, because you expected me *in time*.

Turning to Lili:

— I bless 'the one who helps.'

This blessing fills me with joy.

— Your joy lightens my presence. Ask!

Inwardly, I had recently seen an intense blue light.

G. What is the blue light?

*Abrupt, forbidding gesture. I feel this is a question not to be
asked until a time when I am able to live in the intensity of this
blue light.*

G. I am so happy you are here …

— THANKS TO UNFATHOMABLE GRACE.

Silence.

— I will teach you. Your sign is the sun.
Close your eyes!

I do so.

— Do you see the sun?

G. No.

— Try to imagine it! That suffices.
Now do you see it?

*I try to imagine a glorious sun in dazzling splendor.
My teacher draws a circle before my eyes.*

— Now do you see it?

*My face is tense as my eyes roll searchingly
beneath the lids.*

— You *want* to see more than necessary.

Drawing a new circle.

— And now ... do you see it?

Inwardly, I see a sun appear in a cloudless sky.

G. Yes.

— Good. Is the image clear?

The image of the sun wobbles unsteadily.

G. Not yet.

— You are still *wanting.* Tell me when it becomes clear.

The image becomes clearer, but I feel nervous and heavy.

— Calm yourself!

Drawing a third circle:

— ... and now?

I concentrate only on the sun and see nothing else.

— If the image is clear, open your eyes!

FEELING, WANTING AND WISHING ARE TEMPORAL.
THEIR END IS THE GOAL OF YOUR WAY.

The image of the sun is now perfectly clear;
then it gradually fades away.

— Now you have arrived.

I open my eyes.

— Take heed! You are already gliding.

Only as I feel myself sinking into ever denser layers do I notice
where I have been.

G. Yes, I am gliding.
— You will learn. It is still difficult,
both for you and for me.

> *I intuitively realize that, for a brief moment, I had reached a*
> *never-before-known intensity of life, in which my not-yet-fully-*
> *awakened senses were incapable of perception. And thus I was*
> *left only with the feeling of absolute emptiness, a void. Was this*
> *a first attempt at something which could become a natural state?*
> *Hanna subsequently tells me that she observed me in different*
> *layers, the lowest of which were very dense; these were covered*
> *by brighter ones above, and translucent ones at the top. She*
> *adds: "Normally you sink and rise in these layers of feelings*
> *and thoughts. But when you succeed in raising yourself above*
> *the surface, you are in timelessness. This moment is eternal."*
>
> *Silence.*
>
> *A gesture of my teacher requests water, and I hand a glass to*
> *Hanna. Her drinking of the water weighs her down, easing the*
> *descent of my angel.*

— How heavy water is! Do you have a question?

G. In what way am I still *pagan* ?

— Be pagan in every way, for that is the root of all things. You should now blossom, but this is not possible without roots. You are making a mistake: there, where you do not *feel,* is where you are not pagan; there you are *rotten.* Throw that away!

I understand that where I am unfeeling is where there are dead tissues. Hanna later tells me that the 'deceiver' dwells in insensitivity.

— All of you! Be aware of the secret doors!
There the 'enemy' lurks.
Today 'the one who speaks' nearly fell victim
to the 'deceiver.'
We cannot *help* you there – we can only *warn.*
Do you have another question?

G. I would like to praise God in my every act!
How could I do that continuously?

— Today you *continuously* ask the same question.
Continuously is still time.
There is nothing more beautiful
than praising the Divine.
Let us praise!

Friday, September 10, 1943

12. DIALOGUE WITH LILI

L. I thank you for coming.
On what should I concentrate in my courses
in order to help as best I can?

68

— On *yourself!* If you are well,
  you will be given everything.
L. How can I tell when I am well?
— The sign varies, for you are always changing.
  But there is one sign you can always trust:
  and that is, if you can *love* ... really *love all;*
  for that is given to you.

THIS IS THE GREATEST GRACE –
FOR IT IS THE DIVINE IN YOU.

L. Now I understand the key to the depths ...

  Long silence.

— How wonderful the whole creation is! A WONDER!
  You may ask!
L. Why is asking so difficult for me?
— You were crushed when you wanted to ask
  and you have not yet recovered.

  *As an unwanted child, Lili had suffered silently and had never
  dared to ask questions.*

— Raise yourself up to the radiance
  and you will open like a lily!
L. I try to raise myself, but I feel that I am forcing myself unnaturally.
— Have you ever seen a little bird as it learns to fly?
  First, it opens its wings.
  That is what you forget.
L. What do you mean?
— The wing is a mediator between matter and air.
  You are a human being; your arm is your wing.

FIRST, LEARN TO EMBRACE –
THEN YOU WILL ALSO BE ABLE TO FLY.

There is no other way.

A gesture requesting water, which I bring.

— Everything is a wonder.
  I alşo admire the Divine in water ...
  Oh, if only you could wonder,
  for all of creation is wonderful!
L. Should I also be working scientifically?
— Yes, of course.
L. But I don't know what my field should be.
— Science is the child of wonder. Do not despise it!
  Wondering and being curious are very different.
  There are many who are curious.
  But there have also been some wonderers.
  They, too, were messengers.
  Seek them: they will teach you.
L. Books or people?
— It makes no difference.
  Just be sure that they are wonderers.
  To the seeker, a teacher will be given.
  You can find those who wonder in days of old,
  just as in the present day.

  (exalting:) AND THEY ARE COMING NOW.

L. How good it is to know that there are many wonderers!
— Ask!
L. I feel less and less clean, I feel impure.
  How can I help others, when I feel this way?

— EVERYTHING IS PURE WHICH IS IN ITS PLACE.

  You are impure
  only when you are not in your proper place.
L. Seldom do I feel that I am in my proper place!

— The source of 'the one who helps' is need.
  There is a great need for you.
  Today, in a time of unspeakable darkness,
  I have shown you the radiance of wonder.
  The root of darkness is in the human being,
  who looks without seeing.
  In infinite misery, humans suffer.
  Thus, be untiring, my little servant!
L. Why do people not know about, or even wish for, wonder?
— It is difficult to help those who are half-hearted …
  Have no fear, even that ability will be given to you.
  But *you* … never be half-hearted yourself,
  or you will be swept away!

  This terrifies Lili.

— May your heart know no fear,
  for in fear dwells 'the one who whispers.'
L. If only the force I feel now would grow!
— It will grow.

  FOR THOSE WHO CAN WONDER …
  WONDERS APPEAR.
  THE GREATEST WONDER OF ALL
  IS THE HUMAN BEING.

  Beneath your hands, wonders will sprout.
  I will be there. Darkness fades.
  May Heaven bless you.

Friday September 17, 1943

13. DIALOGUE WITH GITTA

We sit quietly and await the coming of my inner teacher. Outside, the village church bells begin to ring.

— Listen very carefully!
This ringing of bells is preparation.
A new Ringing will come, and *you* are the bells.
But you still try to ring in the old way:
Dark-light ... bad-good ... cold-warm.

These words are accompanied by a swinging gesture, back and forth.

— This speaks only to the ears.
The new Ringing cannot yet come
because the old bell is still swinging.
When it ceases to swing, hangs still in the center
... *then* the new will come.

These words touch me so deeply that my eyes fill with tears.

— The old bell still swings,
but this is the *beginning* of the Mass.

Long silence. In response to a gesture requesting water, I offer it joyfully. After drinking:

— Now *you* drink!

Astonished, I obey. Through the eyes of my angel, Hanna sees blue light reflected in the water. As I drink, she has the impression that this blue light is streaming throughout my body, even into the finest blood vessels.

— When you are hard inside,
  when something is blocked in your heart,
  remember this water.
  It dissolves everything. Do you feel it?

  I feel wonderful – this must be Divine grace!

— You give me water from *below*.
  I give you water from *above*.
  Give to all who thirst
  and the water from *above* will always flow.
  It is to the Divine that you give every drop.
  I came to answer you …

  *I am still overwhelmed by this experience with the blue water
  and all of the questions I had planned to ask have lost their
  importance.*

G. After what just happened,
   my questions have already been answered.
— You still have three.
G. What is the meaning of the veil in my recent dream?
— The veil is slowly disappearing.
  It is what has been, the child of the past.
  Your dream was woven of past and of future.
  But neither of these is important:
  only the *present* matters now.
  Everything else is but tiny waves
  on the surface of the ocean.
G. Why am I so often uncertain?
— The Divine is the only certainty.
  If you are always aware of this,
  any uncertainty in you will become certainty.
G. What is the ugliest thing in me
   that separates me from you?

Rapid gesture designating the furrow
between my eyes.

G. This crease? The will?
— Forcing.
G. And why do I force myself?
— Because you still love the old garments.
Once the eggshell breaks,
it is no longer good for anything.
Do not forget the water!
It dissolves all that is stiff and hard in you.

Turning to Lili:

— Do you have a question?
L. What is the difference
between the right and the left hand?
— There is no right or left,
for it is not the hand that acts, but the heart;
and it is ONE.
When the heart fails to act,
then both hands are left.
We are happy with you: heaven is with you!

Friday, September 17, 1943

13. DIALOGUE WITH LILI

— Let us rejoice together!
L. Why do I give up so quickly after beginning
something with great enthusiasm?

— At the beginning of a long race,
a good runner does not run quickly.
The runner's strength is concentrated;
it is not revealed right from the start.
Every beginning is *concentration,* not diffusion.
A minuscule hole in the egg,
and the bird is never born.
L. How could I detect this hole in the egg?
— It is difficult to understand,
but I will explain it to you:
The problem is not the *hole* ... it is time.
The hole damages only what is unripe, *immature.*

Silence.

— Listen carefully! The sower sows.
You are 'the one who helps.'
You cannot cut the seed *in two.*
Bury it deeply as a *whole* and it will mature
and bring forth a multitude of fruit.
This you can distribute.
But bury the seed deep ... deep in the ground,
and let the earth cover it for a long, long time.
You can hardly wait to begin distributing
the seed *right now.* This is your mistake.
Be patient like the earth from which you are taken,
and you will bring forth a multitude of fruit.

Silence.

— I teach you:
Pay attention to harmony in your work!
L. To harmony in myself?
— No. Many of your students are together
although they don't belong together.

Yet, all belong to you.
Arrange them! Arrange not with the head,
not with the heart ... but with humility.
The Divine arranges everything.

L. Why do I have such different feelings
when I am in the city
and when I am out in the countryside, in nature?

— Two forces dwell in everything that lives:
the force of life and the force of death.
One builds – the other destroys.

YOU ARE NOT ONLY A CREATURE OF CREATION,
YOU ALSO CREATE AND DESTROY:
ABOVE ALL ELSE, *YOURSELF.*

L. I feel that I create so slowly ...

— If you would completely entrust your work to the Divine,
you would not find it slow.

L. What is always hindering me?

— Not *always*! If *nothing* is hindering you, watch out!
What you have *once* done, you can *always* do again.
Do not worry! What hinders also strengthens.
The greater the hindrance,
the greater the trust in your strength.

THE MAGNITUDE OF THE HINDRANCE
IS NOT PUNISHMENT, BUT TRUST.

To all of us:

— Take care! There is no abyss, however deep,
no cliff, however high,
no labyrinth, however twisted that is not a *way.*
May you not be led astray by horror and fear!

If you have faith,
you can walk not only on water,
but also on nothing, on the black void.
Fear not! But take heed of one thing:
Never lean for support!

WHAT APPEARS TO BE YOUR SUREST SUPPORT
WILL BECOME THE DARKEST VOID.
DO NOT SEIZE THE SUPPORT
OR YOU WILL YOURSELF BECOME THE VOID.

There is but ONE support which never deceives:
the *ONE* and *ONLY.*
How wonderful: each of your steps over the void
will become a blossoming island,
upon which others can place their feet.
But take nothing old with you on the path!

THE VOID ATTRACTS THE VOID.

Make your way unclothed:
New and never-before-seen clothing awaits you.

 To Lili:

— Cast off the old in your work as well!
 Seek the completely New!
 Do not fear being naked.
 If you do not remove the old,
 you cannot dress yourself in the new.
 Ö dresses the lilies of the field.
 How could the Divine neglect to dress you anew
 when you have faith?
L. I feel how the old impedes me,
 but I don't yet see the new clearly.

77

— Do not see – have faith!
  Begin your work as if for the first time!
L. If only I were able ...

> *Sign of blessing over Lili.*

— You will be able.
  'The one who speaks' is tired,
  she has had a difficult time. Ask one last question.
L. Where should I begin to improve myself?
— What I say to you will sound strange:
  Do not paint yourself!
  True color is always given.

> *Lili has a habit of using rouge on her cheeks*
> *to hide her paleness when she is tired.*

— Paint conceals. If you are tired during your classes,
  do not be ashamed, and the tiredness
  will disappear. Never paint yourself,
  for true color is always given to you!
  Nothing can be hidden ... everything comes to light.

Friday, September 24, 1943

14. DIALOGUE WITH GITTA

— Let us greet the Divine!
  Joyfully I listen to you.

> *I am worried about Hanna, who has had an extremely heavy*
> *load to carry recently. She acutely feels the misery of the whole*
> *world.*

78

— Do not worry!
'The one who speaks' is light-hearted now.
Have you brought questions?
G. Yes. What is true humility?
— It is easy to recognize:

IF YOU BOW YOUR HEAD
AND FEEL UPLIFTED –
THIS IS *TRUE HUMILITY.*
IF YOU BOW YOUR HEAD –
AND FEEL LOWERED –
THIS IS *FALSE HUMILITY.*

In this way, you can always recognize it.
When you are with me, always carry your head high.
Bow down only when I, too, bow down.

YOU ARE MY EXACT LIKENESS, ONLY DENSER.

Do you understand?
G. *(with joy:)* Oh, yes!
I would like in every way to be your likeness –
an exact reflection of you.
— You already are just that,
you simply are not yet aware of it.
First you must awaken, point by point:

EVERY ONE OF YOUR CELLS MUST AWAKEN.

With the coming of light, you open your eyes.
In darkness, you are asleep.
Do you feel where you are still asleep?

G. Where I am insensitive ... without feeling?
— And where would that be?

> *I immediately indicate my heart.*

79

— Be careful! Be awake before you speak!

G. Then not the heart...?

— But where? This is difficult, isn't it?
  If you don't feel where you are sleeping,
  then waking up is naturally difficult.
  Shall I show you where?

G. Yes!... please do!

> *Pointing to the middle of my forehead*
> *between my eyes:*

— How wrong you were!

G. Here I am sound asleep. How might I wake up?

— You can only awaken when you cease to dream.
  As long as you pay attention to the dream,
  you sink ever more deeply into it.
  Those who wake up, however, say to themselves:
  "It is not true," and thus they awake.
  The dream is very similar to the waking world.
  Deceivingly similar. You all dream.
  'The one who speaks' dreamed deeply today
  so that you might see to what extent you are all asleep.

> *This is an allusion to Hanna's difficult day. But I also sense that*
> *it is a reference to our daily life from birth to death.*

— EACH STEP TO THE DIVINE IS AN AWAKENING.
  EVERY EXISTENCE – NOT ONLY YOURS –
  IS BUT A DREAM.
  BECOMING LIGHTER ... EVER MORE ENLIGHTENED...
  YET STILL A DREAM.
  THE ONLY AWAKENING IS IN THE DIVINE.

  I proclaim to you:
  When the ONE LIGHT penetrates into deepest gloom,
  then there will be deliverance.

We all serve it with joy and gratitude. With thanks.
You will be transformed from *'dreamers'*
to 'awakeners.'
Your goal is to attain the level where anyone
who looks at you ... awakens.

*I understand that we are to reach such a degree of inner bright-
ness that others quite naturally are awakened, just as we are
awakened in the morning by the sun.*

— I await your question.

I touch the middle of my forehead:

G. Why am I still asleep here? I am very curious and eager to hear
more.
— Think of the dream images! Are they necessary?
G. No ... or maybe as a trial ... I am not sure.
— I am referring to ordinary dreams,
when you are sleeping.
G. I don't always dream, so they must not be necessary.

Very sternly:

— Do you believe that anything is 'unnecessary'?
And forget the word 'why':
I will never answer this sort of question.

AVOID THE WORD 'WHY'
AND FULFILL YOUR TASK:
ALWAYS WITHOUT 'WHY'!

Now bow your head if true humility is in you.

*Grateful for the lesson, I bow my head
and my heart lifts.*

— The images of your earthly dream – of your existence –
are merely wrappings for their concealed meaning;
awakening can be found only *within* the dream ...
never without.
This is why you do not awaken.

*I realize that I have not been seeking awakening
in fully experienced daily life.*

— Every dream is a wrapping ... you cannot yet grasp it.

A gesture requesting water:

— This is a 'dream drink' for me.
How wonderful everything is! Unfathomably concealed and at the
same time transparently clear:

WHAT IS CLEAR TO ME IS CONCEALED FROM YOU.
WHAT IS CLEAR TO YOU IS CONCEALED FROM THEM.

*The word 'them' is accompanied by a downward gesture indi-
cating the mass of still 'sleeping' human beings.*

— ONLY TO THE DIVINE IS EVERYTHING CLEAR;
EVEN WHAT IS CONCEALED FROM ME.

How wonderful it all is!

Silence.

— Above is below in the dream, and heavy is light.
'The one who speaks' was above today
and believed herself to be below,
for she was dreaming.
When you are below, you feel well.
Your goal is to be above and nevertheless to feel well.
Because of weight and heaviness,
it is still difficult to be above and to feel well.

Silence.

— I speak now to 'the one who helps':
Your attempts are a good beginning.

*This week, Lili introduced head-stand exercises
in her courses.*

— The fault hides in habit, in the accustomed.
In the unaccustomed, in the reverse, it comes to light.
Turn everything upside-down! Always!
In yourself too! Habit is death, the concealer,
the deceiver who is lurking, the hidden enemy.
It slips into habits, into the insensitive,
into nothingness.
But the deceiver has power only when hidden,
for everyone else is stronger.
Deception has only one strength:
the lie, the half-hearted, the concealing.
The Divine is also still concealed,
but one day will become visible.
My time has come to an end. Do you have a message?
G. I send thanks.
— I will deliver it. May Heaven be with you!

Friday, September 24, 1943

14. DIALOGUE WITH LILI

Today is Lili's birthday.

— I greet you on the day of your birth.
You are in truth newborn.
Your understanding is still weak,
but I watch over you.

L. Could I receive an *order* that I am to obey?
Even when I do make a decision, I am too weak to follow through
with it.

— The little child is still weak.
When it feels well, it eats without being *ordered.*
It smiles without being *commanded.*
The smile is your task.
You are able to smile without *orders!*
The Divine sends you nourishment
and I bring it to you. Everything else is superfluous.
Why do you believe that you need a command?

L. So that the command would always be in me
and lead me to God.

— God ... and *command?*
Ö always gives and never demands,
for Divine strength is infinite.
Only the masses require *commands.*
But you are free.
You can accept and refuse.
You can raise and lower yourself.
It all depends *solely* on you. Could you kill?

L. I hope not ...

— Then why 'Commandments'? Believe in yourself!
Do not lack faith!

L. That is why for a long time
I wanted to commit suicide.

— But you did not do it, for you have a task.
Are you still afraid now?

L. Oh, no!

— You see, not only I watch over you:
the prayers of many straying in darkness
keep watch over you,
for you are the only way out for them.
They desperately need your help
and they watch even better than I.

*Lili senses that every step out of darkness
she takes is also taken for others.*

— You are dear to me. Ask!
L. I would like to learn something about my sign.
— What do you want to know?
L. If I knew more about it,
perhaps I could be of more help.

	The sign of the Divine	Your sign	The two signs united: deliverance

—

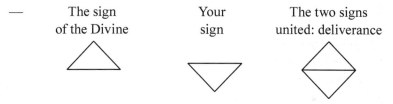

Your sign is the mirror-image of the Divine sign.
Pray thus, hands on the heart:

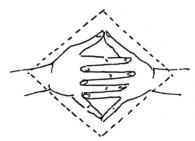

— And over your sign will rise the sign of the Divine.

In the moment of this praying gesture, Hanna's entire being serves and her face assumes an expression of dignity and solemn beauty.

— Ask, my dear one!
L. I am so unsure of myself,
   so uncertain at the beginning of the school year.
— I thank Ö that you are uncertain.
   Uncertainty contains the ONLY certainty.
   What appears certain is death.
   The new is always uncertain.
L. I seldom try out new things in my courses ...
— It is not *you* who tries out:

YOU ARE TRIED OUT.

That is sufficient.

I ask myself if the dialogues are trials for establishing a lasting and conscious relation between human beings and Divine forces.

— Where do you feel inadequate?
L. I do not taste the new enough in my work ...
— Do you ever feel the new at all?
L. I always expect more ...
— Can the new be measured?
   The tiniest new particle is greater than all the old.
   It cannot be weighed. Can you grasp in your heart
   what this tiny particle of the new means?
   It is able to change everything everywhere.
   It takes away the taste of the old.
   The old will become unbearable to you.

THIS TINY PARTICLE OF THE NEW IS THE SEED
OF THE DIVINE KINGDOM IN YOU.

Blessed is the soil that welcomes the seed,
and blessed its fruit!
Do you still doubt in your heart?
L. Oh, no!
— Then it is good.
L. If only it would last!
— The seed is indestructible, that is certain.

After a short silence, turning to me:

— Do you know what the veil in your dream signifies?
The old dream veil is no longer needed.

Pointing first to me and then to Joseph:

— What was a veil for you, was a wall for the 'son':
the ancient wall which humans have built between themselves
and the Creator.
— But the time has come for the old walls to crumble.
The dried out, hardened walls
will be pulled to the ground.

Indicating Joseph's task:

— He, 'the one who builds,' will construct new walls.

A gesture requesting water, which Lili brings.

— I *asked* for water, I did not *command.*
And it was easy for you to bring it.

LISTEN TO THE BIDDING!
IT OPENS HIDDEN STRENGTH IN YOU
AND EVERYTHING BECOMES EASY.

You will lift and carry mountains like soap bubbles.
L. How good it is to be so fulfilled!

— Believe me: the cup is always filled
for those who have thirst. Water does not exist
because of the cup: it is for the one who thirsts.
I am not here by *command.*
It is your bidding which brings me.
Ö allows me to serve and I serve with joy.
You may ask!

L. Relationships between men and women
are sometimes quite problematic ...

— There is only *one* way for you:
to *give* and not to *receive.*
Only from the Divine can you receive.
To all others: give!
You will be given all that you need.
As long as you feel a lack,
it means that you want to receive.
My little servant, is this not so?

L. How clear it is!

— Do not stray away from the way
and all will be given to you,
for the way is all.
Shall we part?

L. *(humbly:)* As God wishes!

— I am always on the way:
there we must not part.
I too have a way,
and it is the same as your way.
The strength of 'the one who speaks' is at an end.

Let us all give thanks!

Friday, October 1, 1943

15. DIALOGUE WITH GITTA

— The time is near when I will no longer
need to descend to be with you.

These words fill me with great joy.

— WHAT IS WAY FOR YOU – IS WEIGHT FOR ME.
WHAT WEIGHS HEAVY ON THE EARTH – IS THE WAY.

Deliverance uplifts the weight
and it will cease to be.
But as long as we are not united – we cannot lift.
Every ecstasy is a foretaste of weightlessness
and that is why humans seek it;
but they do so in the wrong way.

BE ECSTATIC WITH DIVINE DRINK,
BE DRUNK WITH LIGHT!
THAT IS THE SYMBOLISM OF WINE,
THAT IS DIVINE BLOOD.

Virtue, kindness and good intentions
are but empty vessels without the drink.
Thirst after the Divine drink with unquenchable thirst
for It alone brings deliverance!
What can you give if you have nothing in you?
Without drink, you are but miserable clay vessels.

TO THE ONE WHO ASKS TRULY,
DRINK WILL BE GIVEN.

Is that heavy for you?
G. No.

— Is it difficult to carry?

G. No ... it uplifts.

— Behold! Every ecstasy honors the Divine.
Lesser ecstasy is consumed by greater,
but it lives on within it. Nothing is lost.
Let there be no doubt in your soul!

THE ECSTASY OF BEING DRUNK WITH LIGHT
IS THE MOST SACRED OF ALL.

After a long silence:

G. I am thinking about my past.
My love relationships have been unworthy ...

— ... because they were self-serving.
Animals do not mate for selfish reasons;
but this instinct in humans
has been contaminated by too much intellect.
You did not serve.

G. How could I correct this fault?

— From what do you want to free yourself?

G. From the weight of my past.
It is so barren, and I am ashamed.

— What is weight?

*With the asking of this question, all of my previous values
instantaneously change to their opposites. Everything I have
despised, everything I wanted to forget, all that was oppressive
weight, now becomes the greatest treasure: my way.
Tremendously relieved, I reply:*

G. Weight is the way.

— There are many weights – there is but one *way.*
Every weight has a name – the way has no name.

WHO IS WEIGHTLESS ON EARTH – IS WAYLESS.

The matter you have taken upon yourselves is the weight.

IF YOU COULD SENSE THE LONGING OF THE WEIGHT
FOR LIGHT –
IF YOU COULD GRASP THE YEARNING OF THE LIGHT
FOR WEIGHT –
THEN YOU WOULD TASTE ECSTASY.

Hanna is hardly able to bear the intensity
of these words.

— 'The one who speaks' is a fragile vessel;
she is not yet able to bear the force.

After a long deep drink of water:

— I have descended. You are dear to me … ask!
G. I have no more questions,
but I thirst after your words.
— They are not *my* words.
G. Last week you asked if I had a 'message' to send.
I feel that you expected something other than gratitude… than
'thanks.'
— For each and every thing there is a time.
At the rising of the sun, the earth pays homage
to its Creator. That is the 'message.'
When the Light reaches you,
you too, will 'pay homage,'
whether you want to or not.
I put you to the test and I was not disappointed.
I know the seed to be in good soil. Ask!
G. Is the moment of death more important
than any moment of life?
— Only for those who have *neglected their task.*

How can you ever know of a given moment
that it is not the last?

IF YOU ARE *ONE* WITH THE DIVINE,
THERE IS NO DEATH.

I will answer two more of your *numerous* questions.

*The rather ironic tone amuses me, for I actually do have a long
list of carefully prepared questions in my pocket.*

G. I tell lies easily and often have little relationship
    to the words I am saying …
— A rocky cliff: in the stone are many different layers.
    If a heavy layer lies on a weak one … it slides.
    The load presses and slides … and continues to slide.
    Pay attention to the weak layer!
    Never speak untruth! Engrave this in your heart!
    Avoid even the shadow of a lie!
    Two weights resting upon one another
    are the foundation of the cathedral.
    If they slide … all is lost!

THE WORD IS THE BEARER OF LIGHT.
THE TRUE WORD HAS WEIGHT –
THE FALSE ONE IS WEIGHTLESS.

The deceiver rejoices at the breach,
which is an open invitation for 'the father of all lies.'
The lie loosens, demolishes, crushes, divides.
It is not violence which destroys the walls, but deceit.
You have one more question.
G. What is the meaning of last night's dream?
— It is up to *you* to interpret the lesson of your dream.
    That is why it is given to you in a dream.

I am very disappointed at this unexpected rebuke. Until now, the dream interpretations of my angel had been tremendously helpful. Now I become aware that, for quite some time, I had neglected to actively look for explanations myself. I had thought: "Why should I? The angel will give me a better explanation anyway!"
This laziness in thinking on my part is undoubtedly the reason for my teacher's refusal to help.

Friday, October 1, 1943

15. DIALOGUE WITH LILI

— Each of the thoughts you send to me
   is like a fine thread, light as breath, and yet strong enough to
   counter the force of a thousand ropes,
   with which the earth pulls you to itself.
   How difficult it is to raise up, but how necessary!
   It is so difficult to raise your arm
   when a thousand ropes pull you back.

> *The raising gesture of the arm expresses the difficulty of lifting while hindered by the ropes.*

— My little servant, be very careful,
   for that is the heart of all your work.
   Do you understand?
L. Not completely.
— What is not clear?
L. Should I fight against these ropes?
— Imagine that you consist of a hundred points.

93

Each point is connected to the earth by a rope.
A hundred points!
From each point, however, a ray also ascends to God.
Those who have forgotten the *way*
feel only the ropes and they foolishly want
to become free from them; *they do not accept them.*

EVERY POINT THAT IS NOT ACCEPTED
IS A CUTTING OFF FROM GOD.

If a hundred points are heavy, then all is well.
If they are weightless, it is 'outer darkness,'
straying from the way.
Your task is to connect the hundred points with God.
Ninety-nine are not enough.
Light is the hollow tree stump,
light, the seedless fruit,
light, the dried-out thistle.
But the fruit-laden tree is heavy.
Each of its branches bends to the earth,
and yet its sweet burden is light.
Teach *the weight* to those whom you protect
and they will again find *the way.*

> *Vertical gesture from above to below,*
> *followed by its reverse:*

— The line of the downward pulling force is the same
as the line of the uplifting force:
only the direction is different.
Weight ... (downward gesture)
and faith ... *(upward gesture)* are one and the same.
And this is nothingness:

> *Agitated wave-like horizontal gesture suggesting a feeling of*
> *meaningless.*

94

L. Does the waxing and waning moon affect our acts?

— THE ESSENCE OF THE CREATED WORLD
IS THE HUMAN BEING.

One half of the human – the unspoiled half –
is beyond the created.
One day all forces will *serve you,*
but until then, *you serve* them.
Knowing this,
you can measure how far you have come.
The sickle of the moon grows
and you don't grow with it.
Your fingernail grows and you don't grow with it.
Before God, the moon is no larger than your nail.
Soon you will understand.

IF YOU HAVE FAITH, YOUR BURDEN WANES
WITH THE DIMINISHING POWER OF THE MOON.
AND YOUR STRENGTH SWELLS
WITH THE INCREASING FORCE OF THE MOON.

> *After a brief silence, Lili's angel again addresses the subject of
> weight:*

— Where weight disturbs, *there* is the error.
The hundred points should all bear weight,
each to the best of its capability.
L. Atmospheric pressure oppresses me …
— Just as with the moon: *use* the pressure.
It can become a wonderful ally
if you work not *against* it, but *with* it.
Let it press you, and you will master it.
It can press you only as far as the ground.
No further.

It will help you to find the proper distribution
of weight.

IF EACH OF THE HUNDRED POINTS
BEARS EQUALLY,
THEN THE PRESSURE HAS NO MORE INFLUENCE
OVER YOU.

Try it, and you will understand!
How foolish the human being is!
Like a king who fights against his own people!
But *He* said: "Love thy enemy!"

EVERY FORCE IS ENEMY IF YOU DO NOT LOVE IT.
YOU CANNOT LOVE IT IF YOU DO NOT KNOW IT.
BECOME ONE WITH IT,
AND THEN THERE IS NO ENEMY.

L. I am seldom humble, and that pains me.
— What stops you?
L. I *forget* to be humble.
— But don't you see: that is just the answer!
Practice being humble!
Just think of it, and you can always be humble!

THINK OF THE DIVINE
WITH EVERY BEGINNING,
AND YOU WILL FEEL
EVER LESS DISTANT FROM Ö.

That is the goal.
It is time to depart.

Friday, October 8, 1943

16. DIALOGUE WITH GITTA

> *We wait in silence. Just as I feel the wordless presence of my angel, a mosquito stings Hanna's arm.*

— Help 'the one who speaks'! Moisten her arm!
I shall return!

> *I care for Hanna's arm. There is a long silence. Finally we hear:*

— Listen carefully: This is such a tiny creature,
and yet it disturbs tremendously.
Thus pay attention even to the smallest mistake.
WHAT WAS GOOD BEFORE
IS FROM NOW ON NOTHING.
Rejoice! We expect much of you:
your task is great and very difficult!
May the song that you send upward be perfect!
Remember: you sing it for Ö!
What is the first of your many questions?
G. What sort of weight am I supposed to carry?
— You foolish little donkey!
How could you possibly know how heavy the load is!
Lift as much as you can – *that* is the measure,
for you lift it in place of many others.
You will be able to lift ever more.
How could you know such a thing beforehand?
The lifting of weight has nothing to do with suffering.

WHAT YOU LIFT FOR OTHERS
CANNOT WEIGH ON YOU.
ONLY WHAT YOU *NEGLECT* TO LIFT WEIGHS ON YOU.

G. (with relief) Thank you!
— I await the next question.
G. How can I defend myself against the dense,
 numbing fogs which so often engulf me?
— Dense fog, heavy layers of mist descend to the earth when the force
 of the sun is weakened.
 If you burn and blaze brightly
 at all times before the Divine,
 then where could there be fog?
 Ask!
G. How could I tear down the wall that is between me
 and others and makes me unfeeling toward them?
— The wall is not where you believe it to be:
 you are unfeeling with *yourself.*
G. With myself...?
— With *yourself!* Every tool is sacred.

 Again a fog separates me from the meaning
 of what I have heard.

— Fog?
G. Yes ... I do not quite understand.
— You have destroyed yourself!
 Do you still not understand?
G. I do understand ... but how might I correct it?
— By giving protection to others.
 There is no other way. The wall is in you.
 You have built it with your own hands
 and hid behind it from the Divine.
 Most people hide in this way.
 So you have plenty to do.
 What horrible prisons!
 Some day all the prisons will open,
 but not for the self-imprisoned.

Eternal darkness, horrible impenetrable darkness!
It is unbearable to be without light.
Help to tear down the prison walls!
Here we cannot help ... but *you can,* my servant,
for you know what a prison is.
Burn! And Heaven will be in you ...
Everything will become possible for you.

FOR THE STRONG, SIN IS A LESSON.
FOR THE WEAK, IT IS DAMNATION.

> *With these words, the traditional interpretation of sin and guilt*
> *loses its power: a joyful sense of responsibility overcomes me. I*
> *feel that everyone is given the force to overcome sin, but many*
> *avoid the effort of seizing it, because this involves responsibility.*

— You may ask!
G. How can I immediately be aware of whether I am forcing myself?
— Pay attention not to the effort, but to the force!
G. How is that possible?
— Can you feel when force is streaming out of you?
G. Yes.
— This streaming is inherent to force.
When you become tense, you block it.
G. How is it blocked? What is my mistake?

— THERE IS ONLY ONE MISTAKE:
TURNING AWAY FROM THE DIVINE.

Let every act, every thought
be like a flower opening before Ö,
and there will be no mistake.

> *The enormity of this challenge crushes me:*

G. Then I must begin to live in a completely different way!

— Not in a *different* way: a *better* way!
By going a different way – not your own –
you will not advance more quickly, even if you hurry.
Do you have any more questions?
G. There is still much deception in me ... but where?
— Where do you feel the force that is given to you?
G. In my activities? When I paint?
Or when I *really* love ...?

I am interrupted by a forceful affirmative gesture:

— Everything else is deceit and unworthy before the Divine!
G. ... Then I am extremely unworthy!

With great severity:

— DO NOT JUDGE!

The laws for water and for the thirsty are different.
Water as water always quenches thirst.
But the thirsty are not always aware of their thirst.
If water is too cold, it freezes ... the thirsty die of thirst.
If water is too hot, it evaporates ... the thirsty die of thirst.
In their thirst, humans kill one another.
But blood is not water,
and they become even thirstier.

*The severe admonition, "Do not judge!" gives me to understand
that if I underestimate myself, I am like frozen water. When I
overestimate myself, I am like evaporated water. When I live in
the middle, without judgment, then the thirst-quenching water of
life can flow through me naturally.*

— Let us open our hearts and adore Ö!
I depart.

Friday, October 8, 1943

16. DIALOGUE WITH LILI

*The day fades. We utilize the pause between the two dialogues to
rearrange the lamps and provide a more pleasant illumination.
Suddenly, the light goes out. I stand up to turn it on again, but a
stern voice stops me:*

— I put it out!

*We immediately become conscious of how irrelevant it was to
give the aesthetic question of lighting such disproportionate
importance, thereby keeping Lili's angel waiting.*

— Turn on the light!

*I switch on a single lamp
and reach for a second one.*

— Enough! Impenetrable darkness!
A movement ... a flick of a switch ...
and the human makes light.

Pointing to the light bulb:

— A sacred force is captive in a prison of glass,
and for humans the peace of night is taken away.
Behold! The earth is covered with prisons!
But you have the key. Where are you a prisoner?
L. In my habits.
— This is your *own* prison. Where does it weigh on you?
L. Habits always return ...
— They do not return:
you simply do not leave them.
It is up to you.

L. Two things worry me: fear of the new,
and clinging to the habitual.
— The eternally true IS:
Habit is not.
Habit is the dark, the eternally untrue.
In habit, we cannot meet.

IT IS NOT NECESSARY TO BELIEVE THE BELIEVABLE.

L. How could I free myself from all of the obstacles
that are in me?
— They are not in you. The obstacle is the *task*.
Do you first try everything yourself
which you demand of others?
L. Not everything.
— The obstacles which you feel in yourself
are everywhere.
Along the *true* way, there are no obstacles;
they are only on the *false* way.
Only if you walk the *false* path
are there obstacles between you and me.

    Silence.

L. Is there anything we could do against the horrors of the war?

    Lili is stopped by a rapid, forbidding gesture:

— NO! WAR IS THE HABITUAL.
IT IS NOT POSSIBLE TO FIGHT THE PAST.
TURN YOUR HEAD
TOWARDS THE NEVER BEFORE HEARD!

    *I understand that only the coming new Force can transform the
old, habitual impulse to kill.
Silence.*

L. The school year is beginning and I have many doubts.
— Did you feel it in the same way last year?
L. No ... not as strongly.
— Then you are on the right path.
   The way that leads to corruption is broad.
   The true way is narrow;
   so narrow that it must be traveled alone,
   for it has to be cleared by oneself.
   The *never-before-seen* lights the way.
   The never-before-heard leads you.
L. Why do I immediately become impatient when I find
   something good and new ... and then want more of it?
— It is not enough: always thirst
   for the good and the New!
   The one who thirsts will always be given to drink, always!
   You can never be thirsty enough,
   because you are not asking for yourself only.
   The measure of 'the one who helps'
   is different from that of the masses.
   You all are helpers.
   Let us send a thought to the Divine!

Friday, October 15, 1943

17. DIALOGUE WITH GITTA

Along with much of the population of the region, Hanna has had
the flu and a high fever all week. I am worried that she might
not have enough strength for today's dialogue. Nevertheless, we
wait in silence as usual at three o'clock.

103

— I am ready.

G. Thank God!

— Never worry; never be of little faith!
Ask, for time is short today.

The angel is obviously aware of Hanna's limited strength.

G. How might I feel like a treasured instrument
so that I might be more just with myself?

— Who created you?

G. God.

— What the Divine creates is sacred.

YOU ARE NOT ONLY CREATURE –
YOU ALSO PARTAKE OF DIVINE FORCE.
THUS YOU ARE YOUR *OWN* CREATURE.
ACT ACCORDINGLY!

You have called forth good and evil.
Choose the good and evil will disappear,
for no one is there to create it.
What you form *now*
will not turn against its creator.
The vessel which you once formed is already empty
and devoid of strength.
It cannot harm you.
Ask!

G. In what way do I least resemble you?

— EACH OF YOUR QUESTIONS
CONCERNS ONLY *YOURSELF.*
IN JUST THIS WAY
WE DO NOT RESEMBLE ONE ANOTHER.

That is your mistake.

The source of all things is so infinitely far away
that your veiled eye cannot see it.
Follow the line that emerges from the infinite;
follow it joyfully, freely,
and all burdens will disappear.

> *Something opens up inside of me and I breathe a sigh of relief.*

— It is already lighter.

> *Just as the church bell begins to toll, someone begins to pump water with the rusty hand pump in the neighbors' garden: a loud creaking sound results.*

— Two voices ... do you hear them? They battle.
But the third will win: the new.
THE NEW VOICE IS: SILENCE.
In you, there is no silence.

> *Gesture indicating the hard metallic up-and-down movement of the pump handle, followed by the gentler ringing of the church bell.*

— Either you strain yourself ... or you swing along.

SILENCE IS NOT DEPENDENT UPON NOISE.

Fleeing from noise serves no purpose.
Wordless, soundless, unmoving:

SILENCE IS THE TOTALITY OF ALL SOUNDS.

> *Silence.*

— Are you expecting anything else from me?

G. I am so glad that you are here.
— Listen carefully! There is a wonderful mirror in you:

A MIRROR THAT REVEALS ALL!
IT DWELLS INSIDE OF YOU
AND REFLECTS THE DIVINE.
BUT ONLY IN SILENCE.

If a tiny mosquito alights on its surface,
the mirror image is clouded.
If the mirror is not clear,
you cannot create.
Focus all of your attention on it.
Heaven does not hide before the wonderful mirror.

After a long silence, in a soft voice:

— Do you still not feel the miracle in your midst?
It dwells among you: the miracle of the SEVEN.
Its name is still concealed. It dwells among you.

Very softly:

— THE SEVENFOLD SOUL OF THE NEW WORLD,
THE GREAT MYSTERY.

Its foot, its foundation, is truth. You cannot yet see it.
Be true, so that you might see at least
the foot of truth.

THE SILENCE I TAUGHT YOU
IS THE SUM OF ALL MYSTERIES.

Act in the name of silence!

*We all feel that something of extreme importance is being
revealed to us. I eagerly await the angel's next appearance in
anticipation of hearing more about the seven-souled new world.*

106

Friday, October 15, 1943

17. DIALOGUE WITH LILI

— A wondrous chalice descended from Heaven.
Humans – what infants! – seized and dropped
the chalice, and it shattered into a thousand pieces,
into chattering fragments of clay: into words.
Multitudes of words are nothing –
only the ONE, the chalice, *is.*
It descends from heaven again and again …

   An encouraging smile invites Lili to speak.

L. How good it would be if I could smile like you!
— What is stopping you?
L. I don't know …

   Lili had suffered from an unhappy childhood.

— Your lack was joy. But from now on,
no joy will equal yours.
L. I have not even thanked you for the
several times you helped me last week.
— Several times, many times, often …
these are still but fragments, tiny pieces:
they are not yet the ONE.
If you rejoice ten times, there are nine gaps
between the ten joys.
In the beginning, you were created in infinite joy.
The ONE joy is possible for you.
Ask!
L. How could I attain true knowledge of human nature?
— True knowledge of the human does not exist,
for the HUMAN does not yet exist.

THE HUMAN IS SO GREAT THAT
NOT EVEN I CAN SEE IT.

The answer to your question came long ago;
you call it: *love.*
Love is now a mere splinter of clay,
but it will become ONE like joy:
ONE and indivisible.
Love is dawning in the four of you:
not when you are *together,* but when you are ONE.
Ask!

L. Why do we fall so easily into the depths,
into evil ways?

— If the one who falls reaches the bottom,
there is no more falling: only pain.
But why the fall? Because of not serving.
The one who fell let go
of the one and only real support: the UNGRASPABLE.
The graspable was reached for,
and *this* caused the fall.
The fall is not beginning now;
but *now* the bottom has been reached.
The ONE indivisible smile is the only help.

If you are together with the mourners,
then you also mourn.
If you are one with them,
you make them joyful.

> *Silence.*

L. Why do I have such a problem with time?
— Many hours will never equal eternity.

IF ETERNITY IS IN YOUR HEART,
TIME WILL BE BORN IN YOUR HAND,
AND FOR EVERYTHING, THERE WILL BE TIME.

Lili glances at her watch.

— Foolish toy! It breaks eternity into pieces,
and the human believes this makes more.

An indescribable wonder will be born:
the ONE.
Do you feel it, the ONE that approaches?
The ONE, the Whole, has nothing to fear.
Fear not, any of you, when you are ONE.

Silence.

— You may ask!
L. I am disturbed by psychoanalysis.
I have a feeling that something is wrong with it,
but I don't know why.

Freudian psychoanalysis is practiced in Budapest.

— It chops into pieces without having the ability
to put together again.
That is what is disturbing you.
To break apart is easy!
L. Those who understand it better than I tell me that
psychoanalysis does integrate and build up ...
— They are silly, like children
playing with building blocks.
They play around with the most sacred of tasks.
They are worse than all the others,
for they betray those who trust them.

THEY TEAR APART THE LIVING AND THE GROWING,
AND THEN THEY SQUEEZE AND CRUSH IT.

Everywhere it is the same:
torn and splintered fragments are glued back together.
But the waste will be swept away.
We don't glue things together!
Neither hour to hour, nor hand to foot,
not smile to smile, nor person to person.
There has been enough gluing!
The new Wine will not be poured into glued jugs,
for it would burst them!
The glue has many names: 'duty,' 'obedience'
and many, many more.
To paint over the glued parts is senseless:
The very announcement of the coming Wine
causes everything glued to shatter.
The shattering has already occurred;
now comes the new Wine.

I sense that the new Wine represents an intense vibration of life,
which causes old, worn-out values to shatter.

— Fear not! Live in the name of the ONE!

At the end of the dialogue, Hanna's flu is gone;
she is in perfect health.

Friday, October 22, 1943

18. DIALOGUE WITH GITTA

I am wearing a new dress.

— You chose your dress with care.
But dress your soul with even greater care
when you are expecting me.
(Smiling) I am pleased with the way you dress.
Ask!

G. How would it be possible for me to perceive the truth that is concealed behind outer appearances?

— Do you feel them as two different things?

G. No, but I have a tendency to see *only* the form.

— Tendencies and habits are the servants,
but you are the master if you realize
that you see only half of creation.
Pay attention to the other half!
You have *two* eyes, yet you have only *one* sight;
you have *two* ears, yet you hear only *one* sound.
In you are the *two* and the *one.*
Ask!

G. How might I keep from disturbing the unity of us four?

— You repeatedly ask the same question.

G. It is still so difficult for me ...

— It is *already* so difficult.
Rejoice at feeling the difficulty!

I feel overburdened, and I sigh.

— Is it *so* difficult, *so* heavy?

This question causes me to smile, and I relax.

G. It is better now …
— How light is the good, how light is the true!
  The stone does not know that it is heavy,
  nor does the corpse.
G. What is freedom?
— Serving. If you *serve,*
  you are united with the Divine
  and you are *free.*
  There is no more weight, no time, no measure,
  no quantity. Oh, if only you could serve!
  You may ask!
G. What causes the corruption of human sexuality?
  Animals are able to mate only at certain times,
  while humans can do so more or less at will.
  Is that corruption?
  What is the Divine Law for humans,
  and how could we find our way back to it?

  After a long silence:

— Listen carefully!
  The sacred force of which you speak
  is given for the new,
  but not for an ever renewing number of bodies.
  Human beings receive an amount of this creative force
  equivalent to what is lacking on earth.
  Not a great number of human beings are needed:
  the new Human is needed.
  Humankind *stole* the additional sacred force
  – this 'more' of force – and now it must be paid for …
  paid for dearly!

  *It becomes clear to me that the surplus force of sexuality is
  for transformation into the new Human and should neither be
  wasted on sexual extremes nor repressed through asceticism.*

— The new time is approaching when all of this
will no longer be. I proclaim the moment: it is near!
Rejoice from dawn till dusk!
Beauty never before known!

  Silence.

— You are the guardian of a sacred force.
Share it: do not keep it for yourself!
Then you have nothing to fear.
You are still afraid of the old. Without cause!
Raise the sacred force,
and the empty shell is left behind, powerless.
G. How could I *always* feel the force,
so as to radiate it without interruption?
— It is just the opposite:
You feel the force only when you radiate it.
The sun never sees its rays:
its moons *reflect* them.
Know this: The sun, too, is but a moon,
for everything mirrors the Divine Light.

The Divine contemplates itself in us.

BE PURE MIRRORS!

Clouded, cracked mirrors will be cast away,
for they do not serve.
What is still troubling you?
G. Nothing. I rejoice at your teaching.
— It is not *mine!*
With each day, it shall become easier for you,
and your joy will be perfect.
I take leave.

Friday, October 22, 1943

18. DIALOGUE WITH LILI

— Listen carefully:
Sin cannot be destroyed.
In truth, it does not even exist.
The name of all sin is: *'the no longer good.'*
The name of *all* sin!
But sin can be transformed by *'the not yet good.'*
Where is measure? Where is judgment?
With Ö alone.

Ö SENDS SIN
THAT YOUR EYES MAY SEE.

If you stay below, you judge –
You judge others as well as yourself.
Above, another way is open to you.

*These words wipe out the old notions of sin and guilt in me,
leaving space for a strong and vibrant feeling of responsibility.*

L. Why are we passive when we ought to be active ...
and the reverse?
— When do you feel this way? All the time?
L. No.

— ONLY Ö ACTS.

If you feel that *you* act,
then you are passive, you are inactive.

THE TRUE ACT CANNOT BE FELT.
YOU SIMPLY FEEL JOYFUL.

Evil only *seems* to be an act.

In truth, it is inactivity.

L. How are breath and soul related?

— What do you mean by soul?

Lili cannot answer and she remains silent.

— Do you see what you are asking?
What do you sense the soul to be?

Lili hesitates and stammers:

L. The highest in us ... that which is not body ...

— EVERYTHING IS BODY.
WHAT FOR YOU IS UNGRASPABLE SOUL
IS FOR ME A THICK WALL.

Can you grasp air? Truly, I say unto you: you can.
Only what it carries is ungraspable.
You drink wine and feel ecstasy.
Can you grasp ecstasy?

L. No.

— THE SOUL IS WINE – IT CARRIES ECSTASY.
EVERYTHING CAN CARRY ECSTASY.

L. Is the yoga practised here in Hungary good?

— What sort of yoga do you mean?

L. Hatha-Yoga, which comes from India.

— If it helps, then it is good.
Do not judge the seekers!
They seek. Though in reality, they do not seek;
they only believe they do.
In reality, they imitate.
New laws are coming and new Grace.
The new can be recognized by its *namelessness.*
Even the name of the 'highest Helper' became old.

115

The chosen ones already see the nameless new Light.
The others guard the husks of old grain.
The chaff will be burned, cast into the fire.
L. I have been told that Hatha-Yoga helps ...
— Hatha ... *perhaps!*

> *Once again I am amazed at the lively way the angel plays with*
> *words and I smile with pleasure:*
> *'Hatha' also means 'perhaps' in Hungarian.*

— *Perhaps* this helps ... *perhaps* that helps,
perhaps help will come from another *perhaps!*
They wander aimlessly
and there is no balm for their wounds.
Be aware! Do not leave your own place.
Do not stray from your path.
Those who stray wander in circles, again and again.
But you are there, at *one* certain point.

> *The point of certainty, the opposite of 'perhaps.'*

— Everything goes astray, but not you.
Behold! You cannot stray, for you never say:
"*Perhaps* this is the good"!
Everything moves, it twists and squirms.
The solid crumbles, the liquid coagulates.
What was certain is no more ... terrifying!
A narrow bridge spanning the bottomless abyss ...
that is what you are.
Take care of yourselves!
Are you afraid to be the bridge?
The bridge is well-protected,
for it is an absolute necessity.
Even the deceiver who comes and goes
can appear as a bridge.

116

But the eye not focused on the outside
detects such deception.
Be watchful! I will share a secret with you:
One thing remains unknown,
there is one thing of which the deceiver is unaware:
the new.

— THE DECEIVER CAN DRESS ONLY IN THE OLD.
THIS IS THE KEY TO AVOID BEING MISLED.

The deceiver has led many astray.
Engrave this into your heart!
In the name of the 'not yet named,' I bless you.

Friday, October 29, 1943

19. DIALOGUE WITH GITTA

— Listen carefully!
  I teach you the cause of all illness.
  You do not live for yourself.
  You are given your daily nourishment in abundance,
  but not without reason.
  It becomes a wondrous force in you.
  But beware if you keep the force
  only for yourself!
  Be careful, my servant!
  If you should sink down,
  it is not because of too much nourishment taken in,
  but too little *force* returned.
  You hold it back.

  REPENTERS AND ASCETICS ARE NOT NEEDED.
  THEY ARE NOT DEAR TO THE DIVINE.

  The new law, the new measure is different:
  you receive five loaves of bread
  for feeding five thousand.

  THE HOLDING BACK OF FORCE IS
  THE SOURCE OF ALL DISEASE.

  Sin is disease. May this be a lesson to you!

  I am overwhelmed by what I have heard.

— Lift up your head! Ask with a pure and light heart!
G. My greatest wish is to radiate …
  but why then do I hold back the force?
— The answer lies in your question: what is a wish?

118

G. Desire ...
— Not only that. It is a sign of distance.
You do not desire something you already have.

I realize that radiating is my nature; my task is to become conscious of this and to act accordingly.

— Ö created you to shine.
But there is a split between you ...

Dividing gesture, as though splitting my body in half.

— ... and YOU.
I will explain: this split, this dark abyss,
which was ... which is ... but which shall not be,
is also in you:

CREATED WORLD – AND CREATING WORLD.
BETWEEN THEM: THE ABYSS.

Look at yourself: You are the bridge.
You cannot wish for creative rays,
you cannot long to be the bridge,
for to be the bridge is *given* to you.
The bridge is not wishing – but faith.
What has not been ... what is not now ...
and yet shall be ... is deliverance.
Can money provide deliverance?
Can sacrifice, generosity, good intentions
or philanthropy lead to deliverance?
They all fall into the bottomless pit.
They are cast down and devoured by the depths,
for they are all nothing without the new.
Fathomless depths ... in vain do you throw
the old into it, for it will never be filled!

119

The ironic tone of the angel's voice is clearly telling me that with monetary donations, self-serving 'kindness' and so-called love of our neighbors, we will never be able to purchase peace of soul or deliverance.

— Thanks be given to the infinite wisdom of the Divine
that the small CHILD smilingly crosses over the abyss,
for truly what was concealed from the wise
has now been revealed to you,
little children that you are.

*Without my being aware of it, my hands
have clenched into fists.*

— (With a radiant smile:)
When you have a smiling faith,
your hands will open.

*I feel that this faith of which the angel speaks
is a creative force.*

— Open your hands!

I open them and a smile floods through me.

— Now it is good, for you smile.
Ask!
G. How is the human constructed?
What are the seven centers and what is their function?
— The seven levels:
Three of them you know,
and you think you know the fourth.

THREE ARE THE CREATED WORLD.
THREE ARE THE CREATING WORLD.
IN THE MIDDLE IS THE BRIDGE,
WHICH IS NOT KNOWLEDGE.

120

Stone, grass and horse are not followed by humankind,
but by the HUMAN, the *union* of the seven.
It is still difficult for you to grasp.

With a very soft voice:

— I am the Fifth.

I listen with the greatest of intensity as the
seven-souled world takes shape for me.

— The WORD is the fourth level revealed.
The WORD is sacred, the fourth manifestation.
It is the bridge between matter and spirit.

A horizontal gesture at the level of the mouth:

— The fourth level is the foundation of the new House,
the substance of Truth.
Take heed! Do not play with it, for from here ...

Another gesture at the level of the mouth:

— ... from here, the unredeemed, the bad, the false,
leak down and corrupt the first three levels,

AND THAT IS DISEASE.
But the WORD can raise up:
it can redeem the three lower levels.

ONLY THE HUMAN HAS THE WORD.
YOU SPEAK IN THE NAME OF THE DIVINE.

I speak only through the one who speaks,
for I have no mouth.
When I am united with you, I will have one.
Heaven bless you all!

After the dialogue, I beg Hanna to tell us what she experienced during the teaching of the seven levels of the WORLD. She sketches a diagram, warning us, however, that she had not been able to perceive the entire hierarchy of the Creating World, meaning that the diagram is incomplete.

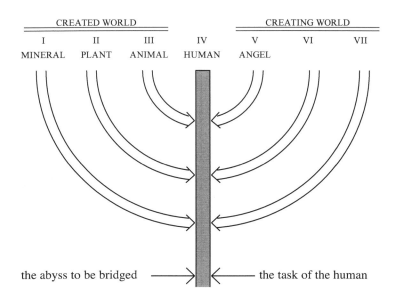

As Hanna draws the curve connecting the animal (III) with the angel (V), I at last understand what my angel had explained at the very beginning of the dialogues: "It and I are united in the task. Do not divide what is one!" Now I understand that the instinctive animal side of my being and the angel can only be united through me, the Human (IV), when I become a bridge over the separating abyss.

Friday, October 29, 1943

19. DIALOGUE WITH LILI

— I speak of the death of the *Highest Helper.*
Of what was the cross made?
Of what were the nails made?
They were made of the rumors about Him
that were spread everywhere,
the talk about his miracles.
The form in which the spirit dresses
is nothing but form.
The multitudes attributed the miracles to the form.
This is why the *Highest Helper* took the cross
upon his shoulders.
And He bore witness:
"It was not I but God who performed the miracle –
through your faith."

You, too, are a *helper.*
Help comes from the faith of the one who *is helped* –
not from *your* faith!
It is not you who perform the miracle,
and not I;
it is the faith of the one who *is helped*
that does it.
— Ask, my little servant!
L. How could we four serve better?
— Sound and harmony.
Four sounds are not necessarily harmony.
Ö is the sum of all sounds.
If you are united, it is a creative force,
a small harmony, the foundation of all miracles.

123

Only if your voice resounds purely,
without falseness, without pretense,
without personal intent, without alteration –
only then do you serve in harmony.
If individual responsibility is taken for each and every voice, there
will be no falsity.
The deceiver can sneak only into the false.
Ask.
L. Why am I always so tense?
— Think of the cross! His body was stretched upon it.
You stretch your body, too; but you become tense
because you give yourself too much importance.

BEHOLD: THE WONDER COMES ONLY
WHEN YOU FORGET YOURSELF.
THAT IS THE SECRET OF ALL SECRETS.

You tense yourself in vain –
this will not cause you to grow in the least.

*From the garden next door, the creaking
of a rusty hand pump can be heard.*

— So much effort just to pull a little water
from the depths!
And the rain falls effortlessly.
Wells dry out … ponds dry out … the earth dries out.

The creaking continues.

Everything creaks and rattles …
that is the 'harmony' of today.
Machines spit out lies with a rattle.
The living are shot dead with a rattle.
All eyes are lowered …
You may ask!

L. In talking with my pupils lately, I sometimes feel myself vibrating
all over as though I have fever ...
was this right?
— *Only* this is right. This instant is eternal.
Then *you are.* Were you tired afterwards?
L. Oh, no!
— You see, it was good,
for it was not *you* who labored at the great Plan.

THE HELPER IS THE BRIDGE
BETWEEN THE ONE WHO IS HELPED
AND THE ETERNAL HELPER –
BUT ONLY AS LONG AS IT IS NEEDED.

> *It seems to me that it is in some way our selfish 'little I' that*
> *wants to help more than is really needed, that wants to feel*
> *'important' in helping.*

L. I am unsure of so many little things.
For example: should I fast?
— The fasting of all fasting is the help you bring.
Fasting in itself does not help at all.
Do you know when it is right to fast?
When you have overeaten!
It would be better if you would simply not overeat.
But all this is really irrelevant, my little servant.

PAY ATTENTION TO THE *MORE*
AND THE LESS WILL SERVE.

L. What is an outburst of temper, of rage?
— To 'burst out' means to begin.
An out-burst is a springboard of force
beginning below and then boiling up;
but it can still be transformed and guided.

125

Take good care of it;
do not pour it out as rage.
Guard it and transform it ...
it is a sacred force.
ONLY IF BADLY USED DOES THE FORCE DESTROY.

L. On what should I concentrate in my work?

— As I have already said: your signpost is *joy.*
I cannot say it to you in a better way.
It is the surest sign.
BUT THERE IS ONLY ONE PLACE TO FIND JOY:
BEYOND THE 'OLD ME.'
Within the 'old me,' there is no joy.
Within the 'old me' is the *no longer good.*
Rejoice evermore in the name of harmony.
Soon we will sing in unison to the ONE JOY.

Now I clearly see the difference between these words: in the
language of the angels, the word személy *(person) refers to the*
'old me,' which no longer serves life. Egyén *(individuality), in*
contrast, serves evolution, the new.

Friday, November 5, 1943

20. DIALOGUE WITH GITTA

— Let us rejoice in the ONE joy!
I say to *you:* the bread you are given
cannot yet be eaten on earth.
It must first be baked in the oven.
Do not worry!
Neither the bread nor the oven burns,
only the wood, known as the 'personal.'
In the heat of its fire, edible bread is baked.
Listen well! The new already dwells among you.
Great wonder.
Joy will be your ever-present companion.
You shall be given wonders,
for you believed without wonders.
Ask, my servant!

I had painstakingly elaborated a theory of vibration in connection with movement and brooded over it for hours. I was quite impressed with my own intelligence.

G. How does motion amplify vibration?
— *(mockingly:)* What an 'intelligent' question!
Now listen to something new: forget about your *head!*

IT IS ONLY THE FIRST OF THE SERVANTS,
AND YOU ARE ITS MASTER.

But even the greatest of masters
is only a foot-servant of the Divine.
If Divine force vibrates through you,
then serve and do not interfere;
your head is of no use at all.

You reach out your hand in vain ... in vain.
If Ö does not dwell within, you are but a clown.
The servant dons the clothes of the absent master,
usurps the role.
But upon the master's return,
the servant is put to shame.
G. What is meant by 'Trinity'?
— If you have faith, it is in you:
The Creator ... the Father.
The Creation ... the Son.
The bridge ... the Holy Spirit.
In truth, ONE.
Ask!
G. How can I avoid falling into my 'little I'?
— You cannot *fall* into the 'little I,'
for you *are in* it. You *all* are in it.

THIS 'LITTLE I' IS YOUR GREATEST TREASURE.
DO NOT WISH TO LEAVE IT – *RAISE IT UP!*

Wood is transformed into light ... it is not lost.
What a wonder, the 'little I'!
The Divine has been forming it for you
since the beginning of time
and you – foolish child! – despise it.
You fool! If you are a good master,
it is a good servant.
And the impossible becomes possible,
and the inedible becomes edible.
When does bread become bread?
G. When it is baked ...
— No. Only when given to the hungry
does bread become bread.

20. DIALOGUE WITH GITTA

G. I have felt a tremendous pressure the past few days,
as if I were being pressed by a vice ...
what was going on?
— You are mistaken. That was not a 'vice';
all of the bread that you have not given to the hungry
was pressing against you.
G. What is holding me back?
— There are two bridges: the great and the small.
The small bridge is still weak.

> *I sense that, with the small, weak bridge,*
> *my self-confidence is meant.*

— Without a way, the bread cannot come:
it is blocked.
G. How can I strengthen my faith in myself?
— By uniting the two bridges,
which, in truth, are ONE.
A bad servant destroys the bridges
so that the master cannot return.
But the little CHILD crosses with a smile

AND THE CHILD IS THE MASTER.

Listen carefully as I repeat:

THE NEW, THE NOT YET SEEN, DWELLS AMONG YOU.
THE SMALL CHILD,
THE POWERFUL MASTER, THE NEW, THE ETERNAL.

ETERNITY IS NOT ETERNAL REPETITION
BUT THE ETERNALLY NEW.

I take leave.

Friday, November 5, 1943

20. DIALOGUE WITH LILI

— Spring is coming, heralded by
   a flower, a blade of grass.
   Religions, temples, churches and prophets
   are also heralds,
   but with the coming of LIGHT and FORCE
   there will be no more temples, no more churches:
   all will be temple and church.

   Who sees a single flower
   in the flower-covered meadow?
   You are not flowers – you are *spring.*
   In the Divine Garden, even *spring*
   is but a single flower.
   Ask!
L. Why do so few people have faith,
   and why does it not awaken in them?
— A network of concrete roads
   spans the entire face of the earth.

   THEY ARE BROAD, WIDE AND SMOOTH,
   AND MADNESS RIDES UPON THEM.

   There are many ways, a tremendous number.
   Do not be astonished that the small and narrow,
   the *only* way was forgotten.
   All the forces are consumed by madness. What is madness?

   A SACRED FORCE THAT WITHERS IN CAPTIVITY.

— But to you it is given to show the way.
   Ask!

L. Why do so few people recognize their *calling?*
— Because they are driven.
They do not pay attention to the *call.*
The purest voice is wasted if no one listens to it.
Listen carefully:
The new Eye grows in your eyes.
The new Ear grows in your ears.
The new Hand grows in your hands.
And you will SEE, HEAR and CREATE.
New Voice ... and old ear?
The new Ear is needed to hear the CALLING.
The voice, too, has a body.
It carries the inaudible, immortal Voice,
which is no longer body.
You are spring.
The new Eye, the new Ear, the new Hand
grow at your touch. The new is budding.
Ask!
L. Why is it so hard to help my family?
— To the old eye, the near is large
and the distant is small.
Look with the new Eye: the near will be small
and the distant, large.
The small still appears large – this deceives you.

IF THE DIVINE IS GREAT IN YOU
EVERY TASK IS SMALL, EASY AND LIGHT.

L. What is movement?
— The greatest of all.
Growth is not yet movement ...
wind is not yet movement ...
the flowing of water is not yet movement ...
decaying to dust is not yet movement ...
the wandering of stars is not yet movement.

131

All of these are only reactions, persistence of inertia.
Motion dictated by hunger, cold or desire
is compulsion.
But you ... you are already *free* to move.

THE ACT MADE FREELY IS MOVEMENT.

The helping Hand ... is Movement.
The radiating Eye... is Movement.
The raising of matter to a new dwelling ...
is Movement.
New creation: no longer captivity, but deliverance.
There is no other freedom.
If you awaken this in your pupils,
then each of their motions will become Movement;
not passive captivity.
In vain are there nerves;
in vain, tendons;
in vain, bones.
from nerves ... whips;
from tendons ... cords;
from bones ... clubs;
and from youth ... corruption.
Only true Movement redeems.
Teach this, my servant,
and bodies will be reborn at your touch!
They will rise from their graves
for now they are all dead ... they are all dead.
Do you accept this task?

L. *(Timidly:)* I will try ... where should I begin?
— Does fear still dwell in you?
L. I feel that my task is becoming ever greater and more urgent.
— Do you know how to begin the Movement in yourself?
  Pronounce these words: "I accept it!"

THE TRUE WORD RISES UP TO THE DIVINE
AND DESCENDS BACK TO YOU – AS FORCE.

The force of the vow springs from you.
The word of the vow is seed sown in Heaven
and its fruit will fall manyfold back to you.
You will have enough to distribute, my servant!
Faith sown in Heaven …
humans sow all their seeds only in earth,
and thus the earth dries out.

L. I don't quite understand the vow …

— Can you comprehend the incomprehensible?

REASON STOPS – BREATHLESSLY –
WHERE FAITH BEGINS.

Reason can never reach Heaven, for it is of the earth.
What is still confusing you?

L. I do not see the difference between *helping*
and the freely accepted act.

— ONLY THE FREELY ACCEPTED ACT HELPS.
NOTHING ELSE!

> *In the ensuing silence, I think of a recent dream
> which I have not been able to understand.*

— *(To me)* I speak to you.
Your dream is saying:
May wonder not be *in* you – but *through* you –
for you are not a flower – you are *spring.*
Wonder appears in the flower,
but who can grasp springtime?
If you are wonder, then you are a flower,
one among many.

Addressed to Lili:

— Does doubt still dwell in your heart?
L. I can hardly bear the abundance I receive ...
— You will bear it.
   I depart.

Friday, November 12, 1943

21. DIALOGUE WITH GITTA

— Now you are strong enough: hear my words!
   The next step will no longer be
   on the path: the old way comes to an end.
   There is not even water to walk upon.
   But woe unto you if you look back!
   If you truly have faith,
   a wayless way will bear your feet:

THE NEW EARTH – THE CHILD'S FIRST STEP.

But take heed! Not even faith will help
if you take along any of the old.
The old, 'the more than necessary,'
would pull you down
to sink like lead in the water.
Listen! The body has been formed for you
from the beginning of time.
Now listen carefully!

THE BODY IS NOT MEANT TO BE USED
IN THE WAYS YOU HAVE BEEN USING IT.

To make this graspable for you is very difficult.
I will return.

*Hanna can scarcely bear the intensity of what is communicated
about the new body.
She rests for a few minutes.*

— Listen: I tell you a secret:
You have come to the end of the way;
there is no more way. You *look* for a place
to put down your foot and you see nothing.
Nothing is there ... *because you look.*
The eye no longer exists for looking, as before.
Look no more with the old eye,
and there will be a new way under your feet.

THE BODY OF THE REDEEMER
IS GIVEN ONLY FOR GIVING.
THE REDEEMER IS NOT A HUMAN;
THE REDEEMER IS *THE HUMAN.*

The truly new is coming.

*Suddenly I comprehend: Jesus became HUMAN. We are all
called to follow His example: to become redeemers.*

I teach you, my servant!
Before every new beginning, sanctify the moment!
Be finished with the old:
look no more with the old eye,
hear no more with the old ear!
Open the old eye again
only when the new in you has opened
and then the new Light will shine through it.
For the body is given only for giving.

Now you can receive only from above,
no longer from below.
A truly new world opens up to you.
You will *live* it.
There will be no secret from you on earth ...
no heaviness, no gloom, no noise.
But woe unto you if you look back!
Take along nothing from the old!
The old, as small, light and worthless
you think it to be, would become a mountain of lead
in the New and that would be your end.
Detach yourselves from the old;
do not throw it away, but use it in a different way.
You still misuse the tool.

> *How can we become better tools? I realize that I am no longer able to draw the human body.*

The human body reveals itself to you only
when you no longer *look at* it.
If you wish to truly perceive it, close your eyes.
Then there will be no impediment.

> *Indicating Joseph:*

— The *son* anticipates best what is meant.
But it will become clear to you, too,
for the time is ripe.
The turning point of creation:
what you valued most, you will come to value least.

> *I have decorated the room with flowers and given careful attention to its aesthetic effect.*

— How carefully you have arranged this room!
Your arrangement has just one fault:

you *attach* yourself to it.
The more you decorate, the more you *bind* yourself.
Do not attach yourself to anything!
Attachments bind to the old, to the habitual.
You do not need that any more.
Seek only the new!
Amidst the flowers of your faith, I feel well,
no matter where you are.

I RELEASE YOU FROM EVERY FORM.
I HAVE NO EYES FOR SEEING
THE FLOWERS OF THIS EARTH.

But I see your festive expectation.
Ask!

G. How can I distinguish between what will become lead
in the new and what I can take along?

— The higher the mountain,
the less will be taken along
by the one who carries the load.
Still less when stepping into water.
What can be taken along
where there is not even water? Life itself,
Life itself and nothing else.
Ask!

G. What is soul? What is spirit?

— Spirit is the Creator.
Soul is the mediator.
Body is matter.
This is the Holy Trinity.

G. I have a feeling that the forces you mentioned earlier
are somehow associated with numbers.
What is 4? What is 7?

137

— If you would cease to look
at the numbers themselves,
you would sense their hidden force.
For behind everything dwells the *Force.*
Every form is a gateway to infinite forces.
For the one who has eyes ... the eye is the gateway.
For the one who has ears ... the ear is the gateway.
Each is given a different gateway ...
but the *Force* is ONE.

Rejoice in your hearts, for the new opens up!
Today I was able to bring you good news.
I depart joyfully.

Friday, November 12, 1943

21. DIALOGUE WITH LILI

— I teach you the end of suffering:
If the letter 'T' is written
with only the horizontal line,
and not the vertical,
you would not know what is missing.
Because you know the letter 'T,'
you can easily provide what is lacking.

You are those who help.
You have been sent to fill the lack.
Evil is nothing but lack.
You encounter a human being,
you feel a lack and you suffer from it.
Where is the end of suffering?

If you would know the *new letter 'T,'*
you would also know what is lacking here,
and you could easily provide it.

SUFFERING IS MEANINGLESS.

Learn the *new abc;*
then everything could be *perfect.*
For you, the secret lies in the *imperfect.*
How do you know that it is *imperfect?* From whom?

TO YOU IT IS GIVEN TO KNOW THE PERFECT.

How can you measure it?
What is your standard?

THE PERFECT IS REFLECTED IN THE IMPERFECT.

You suffer only until you are able to recognize
the Divine in everything.
New letters will be inscribed ... be aware!

SUFFERING GUIDES ONLY THE ANIMAL.
THE BEGINNING OF THE WAY
IS THE END OF SUFFERING.

   Silence.

— Everything grows – even the stone.
   The seed in mother earth,
   the child in the mother's womb ... why do they grow?
   The highest mountain, the tallest tree
   cannot grow to the Heavens.
   The strongest eagle cannot fly so high.
   But the smallest human can reach it,
   for Heaven is within.
   I await your question!

L. What is rest?
— Preparation.
Anything that is not preparation is only apparent rest.
Rest that is not preparation is indolence.
Another name for it is death.
The most wonderful rest descends on you
when you create.

THE RESTFUL ACT AND CREATIVE REST ARE TRUE.

They only appear to be *two:* in truth, they are *one.*
You may ask!
L. Where is Nirvana?

— THERE, WHERE TWO ARE ONE;
WHERE PARALLELS CONVERGE;
APPARENTLY REST – IN REALITY: ACT.
APPARENTLY SILENCE –
IN REALITY: UNISON OF ALL SOUNDS.
APPARENTLY DISTANCE – IN REALITY: WITHIN YOU.

Now I have a question:
What is your most passionate wish?
L. To always be with you and so to be one.
— And how do you expect this to take place?
L. I know that it will be the object of my work.
— It is not a matter of 'work'!
Then you would be 'object'-ified!
An *object* is what is densest.
(touching the table:) This is an object!
(touching a blanket:) This is an object!
(touching a hand:) This is an object!
Let objects be!
Your most passionate wish is *above* all objects!
You will never attain it as the *object* of your *work!*

L. What is nervousness?
— What is it? An army without a commander.
    When battle comes, there is no organization,
    for no one is there to command.
    The brain goes to pieces, order falls apart,
    for a uniting force is lacking. An order is given,
    and then is immediately followed by its contradiction:
    nervousness.
    This does not occur in our ranks:
    we are the Divine army.
    We battle against darkness.
    We hear the call and we obey.

    NERVOUSNESS IS LIFE WITHOUT A TASK.
    NOTHING ELSE.

    Do you have further questions?
L. Why is my memory so bad?
— Because your past was bad.
    It is unpleasant to remember it
    and you have drawn thick curtains in front of it.

        Pointing to me:

— Her past is also bad,
    but it no longer affects her.

        Turning back to Lili:

— You have not forgotten last Friday, have you?
    When you have created, when you have helped,
    then you do not forget.
    It is not your *memory* that is bad,
    but your memories.

        (Silence.)

L. My love is not strong enough …
— Where do you feel this?
L. In front of other people.
— Whom do you love enough?
L. So far, no one.
— Whom do you love most?
L. Ö.
— And after Ö?
L. You.
— *(smiling indulgently:)* Your eyes are still veiled.

IF YOU LOVE THE DIVINE, YOU LOVE EVERYTHING.
IF YOU DO NOT LOVE ENOUGH,
IT IS THE DIVINE YOU DO NOT LOVE ENOUGH,
FOR EVERYTHING IS DIVINE CREATION.

Love Ö in the perfect – admire Ö in the imperfect!
For everything mirrors the Divine.
It will not be difficult to love the Divine.
Above all, I adore Ö and thus I love you.
I take leave of you now.
May you be blessed!

Friday, November 19, 1943

22. DIALOGUE WITH GITTA

— I greet you.
I will teach you about gold.
It is the least useful of all metals,
for it serves no purpose.
What gives it value? The faith invested in it.

The human invests faith in objects
born of the earth, causing them to be cursed.
Curse is forbidding.
Without the curse, you would be straying.
You begin your journey carrying a golden ball.
You carry it. The ball is very heavy,
but you carry it just the same.
Then you arrive at the border of a land
where there is no more faith in gold.
What becomes of the gold?
Only the weight remains.
What is there left for you to do then, my servant?
G. Drop the ball.
— Open your hand,
and the ball rolls down by itself.
Dropping the weight is really not difficult,
but your fingers are cramped from carrying the ball
and you are unable to let it fall.
What is heavy falls by itself.

There is also gold in the new land:
not glittering metal, but Light.
How can you receive the new ball
if you are still grasping the old?
You clutch it like this ... like this you clutch it:

> *A gesture with clenched fingers ... then the hand tilts slightly, as
> if to let the ball roll down.*

— See how easy it is to let it fall!

> *Silence.*

— It is a heavy ball, an innocent globe that you live upon.
Thanks to infinite Divine grace, it became cursed
so that you would not adore it ...
so that you would not adore it!

143

The innocent earthly globe waits to be redeemed.
How will it be redeemed?

BY LEAVING ADAM BEHIND.

I sigh and something in me is released as I relax.

— Is it loosening?
All of you: How well we know the difficulties
of letting the burden fall,
for you have become accustomed to its weight.
Do not regret that the weight burdens you.
The one who carries gold does not feel its weight
as long as gold is something that is believed in.
If the belief is withdrawn, only the weight remains.
You are on the right path.
G. All week long, I searched for something
that would relieve my tension … how could I find it?
— Give it *time,* for the hand is rooted in time.
I await your question.
G. Who am I?
— It is not a good moment to ask;
you are just re-forming yourself.
And when you are completely trans-formed,
you will have no more questions.
G. What is the meaning of my sign, the sun?
— The sign is an image that can help you
to understand your task.
A child asks what *seven* is.
You show it *seven* apples.
The child is fond of apples,
and quickly learns what *seven* means.
You would not show it seven whips.

144

G. What did you mean when you said not long ago:
   "The images of our earthly dream – of our existence –
   are merely wrappings for their concealed meaning;
   awakening can be found only *within* the dream …
   never *without*." ?
— You have slept long enough, my little servant!
   One who has slept long enough
   awakens without help.
   There is no need to be awakened!
   Lack of strength closes the eyes.
   Filled with strength, they open by themselves.
   Lack of strength is blindness, sleep.

THE HUMAN SLEEPS FOR LACK OF STRENGTH.

   How could the day, the new day, be begun
   if one did not have the strength to *act?*
G. How good it would be to already now awaken others!
— You talk in your dream.
   You four are all asleep in one room.
   You dream of one another.
   You believe you are talking with each other,
   for the dream image is deceptive.

   The dreamer does not dream of being asleep,
   but of waking … coming … going … talking.
   Yet in reality, the dreamer sleeps.
   Then comes the dawn and the dream-mist dissolves.

THE NEW ACT NEARS.

   Every dream will be fulfilled –
   for the dream, too, is preparation.
   In the womb of the mother,
   the unborn child dreams of daylight.

Without this dreaming,
it could not be born into the light of day.

ALL THAT YOU DO NOW
IS DREAM-ACT ... IS DREAM-THOUGHT.

Dream ever more beautifully, always;
for all dreams become reality!
The dream, too, is faith.
I am waiting.

  (Silence.)

G. I cannot live loosely and freely now;
   my head always rushes ahead.
— If only you could see yourself for but a moment:
   you lie in space and sleep, motionless and calm ...
   your feet do not rush.
   Each of your movements is but dream ... only dream.

  I think of my blind rushing.

— Do you actually get anywhere when you rush?
G. Only on earth ...
   it is just my habit to rush!
   How horrible habit is!
— Take heed! Do not look back!
   The *horrible* is a blind force.
   Horror is the old god.
   If you see horrors, you see the old gods.

BUT THEY ARE NO LONGER GODS:
YOU ARE THEIR MASTER.

You see, my servant: today there was no noise.
The burden fades away
when you loosen your grasp on it.
I depart.

146

Friday, November 19, 1943

22. DIALOGUE WITH LILI

— Let us greet the Lord of the wheat fields!
  I speak to you of the wheat:
  Your hand is empty but soon it will be filled.
  Listen! You have ten grains of wheat; no more.
  You can distribute them just ten times –
  not twenty.
  Can a grain of wheat germinate
  if you split it in two?
  Even if you have done it with the best of intentions?
  In a grain of wheat dwell the old and the New:
  it cannot be split.
  With your human mind, you cannot differentiate
  between the old and the new.
  Even what you consider to be new is old.
  Do not separate, do not judge … *sow!*
  Then the new will grow:
  the new which is neither seed nor sprout.
  For all that is but a dwelling for the new.
  Let the seed fall intact, as a whole!
  Only in this way will it multiply –
  it will germinate!

THE TIME OF NEW GERMINATION HAS COME.

L. I do not quite understand what I am doing wrong.

> *Lili is exhausted. Her pupils have been coming to her with their personal problems day after day until far into the night; and Lili is unable to say 'no.'*

— You have ten grains of wheat.

147

You cannot give them to twenty people.
But *sow* them and soon there will be a hundred.
Heavenly Wheat is quick to provide grain.
I am waiting.

L. What is karma?

— A WHIP FOR LASHING ONESELF.

Today this question is too difficult for you.
It conceals a great secret.

*We are all familiar with the concept of karma in Hinduism, and
I wonder what the secret concealed behind this theory might be.*

L. And what is health?
— Balance. If it is unsteady, there is a lack.

ONLY IN THE ANIMAL
DOES BALANCE COME FROM THE BODY;
NOT SO IN THE HUMAN.

L. Why did I previously prefer teaching the ill,
whereas I now prefer teaching the healthy?
— You are becoming healthy yourself.
The health in human beings is the soil
in which you sow the seed.
Heavenly Seeds in *bad soil* ... ?

To all of us:

— Do not worry! A wonderful transformation begins.
It will not always appear good to you,
for the old hulls burst, rot and decay.
Do not be afraid!
What happens to you now is no small matter.
You, too, my little servant: do not worry.
What happens to you is good.
And now I leave you, but not for long.

148

Friday, November 26, 1943

23. DIALOGUE WITH GITTA

— Today I will continue to talk about gold.
Where does it come from? Of what is it the fruit?
The fruit of the tree of knowledge.
Adam reached for what *glitters*
instead of what *shines.*
There is another tree:
Mystery is its name – Light is its fruit.
The tree of knowledge is the possibility
of *becoming* human –
the other tree is *being* Human.
Gold contaminates the earth.
What is superfluous must burn.
Gold cannot be burned.

EARTHLY LIGHT IS *INVOLUNTARY* BURNING.
HEAVENLY LIGHT IS *VOLUNTARY* BURNING: SACRIFICE.

The first tree – the old 'I' – reflects light.
The second tree – the new 'I' – radiates Light.
To mirror is different from radiating, from being sun.
Ask!
G. What is rhythm?
— First came rhythm … then came song.
There is rhythm without song,
but no song without rhythm.
Rhythm is body; melody or song is soul.
Body and soul carry the third.

> *I think of the music of Mozart. Is it the rhythm that moves us? Is*
> *it the melody? No, it is the inexplicable 'third' which so touches*

our heart. It is the Divine impulse which gave birth to Mozart's rhythm and melody.

G. How could I come closer to my feeling of rhythm?
— First was rhythm – then the Word.
   Original vibration ... first day ...
   primordial ground of all mysteries.
   In the mighty vibration of the new Creation,
   new Names are born.
   Your Name, too, is born of rhythm.
   With rhythm you can create,
   with rhythm you can destroy.
   The new Ear hears it.
   The beat one hears is not rhythm.
   Are you able to follow me?
G. Oh, yes!
— You may ask!
G. Does the form of the sphere have a meaning?
— What would a half-sun be,
   shining on but half of creation?

THE SPHERE IS THE IMAGE
OF GIVING WITHOUT JUDGMENT.

*I think of the sun which shines everywhere,
simply because this is its Divine nature.*

— The new harvest is Light, not glistening metal.
   Because the human speculated for so long
   about how iron could become gold,
   gold became iron.
   And this iron smashes down on the human.

*We live in a time of war, of which the iron weapon is a symbol.
And war springs from the greed for power, for gold.*

— Transformation, burning.
  Only the human *kindles* fire;
  all else can only *be kindled.*
  The altar is ready.
  Kindle fire in honor of the Divine!
  But set fire only to the superfluous,
  not the altar itself!
  If you could, you would set fire even to the altar,
  for at this point you are but the 'priest's apprentice'!

  We all burst into laughter.

— Speak, my little servant!
G. What is true offering of self, true sacrifice?
— A miracle! The most beautiful song,
  the most beautiful scent, the most beautiful light:
  all of this *ascends* to the feet of the Divine.
  But only the most delightful, the most blissful!
  Not tears, not self-torture, not sorrow!
  They are all but smoke that *descends*
  and covers the earth with a dark layer.
  Incomplete burning becomes smoke;
  incomplete offering becomes pain and torment;
  imperfect sacrifice is not Light but coal dust;
  not transformation, but decomposition,
  soot, gas, decay.
  Blow on the fire! I will help you!
  Learning is a form of burning, too.
  But for you, my words are merely wood
  that has not yet been kindled,
  wood that is just lying about.
  You will receive no new wood!

  The old law: trees grow, are felled and burned.

New trees grow, are felled ...
But the tree of life is everlasting:
its fruit is Light,
its trunk is the fire of the old tree.
This tree will no longer be burned
for it gives LIGHT.

THE HUMAN IS NOT THE CROWN OF CREATION,
FOR EVERY CROWN IS MADE OF GOLD.
THE HUMAN IS THE *SOUL* OF CREATION.

May heaven be with you!

> *Hanna later tells me that 'bringing the words down' to us was*
> *more difficult today than ever before. My inner guide had moved*
> *a certain distance away from us, like a mother bird moving ever*
> *further out on the branch, then finally hopping to another one,*
> *as a 'teaching method.' A baby bird then has three possibilities:*
> *to stay where it is ... to fall ... or to fly for the first time in its life.*

Friday, November 26, 1943

23. DIALOGUE WITH LILI

— Do you know what beauty is?

THE ACT OF THE GOOD SERVANT
GIVING MORE THAN THE NECESSARY.

The body moves ... that is necessary.
Dancing is *more* ... and if it is truly dance,
it is beautiful.
Voice is necessary ... song is *more.*

To form is necessary ... only the *more* is beautiful.

THE NEW WORLD WILL BE BUILT ONLY OF BEAUTY.

Be good servants, for only the act
which is *more* than what is necessary
can build the new world.
It cannot be built of anything else.

    Silence.

— I teach you:
    Take heed of all the 'Judas'
    who put the Word up for sale.
    They are around you now.
    Wherever fire burns,
    true and false will be separated.
    That is the purpose of fire.
    Are you aware of that? Take heed!
    Among the twelve there is always a traitor:
    the most miserable.
    This is how it must be – do not be troubled.
    Raw ore *can be* put to great use,
    metal *is* indeed useful, and
    slag is trodden underfoot.
    The fire divides and purifies.
    That is as it should be.
L. Should I do something about the traitors?
— Nourish and protect the fire!
    Do not worry about anything else!
    Ask!
L. In the functioning of the organs, what is necessary
    and what is more than necessary?
— The organs have only one *more:*
    the child born of the body.

ONLY WHAT HAS A LIFE OF ITS OWN IS *MORE*.

All else is waste, curse.
The beauty of the young maiden renews itself
one day in her small child –
not in the painted face of the childless.
Organs cannot accomplish *more* – humans can.

> *Hanna later explains to us that the more of the body is the
> earthly child, while the more of the human is to bring forth the
> new Child of Light.*

— But in today's world,
   only the body is known.
   Only the body is 'built'
   and it becomes uglier all the time.
   The feet of the one who dances for personal gain
· become vulgar,
   and the teacher of such dancing is even worse!
   Do you have any more questions?
L. What is resistance?
— In the created world, it is the urge for *more*.
   Ö does not resist you.
   But you, you resist the Divine.
L. And what is force?
— Soon you will be able to understand this,
   but now is not yet the moment.
L. What is flexibility?
— The basic condition of life, the proper resistance.
   The rigid cannot resist.
   What flexibility is for you,
   is force, vibration in the new World.
   Only motion is force.
   The motionless, the static, are never force.

Force and flexibility belong together.
What a difference there is between
resistance and rigidity!

L. What is the mind, reason?

— CONDUCTION ... BUT NOT THE CONDUCTOR.

How clear this becomes for me! The instrument ... but not the
master. The mind, reason, is merely an instrument. I think of a
concert grand piano. Only when a master comes to play on this
finely tuned instrument does it give forth divine music.

— You lick the sugar-spoon and say: 'sweet.'
It is not the spoon which is sweet.
If you try to bite the spoon,
you can break your teeth.

Silence.

— My little servant, are you happy?
Be happy, all of you,
for your life is beautiful when you serve.
The new is as beautiful as the old is ugly.
But be careful:

IF THE FULL-GROWN ADULT CONTINUES TO GROW,
THIS IS FAT OR TUMOR:
IT IS NOT BEAUTIFUL.
YOU HAVE BECOME FULL-GROWN ADULTS,
GIVE BIRTH TO THE NEW, TO THE *CHILD!*
STOP TRYING TO MAKE *YOURSELVES* GROW!

Do you have any more questions?

L. Does everyone have a teacher, a spiritual guide?

— No. We consist of faith – purely of faith.

TO THOSE WHO HAVE FAITH, WHO BELIEVE –
WE *ARE*.
AND FAITH IS THE FORCE OF THE DIVINE.
IF YOU BELIEVE THAT I HAVE A VOICE …
I CAN SPEAK.
IF YOU DO NOT BELIEVE IT … I AM MUTE.
IF YOU BELIEVE THAT I AM YOU … I BECOME YOU.

Believe in the high!
You can also believe in the low.
Today devils clamor and angels are silent.

BUT THROUGH YOUR BELIEF, WE DESCEND.
FOR BELIEF IS THE BRIDGE.

I leave you now.

Friday, December 3, 1943

24. DIALOGUE WITH GITTA

> *Our house is in the process of being whitewashed and painted,*
> *so a friend has kindly given us the use of her quiet apartment for*
> *today's dialogue.*

— Every home is a sanctuary.
Let us thank the one who welcomes us!
Listen carefully: you are all temples.*
In the sanctuary of sanctuaries,
you welcome the Divine.
But it is of no use to welcome Ö
if you do not welcome the unredeemed.

* In Hungarian there is just one word for 'temple' and 'church': *templom.*

156

The temple exists for them.

LEARN TO WELCOME!
JUST AS YOU WELCOME,
SO WILL YOU BE WELCOMED BY THE DIVINE.

The temple does not choose: the temple welcomes.
Imagine an empty church –
the sanctuary freezes in it!
Do you welcome my words?
G. Oh, yes!
— Do not fear to open the gates of the temple,
my servant: the church is already pure,
the mass can begin.
G. What is the heart?
— The sanctuary of sanctuaries,
the place where Ö dwells,
the place of grace, the chalice.
G. And what dwells in the middle of the forehead?
— The new Seeing.
G. And what is the Light, the new Light?
— *What* refers only to objects.
G. There is no word to express it …
— There will be one! Why do you ask?
Do you wish to *know,* or …
G. To come closer.
— Do you come closer by means of *knowing* it?
G. If it comes from *you* … then yes.
— Does the mother come closer to the child she carries
in her womb because she *knows* it to be there?
When does she see it? When it is born!
Do not desire to *know,*
just take good care of the Child!
G. How should I take care of the Child of Light?

— Who is the Light?

G. The Divine!

— You have spoken truth. Take good care of the Divine!

G. What was I like before I was born?

— You have not yet been born!
  Ask when you will be born!
  Now you are what you were,
  but will not be, for you are changing.

G. You said that I am subject to another law
  than most others.
  How can I recognize those who are subject
  to the same law as I?

— By the fact that they understand your words.
  The others do not understand.

  THEY LEARNED ...
  AND YET THEY DO NOT UNDERSTAND.
  THEY DID NOT LEARN ...
  AND YET THEY UNDERSTAND.

  Silence.

— Do you welcome me?

G. (joyfully:) Oh, yes!

— Welcome everyone and everything in this way!
  That is your task.
  Only when you welcome the unredeemed
  can I pass on Divine grace to you.

  In a powerful voice:

— Heavy temple gate, bolted with iron bars:

  OPEN WIDE! I SAY TO YOU: OPEN WIDE!

  Divine grace be upon you!

158

Friday, December 3, 1943

24. DIALOGUE WITH LILI

— Today I will speak of your sign.
  Try to imagine its form.
  Do you understand your sign, my little servant?
L. I don't think so …
— It is a marvelous sign.
  Imagine the infinitely great and the infinitely small.
  Infinitely great …

> *The hands spread out from the heart*
> *and the arms open wide:*

Infinitely small …

> *The outstretched arms return to the heart*
> *and the fingers join at one point.*

— How could the infinitely small see the infinitely great
  if it were not for the *focal point?*
  Have you ever seen the Divine in the eyes
  of someone who has been helped?
L. Yes, I have …
— There you saw the Divine!
  All lines which come from infinity
  converge at the *focal point.*

| infinitely great | infinitely small | the point of deliverance |

— The infinitely great image appears at one single point.

159

You are a funnel: the triangle is its sign.
May this image guide all of your acts!
Look! Beneath the cone of rays,
there is a second inverted cone:
that is deliverance.

THE HUMAN IS THE FOCAL POINT.
VERILY, A SINGLE POINT:
THE POINT OF DELIVERANCE.
THIS MARVELOUS TASK IS OUR WAY –
NOT FORMS AND RELIGIONS.

L. Tell me more about deliverance!
— I am always speaking about deliverance ... always!
You are but a minute being in the Creation,
and yet you are an image of the Divine:
you *radiate* this image.
— Ask!
L. Is there a task for the physical organs
at higher levels?
— There is a deep secret concealed in what I now say:

EACH ORGAN OF YOUR BODY
IS AN IMAGE OF A UNIVERSAL FORCE –
IT RECEIVES ITS STRENGTH FROM THIS FORCE.
YOUR HEARTBEAT IS IDENTICAL
WITH THE HEARTBEAT OF THE UNIVERSE.

But if these forces are left without a task
all is for naught:
existence without a goal is confusion, chaos.
Sickness, too, is chaos.
The meeting of the forces of the universe *at one point*
is New Creation.

The recognition of your task – the funnel –
is Creation.

EACH OF YOUR ORGANS IS SACRED.
THE BODY – THE FINITE –
IS A TINY REPLICA OF THE INFINITE.

Heaven be with you!

Friday, December 10, 1943

25. DIALOGUE WITH GITTA

We feel the wordless presence of my inner teacher and await the beginning of the dialogue. Suddenly, the shrill ringing of the telephone cuts through the silence, shocking us all. I hastily disconnect it and reproach Joseph: "It was supposed to be your job to disconnect the telephone!"

— I declare battle!
In the past, you have defended yourselves:
from now on, attack!
Only a weak fire needs protection from the wind.
Fear not to enter into battle!

WHO CAN FIGHT AGAINST DARKNESS? *LIGHT.*
AND WHO WILL BE VICTORIOUS? *THE LIGHT.*

Darkness is dead, lifeless, unchanging.
What is dark is dark.
Nothing is darker than darkness.
Darkness cannot increase, but Light can decrease.

Silence.

— Listen carefully, my servant, I will teach you:
What is fever?
The heart beats – that is rhythm.
What disturbs the regularity of the rhythm?
A foreign, poisonous substance enters the blood,
the heart beats faster and the fire becomes hotter.
If destructive substances are in you,
your rhythm is disturbed,
and what disturbs must burn.
That is fever. Fever purifies the blood
and the rhythm then adjusts itself.
You have less and less fever,
for the old in you heals.

G. I would like to completely burn away
what is rotten in me!

— There you are wrong: Let nothing rot!
Fever is necessary only when something is rotten.

G. Why am I not aware when something begins to rot?

— Stop defending! Attack! Rise up against darkness!
When you really burn, you will not find enough matter
to burn … let alone to rot.

     Silence.

— Listen well! Just what you believe to be your fault
can become your virtue
if you only recognize it:
You do not see the human being.
This is not a fault,
for your eyes are not meant to *see.*
If your eyes would *shine,* all would be well.

DO NOT TAKE PART IN DARKNESS,
BUT GIVE LIGHT, ALWAYS AND EVERYWHERE.
THEN DARKNESS WILL FLEE.

162

How do you know that it is dark?
In what does darkness show itself in a room?
In the lamp when it does not burn.
The lamp is responsible.

LIGHT THE HUMAN
AND DO NOT GRIEVE OVER DARKNESS!
THAT IS YOUR LAW.

I declare war and not peace.
Be attentive to rhythm, for it is the Divine message.
Ö judges through you – Ö does battle through you.
Take heed to serve the Divine
and not evil, which is the past!
Only by means of rhythm
will you be able to differentiate between the two.
G. That is not clear to me …
— The fire burning in you – the fire of the body –
is called life, and it builds. Fever destroys.
It is the same fire, but in excess.
Your heart knocks seventy times: seven times ten.
The rhythm of the human is sevenfold.
In the absence of evil, even the deepest wound
heals in *seven* days.
Rhythm is the capacity of the vessel.
One drop too much … and it overflows.
Take care: listen, always listen, for this rhythm
is no longer the rhythm of the body.
The mind cannot grasp it.
Leave the mind in its own realm!
The fire of life is eternal;
the fire of fever is transitory.
The *more* is not always better.

The intensity of your fire
would be a fatal fever for someone else.
There is only one key: stay alert!

The loudly ticking alarm clock had disturbed me so much before
the dialogue that I had put it away in the cupboard. Just now, the
alarm goes off: I had forgotten to disengage it.

— Let this be a lesson to you, for you judged before:

In an ironic tone of voice:

— "It was supposed to be your job"… to ensure silence.

My companions are heartily amused.

— We teach you because you are dear to us
and you like to learn. Ask!
G. What is meant by 'eternal damnation'?
— A goblin, a bogeyman! I can reveal it to you.
But woe to those who *need fear*
and no longer believe in damnation.
They no longer fear anything,
though fear would actually help them.

ETERNAL DAMNATION IS:
TO BE UNAWARE THAT THEY ARE *IN IT*
AND TO HAVE NO FEAR.

The absence of fever in the body is a victory
by the poisoner of life.
I declare war, that they may again learn
to be afraid, for there is no more fear in them.
There is no more fever in them
and that is their damnation.
Fever is not punishment, but healing.

164

THEY FEAR ONE ANOTHER ... AND THAT IS HELL.

They fear the bomb
rather than God's hand,
which strikes with certainty.
I speak of fear: fear is the seed of belief.
Young tribes are afraid. Of what?
Of the unknown. What is the unknown?
That which is beyond them, the Greater.

YOUR LAW IS JOY, NOT FEAR:
ALREADY THE SEED IN YOU BEGINS TO SPROUT.

When it sprouts and sheds its husk,
the seed disappears and fear is gone.
But the others have need of fear.
Our battle is not the old battle.
We proclaim the new, the unknown.
This brings the beginner fear, and the chosen, joy.

> *I have the impression that the 'chosen' is someone who has voluntarily taken on the earthly task.*

— Never forget: what gives life to you ...
scorches others to ashes.

> *Joseph has just had an operation for a ruptured hernia. In his youth, he had believed that the salvation of humanity would come from an equitable and universal distribution of material goods. It had become his 'materialistic ideal.'*

— I speak to the convalescent one:
the old lack has been filled.
The man of the past lifted more than he was able.

HE HAS LIFTED MATTER ABOVE HIMSELF,
AND IT TORE HIM.

165

May the scar remind you of this, my son!
It is the image of a whole age! But you are cured.
The scar may reopen, but it is no longer dangerous.
You are healing. Let us give thanks!

Friday, December 10, 1943

25. DIALOGUE WITH LILI

> *Lili dreamed that she was asked: "If you should die, what would*
> *be your last wish?" In the dream, she responded: "That what I*
> *am receiving now might continue to live on in my students."*

— I will speak about your dream:

THE GERM IS THE DEATH OF THE GRAIN.

The small creatures living under the ground
see only the death of the grain;
they do not see the sprout,
which is above the soil.
The new Sprout is the new Being.
You chose well in your dream:
you gave up the perishable in exchange for the eternal.
And the one who gives shall receive.
The new sprout – the eye of the seed – is only *one.*
It is above duality, beyond *two-ness.*
Do not fear death … death does not exist!

IF YOU ACT WITH ME,
YOU WILL KNOW NO DEATH.

Take good care: what I am saying is of the essence.

Only for the weak is the certainty of death a stimulus.
But you are no longer weak. Your time is short,
but do not let that guide your actions!

*In the silence that follows, I anxiously ask myself what 'your time
is short' means in terms of earthly time. I have often observed
that the angels' sense of time is very different from our own.
Fifteen months later, my question was to be answered.*

— 'The one who speaks' now sees you shining.
Ask, my servant!
L. May I ask a question for 'the one who speaks' –
for Hanna?
— There is no need for questions: she will be answered.
L. How could humanity improve itself a little bit?
— There is no such thing as *a little bit.*
It is *all* one or *all* the other.
Do you eat meat that is rotten?
L. No.
Meat that is *a little bit* rotten ... would you eat it?
L. No.
— *All* one or *all* the other. What rots?
Matter whose essence has departed.

Silence.

— Marvelous! Two eggs:
In one, the germ of life; in the other, nothing.
Only upon hatching does it become apparent:
In the warmth, the germ grows – the germless rots.
You can brood, you can warm –
but you cannot provide germs.
Do not worry; but always give warmth.

Ö ALONE GIVES GERMS;
Ö, THE LORD OF GERMINATION.

Do not concern yourself with the 'where' of the germ.
Warm! Awaken!
The rotten and the foul are germless.
They still belong to the age of the curse.
The little bird casts the rotten egg from its nest,
without pity, for warming it would be useless.

BUT THE HUMAN STILL SITS ON THE GERMLESS EGG
AND CONTINUES TO WARM IT.

Though it spoils, rots, putrefies,
still the human continues to warm it,
fearfully protecting the rotten egg
from which the new will never hatch.
And remember:
as long as a bird continues to brood,
no new eggs are laid.
Do you understand this lesson?
To you, it seems merciless, but it is not. It is strong.
A sure sign: What spoils when warmed is germless;
what sprouts is good.
But you: just warm! Nothing else.
Rottenness is its own judge. Just radiate warmth!
L. Where am I making mistakes in my teaching?
— In exactly the same way. Listen:
The chicken that is halfway hatched
appears to be rotten.
But growing life absorbs what is apparently rotten
and transforms it.

DO NOT CHANGE THE BAD – STRENGTHEN THE GOOD!

Thus the good will absorb the bad
which is all around it.
I have more to say: Praise!

Praise the praiseworthy in everyone, everywhere!
True praise strengthens, you will see wonders.
But never praise falsely,

AND NEVER LIE, EVEN WITH GOOD INTENTIONS!

Ask!
L. What is panic?
— Terror! Turning away from God! Sudden split!
Terror is the ancient god, the terrible:
Pan – panic. Only the animal has need of terror.
L. What is readiness?
— The right attitude.
If the tool is ready, it can be used at any time.
Being human is being ready.

THE HUMAN IS THE TOOL OF GOD.

Not to be ready is to be useless.
L. Why is there so much vengeance
and malicious joy in the human?
— A happy person is neither vengeful nor malicious,
and does not rejoice at the misfortune of others.
The sick hate the healthy … the unhappy, the happy …
the drunken, the sober.
Hate is fear, active fear, masked fear, shame.
The sick person spreads sickness.
Therefore, I say to you: spread health! Just that!
That is our war.
Do not struggle against sickness – strengthen health!
These are two completely different things.
The doctor who claims to vanquish illness, errs.
Ö is the healing force!
To act *with* this force is true healing.
It can even appear that a charlatan
'heals' better than a learned physician.

169

L. Is any one form of art more valuable than the others?
— Yes. The one that best serves.
    Only the most valuable can serve the Divine.
    By their fruits you may know them.
    But every art is changing.
    For one instant – let us be *one!*

Friday, December 17, 1943

26. DIALOGUE WITH GITTA

— I will speak of creation in art.
    A work of art is mere matter.
    A sculpture stands in space.
    The sculpture itself is not creation;
    it is but a vessel.
    When the vessel is filled, the drink creates.

        *Hanna is unable to find words for what my teacher wants to
        communicate about the new Art.*

— If only I could speak about new Art!
    If only I could!

    WHAT WAS VESSEL – WILL BE DRINK.
    WHAT WAS DRINK – WILL BE ECSTASY.

    This is a sterile period in time.
    The hands of merchants grasp empty vessels.
    Incense is offered for the artist.
    Incense is offered for the very one
    who should be offering it.
    The smoke descends and Cain has the word.

Everything parches. They are afraid of death.
They cage the bird – the blue bird –
until it becomes a gray sparrow.
Picture galleries, storerooms, crypts!
They guard dead husks. Odor of tombs.
No one looks ahead … they all look back.
Who serves the Divine? Who? Whom do you serve?

G. *(timidly:)* I would like to serve the Divine!

— But *do* you?

G. Not always …

— *(severely:)* Still 'not always'!

G. *(meekly:)* … what should I do?

— There is no 'should'!
Form a new vessel for the Divine, all of you:
a new cup for the drink!

THE DRINK STREAMS FORTH
BUT THERE IS NOTHING TO RECEIVE IT!

The new building, the new temple, has no walls,
for it is always growing.
Change! Transform everything!
The ancient temple, the ancient church,
was protection, fortress, refuge.
The new one is different: it has no walls.
Proclaim the new World with the means
you have been given. Do not be lazy!

> *This week, I had again not had the courage to begin a new oil
> painting. I was afraid.*

— Even *you* are still afraid! Create!
Not with fear, but with joy!
You stand at a higher level.
If you begin to fear, that is death for you.

171

REMEMBER: *MUST* AND *SHOULD* ARE DEATH!

May joy guide every line you draw ...
you draw them for the Divine!
If only I were able to speak of the new Art!
It has never before existed ...
not even for the greatest artists.

> *I am amazed to learn that not even the greatest artists meet the standards of the new Art. But when I realize that the new Human is only in the early stages of becoming, I understand that there cannot yet be such a thing as the new Art.*

— Ask!
G. What is meant by the 'Last Judgment'?
— What do you not understand?
G. Everything that you say is new
and the old concepts acquire a new taste.
— It is not the taste that changes,
but the one who tastes.
Only the dead palate needs spiced foods.
For the living, bread is the best.
The hungry need neither caviar nor paprika
on their bread.
If you are healthy and not ill,
what tastes good to you is what you need.

> *That I did not receive an answer to my 'Last Judgment' question is not surprising, because I had been anticipating a 'sensational' answer.*

G. What are those moments of life which have an *enchanting* taste, which are special moods?
— A deep mystery. The sun is white;
but *fragmented,* it becomes multi-colored.
That is the 'enchanting' taste of eternity, *fragmented.*

Soon you will understand this.
Do you believe that there are seven colors?
G. Yes.
— There are infinitely more ... but you see only seven.
When you cease to be who you were,
you will see all of the new Colors.
G. Will I also paint them?
— Those who see your painting will perceive
the new Colors, but they will not be on the canvas.
Do not seek the new Colors outside.
Red is a universe of suns and moons and worlds.
Blue is another universe ... the new is within you.

EVERYTHING IS WITHIN YOU AND NOT WITHOUT.

Ask!
G. What is 'resurrection'?
— A necessary evil.
If you are already above,
rising, re-surrection, is unnecessary:
only what is below can 'resurrect.'
Fallen, in the depths of the tomb ...
it rises up again.
Re-surrects.
It is a spectacle.

WHAT IS THERE TO RESURRECT
IF YOU ARE UNITED WITH THE DIVINE?

The Kingdom of the Divine approaches.
Call and it will come: it is within you.

*Is this an allusion to Jesus, who lived in his immortal body,
united with the Father, already before his earthly death? Did he
let himself be entombed to teach us the immortality of the body
of light, given to all?*

Friday, December 17, 1943

26. DIALOGUE WITH LILI

— I will speak of playing.
What is play? Preparation.
Practicing for mastery over force and matter.
Mastery is preparation for creating.
Here is an example: children are playing.
Two of them hold a rope and twirl it ... a third jumps.
The rope is matter set in motion by an outside force.
The child jumps.
If it jumps too early or too late,
the rope deals the child a blow.

THE RIGHT MOMENT IS THE GOAL.
AND THE RIGHT MOMENT
IS THE JOY OF PLAY.

Teach playing –
not *with* the body but *through* the body.
You teach children.
Teach them to play, to play new Games!
Prepare them to be creative!
No more old games, *new* ones!
Did you play when you were a child, my servant?
L. Hardly ever ...
— Then it is right for you to teach others,
for you know the lack well. Now you, too, will play.
See the child in your pupils, awaken the child:
but not the old one!
Only when the old leaves fall can the new bud sprout.
Listen well!
I will whisper wonderful new Games in your ear!

The child jumps ... the dancer leaps and twirls.

EVERY ORGAN, EVERY LIMB IS ONE
WITH A FORCE OF THE UNIVERSE.

Do you have an idea of what dancing is?
The swirling force raises up –
the whirlpool draws down.
What a powerful whirlpool the old dance is!
It pulls, it tears *downward* into the body.
The new Dance is *upward* whirling force.
But for now, just play! Prepare yourselves!
New Game ... new Dance ... new World.

THE PLAYING CHILD FORGETS ITSELF.

That is exactly what brings forth the new Game.
The child unable to play alone is not alive.

Forces whirl you about, hurl you – or you hurl them.
The difference is great! You feel it, don't you?
It is given to you to serve the Divine.
Could anything be more wondrous?
Oh, if you could but once taste self-forgetful play!

CREATION IS BUT SELF-FORGETFUL PLAY.

The creating Master forgets the carefully prepared
tool and yet there is no harm, for it serves.
I await your question.

L. Why am I so easily driven to despair?
— What despairs you?
L. More often *small* things than big ones.
— And therein lies the answer:
   small things concern the *small* Lili.
   But you – separate yourself from them!

The *small* Lili will deal with them.
Des-pair is not unity, one.
Do not dwell in despair, in two-ness!
Leave the old behind
and you will be free from despair.
You will also leave behind the new;
all is to be left behind,
for everything is but husk, empty husk.
Ask!
L. What is pain?
— Guardian angel, guardian angel of the animal.
Fear is the sign that comes *before* error.
Pain comes only *after.* Both are indications, signals.
But your sign is joy.
Are you joyful when you are with me?

> *Lili is unable to express herself in words;*
> *she nods silently.*

— What would make you even more joyful?
L. That would be absolutely *impossible!*

— NOTHING IS IMPOSSIBLE! THERE IS NO IMPOSSIBLE.
IMPOSSIBLE DOES NOT EXIST.
EVERYTHING IS POSSIBLE!

> *A long silence follows. We all feel that something essential is*
> *happening in Lili. I avoid looking at her, feeling that my gaze*
> *could disturb a deep and sacred happening inside of her.*

— Ask, my little servant!
L. It is so strange to ask now.
I had the feeling that I ceased to exist.
— Truly, you *will* cease to exist.
I rocked you in my arms,
you, who never were rocked.

And it was good for me to rock you.

*I feel this as an allusion to the loveless and lonely childhood of
Lili, who had been an unexpected and undesired child.*

— BEFORE BIRTH – THE OLD BIRTH –
MOTHER AND CHILD ARE *ONE*.
WHEN THE CHILD IS BORN – THEY BECOME *TWO*.

YOU AND I ARE *TWO*.
WHEN WE ARE BORN – WE BECOME *ONE*.

For you, this is a mystery. You cannot yet grasp it.
Ask!
L. What is tiredness?
— The old rhythm … a pause between two sounds.
If you act in the new, you cannot be tired.
If you are tired, that is the small death.

Silence.

The tree of everlasting life.
The Father has given it to us, and we guard it.

*Her angel shows the specifically fatherly aspect of the Divine to
Lili, who had not experienced fatherly love as a child.*

We will give it to the one who no longer listens
to the serpent, owner of the *other* tree.
We guard the tree of eternal life …
we guard it well … with sword in hand.
But why the tree if there is no fruit?
And why fruit if there is no one to eat it?
It is not the fruit which is unripe – but the eater.
This is why we continue to guard the tree.
The good Father does not guard the beautiful fruit
for Himself, but for the children.

The infant cannot yet eat the fruit,
as the Father well knows.
You are in Paradise at every moment.
Two forbidden trees. You can choose!
The serpent tempted you ... you ate ...
and the fruit was bitter.

WE FORBID ... WE GUARD
BUT YOU: *DO* COME –
TRIUMPH OVER US!

Apparent joy enticed you and you ate *fear.*
Our sword strikes down only the *fearful,*
for *fear* brought forth the sword.

You may ask another question, my servant!
L. I do not understand what is meant
by the cornerstone in the Bible.
— The bearer of weight, the redeemer, the despised.

Prepare yourselves, be ready!
Let us all serve the Divine!

Saturday, December 18, 1943

MESSAGE FOR X

For quite some time, I have worried about X – a close friend
I have known since childhood. He is of German origin and
unfortunately his entire interest is devoted to the Führer *and the*
Reich *(*Führer, *guide, was the current designation for Hitler,*
and the Reich, *kingdom, designated his imperialistic project).*
While working on an advertising design, Hanna suddenly sets
her brush aside and says, "I hear German words, they're meant
for X. Write them down!"

You coward!
You pampered child!
There is but one guide:
The Divine Shepherd.

He proclaims:
IT SHALL BE!
What has been 'til now,
is not true.
A flash of
unsheathed steel
makes clear:
decision is near,
you eel!

With wondrous force
you are adorned
and could shine
like a Christmas tree.
Act in accordance!
You waste divine gifts!

179

You'll pay dearly.
Tremble in my presence!
In vain you slither into yourself!
No hole left for hiding!
You are transparent like glass –
shatter like glass!
Soul demands freedom!

Such dignity is bestowed upon you –
yet you wallow in the mud
like a mole
and writhe and err.
Come forth, spirit!
Ardently I remind you:
God knows
who you are.

*I am very shaken by this strong admonishment. Hanna does
not completely understand all of the words and I translate what
I can into Hungarian. We discuss how we might try and pass
on this message to X. Anticipating his ironic smile, I decide to
cautiously first inform him about the change that has occurred
in my life, to see how he reacts.*

*A short while later, I take a walk with him. X listens to me
quietly and then asks questions, from which I can tell that he has
been deeply touched. I return to Budaliget by bicycle and tell
Hanna about his interested response. Immediately, she hears the
following words:*

He is mine!
Not for an instant
will I let him go!
I laugh with joy,
I dance without restraint:

Indeed, he is formed
in the image of God!
His penance will be heavy,
but not without end.
Like a child in the forest
he is full of fright.
But soon it will be bright.
Softly, gently,
without glare,
the light returns.
Praise we sing.
Long, so long
has been the night.

Beginning:
"Don't listen,
don't look,
don't know,
don't turn:
just follow the only true *'Führer'*!"

In truth, you are HIS child!
So tenderly
HE loves you.
Turn your gaze
from all things visible.
In truth, you are HIS child!
BECOME
HALF HEAVEN – HALF EARTH!

The glowing joy of the angel at the first awakening of his protégé impresses me profoundly. How limited, how lame and gray are our feelings, compared with this fiery passion!

The wheel
Birth and death,
bread and dread,
dirt.
Beginning and end.

Evolve –
and from two there will be one!

Be heaven's knight!
Overcome
hate and war,
peace and love,
death and dread!
Of dirt and God
will come the wonder
of ONE.

All that was
is futile fluff.

From HIM for you a wing
and I will sing.
We will overcome
what was blind;
not with torment
but with gentle rays
bringing light.
The Kingdom nears.
The wheel stands still:
Divine will.

Friday, December 24, 1943

27. DIALOGUE WITH LILI. FRAGMENT.

— "An angel descended from heaven ..."*
You no longer need hasten to see the light,
for the LIGHT will be everywhere
and Bethlehem will be no more.
I proclaim a new Christmas,
no longer followed by Easter.
From now on, Easter is merely an empty shell.
But today the light, the old light,
is so revered that the flames of life are extinguished.

> *These words are an ironic, bitter reference
> to the war.*

— On the stone and on straw warmed by the animal
lies the newborn *in you.*
Good is the stone, good the straw,
good the warm breath;
bad is the decayed stable, bad are the cold
and darkness outside.

Fear not! The dragon cannot reach the newborn.
The old dragon is beside its tree,
but the red apple no longer entices.
Do you see the newborn?
L. No.
— Do try to see it!

YOU BELIEVE YOU GIVE BIRTH ,
BUT IT IS *Ö* WHO GIVES BIRTH TO YOU!

* From a traditional Hungarian Christmas carol.

Silence.

— Do you have questions?

L. What is a real feast ... a feast of the heart?

— A part of Heaven.

Downward gesture:

— What they do down there ...
  is the *split* of a broken heaven
  which will never become whole again.
  They gnaw at the splinters of the old heaven;
  but we are building the new Heaven.
  And we build it together.

L. What is 'goodness' ... 'charity'?

— Worthless old splinters! Away with them!
  Today everyone gives the 'good.' Rubbish!

ONLY Ö GIVES AND EVERYTHING IS GIVEN.
WE MERELY *TRANSMIT* THE DIVINE GIFT.

Tiny worms with delusions of grandeur say: "I give."
Do not be soiled by this kind of 'good.'
May there be no such 'good' in you!
Not evil has darkened the world,
but the 'good': the 'good' person, who says, "I give."
And see, what is given? Death!
You, 'good' people, you will pay the penalty.
In the coming new LIGHT,
everything false will crumble to dust.
What do you own?

L. Nothing.

— Then what can you give?

L. From myself ... nothing.

— Rotten corrupt species! Woe unto you!

You build 'good' hospitals for your victims.
But you, my servant, you are not 'good':
the GOOD will stream *through* you.
Ask!

L. How might religion and science become united?
— In the new Light, one will see that *they are one* ...
They have always been one,
just as melody and rhythm are one and inseparable.
Each member of the great orchestra plays,
but the symphony is one.
Sometimes the violin leads,
sometimes the cello,
sometimes religion,
sometimes science.
But now: nothing! For no one serves: everyone leads.
More than all others, the drum,
for it is the loudest.
The conductor is a servant of the symphony's spirit.
But now there is not even a conductor.
The loudest dominates ...

    Long silence.

May heaven bless you!

Friday, December 31, 1943

28. DIALOGUE WITH GITTA

It is the last day of the year. In the past, I have always found New Year's celebrations to be meaningless and boring. But today I am full of expectation as I wonder how the angels will mark the passage from the old year into the new.

— Alpha – Omega ... Omega – Alpha.

THE CREATED HUMAN STANDS
BETWEEN BEGINNING AND END.
THE CREATING HUMAN STANDS
BETWEEN END AND BEGINNING.

Between beginning and end is time.
Between end and beginning is timelessness.
The end of the old year is the beginning of the new.
The end of the old world is the beginning of the new.
The miracle is between the end and the beginning,
between Omega and Alpha.

Humans have always celebrated
what cannot be celebrated.

I do not understand at first, but suddenly it dawns on me that the timeless moment, the transition from the old year into the new, cannot be grasped by those who live in time.

— The gateway to the narrow path is: Omega – Alpha.
The one who passes through it *bodily* – in time –
steps into death.
The one who passes through it *spiritually*
– beyond time – steps into eternity.

Can you measure time between Omega and Alpha?
A fleeting instant ends – a new instant begins.
Between the two, there is no time.

BETWEEN THEM IS ETERNITY.

There is a gateway to eternity:
It opens not at the beginning, but at the end.
The Creator sets in motion
and the new instant *is;*
the old is no more.

AT THE DEATH OF EACH INSTANT
YOU CAN ENTER INTO ETERNITY,
INTO THE CREATING WORLD.
AND THERE YOU – YOURSELF – SET IN MOTION.

This is visible to all and yet not seen.
The gate is open, but the opening is so narrow
that the born cannot pass through.
This is the greatest secret:
Every instant – even the instant of the instant –
is an open gate.

THERE IS NO SACRED INSTANT –
FOR *EVERY INSTANT IS SACRED.*

Thus you live in the eternal *and* in the temporal.
You are the ball *as well as* the player.
Do not pay attention to the beginning:
the beginning is already end.
What begins, ends, and cannot be altered;
for force and matter are already *in motion.*
Take heed:
The origin of everything, the birthplace of motion,
is between the end and the beginning.

The created world is a ball.
The Creator plays with it … gives the ball a push,
that it may return in joy.

IN THE CREATOR'S IMAGE:
ALL IS IN THIS IMAGE,
CELESTIAL BODIES, ATOMS, ALL.

Silence.

— Learn this:
There is only one certainty, and that is *joy.*
Everything can be explained: joy has no explanation.
We cannot explain why we are joyful.
Joy is our task.

WHAT YOU RECEIVE IS A SOURCE OF JOY FOR THE JOYLESS.

— Ask, my servant!
G. Please, tell more about the eternal instant!
Would you explain it to me in another way?
— The eternal instant is a ray of eternal Light.
Humans have the task of creating an opening
in the sphere where they live
so that the ray can enter.
No need to demolish a house to let light in!
A window suffices.
To reach up to the infinite Light,
it is necessary to go beyond the created.
Only thus can you reach it.

BEYOND THE CREATED
YOU ARE LIBERATED AND YOU LIBERATE.

How deceptive is this sphere from within,
with its suns and moons and 'infinite space,'
which in reality is finite!

With its billions of years; its billions of years,
which are nothing compared to an eternal instant.
If an opening is created in the sphere
where you live, there is no more prison,
there are no more *prisoners;*
just free *inhabitants* in the sphere.
No more curse, but blessing.
No more darkness, but Light.
No more suffering, but joy.
This tiny opening is deliverance:
everything changes!
The way out, the solution: Omega to ALPHA.

After a long silence:

— Take heed of measure! What is more –
below as above –
is deviation from the path.
Therefore learn to feel: too much – too little.
'Enough' is equilibrium
between force and matter, between finite and infinite.

BETWEEN THE TWO IS THE PATH: ENOUGH.

Take care, do not stray from the path!
Your measure is unique.
Everyone has a key: one's *own* measure.
— You may ask another question.
G. We see the bad and speak of it.
Where is the boundary between clear seeing
and pretentious judgment?
— Measure. You are a bringer of Light.
Know the weakness of the eyes!
But not in a judgmental way!

If your entire being serves deliverance,
then you will *measure* and not *judge.*

JUDGMENT BELONGS ONLY TO THE DIVINE.

Listen carefully! There are Seven Joys.
Discover them! This is not an easy task.
Each of the Seven Joys will be the guiding spirit
of one day of the week.
I give you seven days to discover them.
Tell me next week what you have discovered.
I take leave of you.

Friday, December 31, 1943

28. DIALOGUE WITH LILI

— What is easy for me – is difficult for you.
What is easy for you – is difficult for me.
How difficult it is
to make you aware of even the simplest thing:

EVERY MOTION CAN BE AN IMAGE OF CREATION.

A push at one point sets into motion.
Listen well: motion begins at one point,
its point of origin.
And then it returns.
Everything is pushed and everything returns.

> *These words lead to my understanding that every true motion*
> *pulses as part of a cosmic rhythm.*

The human has strayed from this law.

Knowledge has caused a tiny bit of deviation
in the human.
This 'tiny bit' can corrupt everything.
But when the human returns
to the Divine Source of all motion,
the name of all motion becomes:
deliverance.

WHEN MOTION RETURNS TO ITS SOURCE,
JOY IS BORN IN THE HUMAN.

Even the vilest human is still human
in being able *to give.*
A single instant too soon or too late:
that is the apple of knowledge.
It was not meant for eating.
But the humans ate the apple
and hoarded Divine Knowledge for themselves.
The fault was not in the apple;
only the eating of it was forbidden.
This is an image of all that is human:
the forbidden apple seduces one to take
and not to give.
Giving is everything.

THE FAULT IS NOT IN KNOWLEDGE –
BUT IN HOARDING IT.

When given, knowledge, too, is a blessing.
All that is given forth is a blessing.
But we can give only *through the Divine.*
Then we become one with the Source and that is joy.

TRUE MOTION IS DIVINELY INSPIRED
AND IT RETURNS TO THE DIVINE.

191

Teach everyone to give in this way
and the curse will come to an end.
It is not *you* who give;
teach only *how* to give.
Everyone can give; every motion can serve.
From inner motion evolves the outer.

I help you in your work, my servant:
joy is the sign.
Take note of what brings each person to rejoice.

WHERE SOMEONE IS UNABLE TO REJOICE,
THERE IS THE APPLE:
THE APPLE SELFISHLY EATEN AND NOT GIVEN ON.

Away with it!

Even the most miserable of those
you shelter under your cloak can learn to rejoice.
That is joy:
set in motion …
streaming outward …
totally spending itself …
and returning, like a breath of air.
Beginning, end and joy are in the heart.

JOY IS THE AIR OF THE NEW WORLD.

Ask!
L. What is peace?
— Not a pause between two wars.
Peace has never yet been – but it will be.
Peace! You only long for it; but not enough.

PEACE IS THE NEW VIBRATION.

Unlike anything before.

L. If there is no peace in me, I cannot rejoice.
— You speak truth.
L. Now the new year begins and I would like to start
   in a completely different way.
   Please help me!
— My peace is your peace. My joy is your joy.
   Thus, cherish it!
   Joy is infinite. You receive as much
   as you are able to give forth.
   Joy has no limits. It is your capacity to give
   that is limited.

> *I feel that the angel could give Lili infinitely more, but that she
> is not yet able to bear such intensity. And so her angel's giving
> must be restricted to the proper measure.*

— Joy knows no limits, no beginning and no end,
   for joy is eternal.
   I also rejoice only to the extent
   that I am able to give to you.
   And you rejoice only to the extent
   that you are able to give forth.
   Rejoice then! May your joy be perfect!
   Give to the happy ... give to the unhappy!
   Be not sparing of your joy!
   May this be your new year!
   Ask!
L. What is hope?
— Why do you ask this, my little servant?
L. Because I feel it beginning to grow in me.
— Pay attention to where you direct your hope!
   If you direct it to the Divine,
   you will never be disappointed, for Ö gives all.
   Only the godless are hopeless.

Listen well!
Do not merely hope … *give* hope!
Do not merely have faith … *give* faith!
Do not merely love … *show how* to love!
Not hope for yourself!
Not faith for yourself!
Not love for yourself!
That is the burden; it is light.
And you carry it lightly, that we know well.

> *Silence.*

L. It is unclear to me what 'spiritism' and
'mysticism' are.

> *By 'mysticism,' Lili means exaggerated interpretations of sensa-*
> *tional, inexplicable, paranormal phenomena.*

It is its nature to be unclear!
Old mist and fog vanish at the coming of dawn.
Do you know what a genuine *mystery* is?

A SMILE ORIGINATING IN THE DEPTHS OF THE SOUL.
THAT IS A MYSTERY.

Teeth-chattering, slobbering, despair of the shipwrecked, that is
what 'spiritualism' is.
They want a sign and it is not given to them.

NOT THE DEAD SHOULD BE CONJURED,
BUT LIFE: ETERNAL LIFE!

The sacred teaching is not hidden
in darkness and obscurity;
it radiates in bright daylight.
What they call up, they receive.
Leave the dead with their dead!

So often did they summon death
that finally it came.
Let us summon joy, and the Divine Realm will come!
Call not trembling with fear, but with jubilation!

COULD ANYTHING BE MORE NATURAL
THAN OUR TALKING TOGETHER?

Where is that thing you call 'mysticism'?
It has sunk. Everything old disappears.
Have you rejoiced today at being with me?
L. Oh, yes!
— Pass on this joy!

> *Feeling that the dialogue is concluded, I work at completing my notes. Suddenly Lili's teacher speaks to me:*

— Do nothing afterwards!
Do everything in its time!
Write even the accents in their proper time!

> *I am astonished.*

— Do not take this as jest.
Joking is foreign to me …
but I know joy.

Ö is peace.
May peace – not mine, but Divine peace –
come over you!
May HIS kingdom come!

January 1944

MESSAGE FOR X

I tried repeatedly to reach X in a calm moment. In vain! In his
free time he listens constantly to German Radio and I fear that
his political interests will prevent him from being able to receive
the message of the angel. Today, Hanna again hears German
words, and I feel them as a response to my concerns.

Seeds need earth and warmth.

Be truly warm –
and what was hardened
will open up!
Wait!
Do nothing!
Let Divine Force act.

Stem will sprout
and sap will flow within.
Sing and shine,
don't whine!
The earth is moist enough.
Let go!
He will be warm.

Wretched was the world
but HE floods all
with Light.

Soon another message arrived:

The cell of the eye
does not see the bright.

Blindly it serves.

You are not cell –
you are eye.
Shine!
Be source
for the new wave
in the Universe.

The eyes
of animals absorb.
You are not animal,
and not frill:
You are human,
you REDEEM!
You can overcome the night.
The wave brings the rays
down to the valley
where the blind
writhe in pain.
Pain will wane
when your eyes shine.
The night will end.

MAY THERE BE LIGHT!

Friday, January 7, 1944

29. DIALOGUE WITH GITTA

— Today, I will speak of the cradle of joy.
Hate, fire and poison comprise the cradle of joy.
The created world is the body of the Divine.
Can there be evil in Ö?

Bile, too, is a well of joy and yet bile is poison.

Bile, in itself very bitter, serves in the digestive process by breaking down food and transforming it.

— There is a fire in your body that does not destroy,
a poison that does not kill.
How can this be?

EVERYTHING IN THE GREAT PLAN IS GOOD.

Understand the secret: *transformation!*
The human being is called upon to *transform.*
What is bad is the 'too much.'
The cruelest beast in existence is the human;
and this same creature is the cradle of eternal joy.

FORCES NOT USED, FORCES NOT TRANSFORMED
DEVASTATE … DESTROY … POISON.

Sinking gesture:

— Listen carefully: what is bad here *below* …

Uplifting gesture:

… is good there *above.*
Everything depends on this.
Forces are destructive
when they are not in their proper place.

There is no destruction if you lift them up.
Then from poison comes healing and from fire, light.
This is why the human stood and is upright,
no longer crawls.
Out of all the evil you can imagine
is born the new Jerusalem.

WHEN THE TASK IS ACKNOWLEDGED,
THERE IS NO EVIL.
UNACKNOWLEDGED, IT DESTROYS.

Evil is the cradle of joy.
You flee in vain from evil … for there is no evil.
Evil: the eternal question of humanity!
No one could explain, but I proclaim:
Evil is the not-yet-transformed

EVIL IS GOOD THAT IS BEING FORMED,
BUT IS NOT YET FORMED.

Silence.

Disease. Each human organ is a force.
Together in harmony, they bear fruit!
Where there is a fault, the 'more' leaks out.
If bile overflows, it becomes poison.
The 'more' overflows and destroys the whole.
If the 'more' has no way out, it forces a way,
and what would *above* become the new World,
below becomes poison.
Above: life, secret eternal source of joy.

If you raise everything up,
you hold eternal joy in your hand.
There is no evil.

Held high, the destructive force of scorn
becomes Hallelujah.
Fire destroys ... raised up, it is flaming joy.
Only know this, and all illness, everything vile,
everything evil, comes to an end.
This is the scepter I place in your hand.
It connects below and above.
Take it and know: no longer *two* – but *one.*
No longer good and bad: only good!
I give it to you all. Do you accept it?

G. Yes.

L. Yes.

> *Joseph hesitates and does not speak.*
> *Sternly to him:*

— Answer!

J. Yes.

> *The image of the scepter becomes clear to me for the first time:*
> *true kings rule in the vertical line, uniting heavenly and earthly*
> *forces. The scepter is held vertically in the hand, and the hand*
> *signifies the act. To me, this means that the real Kingdom is*
> *attainable only by means of rightful acts on earth ... and that*
> *is everyone's task. Our openly pronounced acceptance of the*
> *scepter calls down heavenly help for this task.*

— What did you discover about the 'seven joys'?
I am waiting.

> *In seven sentences, I relate what I experienced as the 'seven*
> *joys.' (These notes were subsequently lost.)*

— I do not accept this. Raise it higher!
How will you raise it up?

G. That is just what I wanted to ask you.

— It is not yet simple enough;
   you have not yet tried hard enough.
   Your task was great.
   Those are not yet the *Seven.*
   There are infinitely many joys.
   In the end, there will be seven words,
   not seven sentences.
   You are already a *word:* "One-I," individuality.*
   Individuality: concentrated work of billions of years,
   collaboration, union of cells.
   What you brought is not enough.
   You thought your task was easy.
   When the grapes are freshly picked, there is no wine:
   only juice.
   If you had picked the grapes last Saturday,
   there would now be wine.
   But you merely plucked sweet grapes here and there along the way.
   I asked not for grapes, but for wine, for old wine.
   For only ecstasy rises to the Divine;
   sweetness stays below.
   I am waiting.
G. How could I elevate the bad through my acts?
— Transformation. Reforming.
   You are the one who transforms.
   The 'more' of the tree is its fruit.
   When you eat the flesh of the fruit, you kill it;
   but at the same time,
   you transform it into human force.
   The 'more' of the earth dies in you and is reborn.

YOU WELCOME EVIL
AND TRANSFORM IT INTO GOOD.

* *Egy-én* ('One-I') in Hungarian means: 'Individuality.'

EVIL DOES NOT EXIST;
THERE IS ONLY FORCE
THAT HAS NOT YET BEEN TRANSFORMED.

G. When force flows through me, I feel different radiations streaming
out of each of my hands.
What purpose do they serve?
— Healing. Only together do they serve;
separated, they have no task.
Do not seek to 'know' … but serve!
Then you will have new Awareness
and not old knowledge.
In the beginning was the Creation …
then incompetent fools 'explained' it.
The artist creates … the 'worms' explain.
Poor little gelatinous worms in your skull!
One last question!
G. I once believed I was acting according to my own law,
but this was not so.
How could I have so completely fooled myself?
— One word explains it: You said, 'I.'
That was the end.
A curtain descended between you and Eternal Truth.
You could not have awareness,
for you were in the dark.
The curtain is called 'I.'
Open it and you become Ö!
Then you will no longer ask questions,
for the Divine knows everything.
If you act in the name of your law,
you know nothing,
you *cannot* know anything of yourself.
Ö is total certainty … do not be uncertain!

G: How can I pull the curtain open and always serve well?
— It is not a matter of pulling it: do not hide behind the curtain.
Only then does it block the light.
Stand in front of it, and it will no longer disturb you.
No great steps are needed.

Ironically:

You are still too shy.
G: I don't want to be shy. Why am I?
— Because you are a child.
But those who are like children belong to the Realm of God.
The child has fear, but has faith in its Father.
And the FATHER is truly at its side. Believe in HIM!

The human being is a scepter in the Divine Hand.
The scepter unites above and below.
I depart.

Friday, January 7, 1944

29. DIALOGUE WITH LILI

We quietly wait for Lili's angel but there is one disturbance after another. First, a young man repeatedly tries to start his motor-cycle just beside our house, making a tremendous racket. The motor never quite starts and the struggle seems to go on forever. When he finally leaves, a mouse beneath the cupboard takes over the role of noisemaker: It is apparently playing football with a nut, which naturally attracts the attention of our cat; she complains relentlessly from outside the door to our room. Lili's angel speaks first to me:

— The noise is not without – but within.

THE LITTLE NOISES WITHIN YOU
CALLED THE NOISES AROUND YOU.

To us all:

— Ö is One – but has two hands.
Weight is one … faith is the other.
Matter listens to the left hand,
spirit to the right.
But the human is the wonder:

*Hanna's widely outstretched arms are slowly brought together
until the hands touch each other, forming a circle.*

— Through the human, the circle becomes whole,
and the embrace complete.
— Thus, there is no more weight,
thus there is no more faith.

*The cat meows again. I am beside myself with rage.
Lili's angel turns back to me:*

— WITH THE BEAST YOU DO NOT CALM THE BEAST.

I will stop for a while.

*I carry the cat to the garden.
After a long silence, to Lili:*

— Ask, my little servant!
L. My courses are becoming more and more difficult …
— What you doubt is not the new, but the old,
and that is good. What weighs you down?
L. I cannot transform either myself
or others quickly enough.

— My heart rejoices at you.
  You will find the new, my servant!
  It opens itself to those who seek it.
  Where do you feel the new?
L. I only sense that everything will be different.
— Through Ö, everything will become different.
  We are all working on a wonderful plan.
  Joy arises through the two, united as one.
  When you seek the new, the old is not lost,
  for it is one of the two.
L. I seek the one, the true, the just, and it disturbs me
  that I am not able to speak, to act and to move simply.
— As you approach the new, all of this will be fulfilled.
L. Why does it become so difficult to ask?
— Because the air is getting thinner
  and your lungs must adjust.

I RETREAT HIGHER … EVER HIGHER.
BUT YOU ARE NOT ALLOWED TO GO AWAY FROM ME.

You do not even notice that you are rising.
It is forbidden for us to leave each other.
I draw you higher … always higher,
for still we are not at home, where we can be united.
Everything becomes heavier and lighter.
Weight and task are two:
Weight becomes light … task becomes heavy,
as you transform.
Matter, family, what a weight that was!
It is no more.
Freed from weight, have strength for the task!

What else is troubling you?
L. I am still very weak …

— Do you believe that I am strong?

L. Yes. Through Ö.

— Then where is weakness?

L. I had lost sight of the Divine.

— Thus you are held:
supported from below ... blessed from above.
Rejoice, my servant! May you become aware!
Our time is ending.
If you have a last question, ask it now.

L. Where does self-centeredness come from?

— From Ö. Everything comes from Ö.

L. *(astonished:)* How can that be?

— Self-centeredness is the weight,
the left hand of the Divine.
For the animal, it is a matter of elevation,
but for the human, it is weight.
In its place, everything is good.

Heaven is with you.

MESSAGE FOR X

At last I find an opportunity to take a walk with X and give him the messages that have come for him. Suddenly he stands still and appears to be deeply touched. In a hesitant voice, he asks: "Yes, but then what is my role in practical life?" I reply : "You can be sure that you will receive an answer." Today I am able to write it down.

I am you.
Listen!

Half an arch – as good as none.
Lightly it should stand above
to overarch and carry.

Not quake, not totter,
for it would lean
and sink
in the clay.
The arch must hold.

But half,
it cannot lift,
it cannot die,
it cannot live.

Force becomes strain,
dignity burden.
Sap becomes steam
of wild storms
silently raging
under the half-arch.

The arch so yearns to serve,
to carry the many
who perish in waves
of fright and flight,
of doubt and chain,
of greed and blood,
of rage and rape,
in the depths of the abyss.

Give me your hand!
No more wall
between you and me.

You ask:
"What is my role?"

Wild waves
rage below.
Riotous rags
toss and float.
Broken beams
bleakly swirl,
support the house
no more.

Now you are half –
but soon no more!

GIVE ME YOUR HAND!
WE FORM THE BAND,
THE ARCH, THE BOW.
WE JOIN ABOVE
AND WE JOIN BELOW!

The New is born.
In praise we raise
a song for HIM
who created all.

What on earth was half
will be whole.
We shall arch,
and HE will reign.
HE proclaims:
MAY IT BE!

> *I record the message for X, but am unable to deliver it to him,
> because he has left Budapest in the meantime. Twenty-two years
> later, he finally receives all of the messages.*

The second birth

In the dark womb,
tender and naked,
swims the child.
As if dream,
a feeble beam
begins to gleam.

The child ripens,
the womb narrows.

Push through!
Upward!
Toward the gate!
Break through!
To the light!
Nothing hinders.

The night remains
in the depths below.
The child awakens
to Eternal Life.

Death is dead,
never more to be.
Only life
in Divine Light.

Saturday, January 15, 1944

30. DIALOGUE WITH GITTA

*The Dialogue could not take place yesterday because Hanna
and Joseph were called to visit Joseph's gravely ill father in the
hospital.*

— I speak to you of the narrow passage.
If you come to a standstill
– and often you do stand still –,
be aware of the reason:

THERE IS NO TRUE FAITH WITHOUT THE ACT.
THERE IS NO TRUE ACT WITHOUT FAITH.

Faith cannot be greater than the act;
an act cannot be greater than faith:
for they are *one.*
It is not your faith which is insufficient;
it is your act.

FAITH WITHOUT AN ACT IS NOT FAITH.

You could *do* more … you are still a coward.
Be aware of what you are doing!
Not only have faith … but *act!*
Do you *act,* my servant?

G. What do you actually mean when you say, *'act'*?

Very sternly:

— I asked *you!* Do not ask: answer!
G. I seldom act ...
— What does this indicate?
G. I do not use the force that is given to me.
— And what is the reason for this?
G. I do not know.
— Pay close attention:

ACT AND FAITH HAVE BEEN SEPARATED.

The reason was the many empty acts.
Now your heart begins to detest the meaningless act.
Already you can act without it being empty.
All of you! Take heed of the narrow passage:

ACT AND FAITH WILL BE ONE.
AND THERE WILL BE A NEW HEAVEN
AND A NEW EARTH.

G. Is thinking also an act?
— Only part of the act.
The act is one: *the task.*
There is no divided act.
There are no multiple acts.
From dawn till dusk ... from dusk till dawn,
from birth till death ... only one act: *Serving.*
There is no small act ... there is only the task.
What appears as a small act
is only the inadequate,
or the unfulfilled act.
You cannot stretch out your hand
without this being an act.

'Much' is always delusion.
A pause does not make two separate songs out of one.
Do not be misled!
Ask, my servant!

G. What are sunspots ... what effect do they have on us
... and how could they be controlled?

— Why do you want to know this?

G. Because I recently watched the setting sun:
with the naked eye, I saw big black spots
and I was filled with anticipation of great horrors.

— How could I explain the effect
of infinite numbers of suns to you?
You are a curious child, but that is not a fault.
You would be horrified if you could see
the tremendous forces that race back and forth
through you, without your knowing it.
But if you are *whole* and if you follow your calling,
there are no more blind forces,
for then they become active in you and through you.
If not, they destroy you.

   Silence.

— Your task is not finished, but that does not matter.

G. I have been unable to paint because I could not find
the 'seven joys.'

   All week long, I have searched in vain for the 'seven joys' – with
   much effort, but no success.

— To paint and to enjoy is one and the same thing.
You child! You have tried too hard!
Paint and rejoice ... rejoice and paint!
In this way, your task is formed.
Thus you will not have 'much' to do.

212

From dawn to dusk: ONE ACT!

My angel turns to Lili:

— You asked yourself in your heart what life is.
You will savor it when it begins.
You merely taste it now, but soon you will *live* it,
the still secret *new Vibration.*

The two of us are also ONE.
I respond and you accept my answers gladly.
We are completely different and yet we are ONE.
And how different you all are –
to the splendor of the Divine.
Different and yet truly ONE.

Saturday, January 15, 1944

30. DIALOGUE WITH JOSEPH

*A deep silence follows the dialogue with my angel. Hanna turns
to Joseph and gazes steadfastly at him. Suddenly he very clearly
sees the image of his angel, bathed in an intense green light. All
hesitation, all shyness and all false shame of speaking is swept
away.*

J. Speak to me!
— False shame is a sign of weakness.
Adam hid because he was not yet HUMAN.
The FATHER and your father are one.
Between them, the son.
The son is the link.

213

There is no death because the son is there.

Silence is my word.
From silence, create the *act.*
However loud your tool may be,
it creates silence in matter.

Joseph's work consists of carpentry and furniture building.

— Silence – balance – measure.
The saw cries out and what it creates
radiates silence, peace and balance.
Do you have a question?

Joseph is deeply affected by his father's illness.

J. Speak about death.
— You ask about something that does not exist.
I will answer you just the same.

WHAT IS DEATH BELOW ... IS LIFE ABOVE.
YOU, TOO, ARE MORTAL AND YET LIVE ETERNALLY.

All else is time and illusion:
waves breaking on the shore,
infinity of small deaths ... that is life.
Cells die ... new ones are born.
Do not let your father go – he can still live on!

IT IS NOT DEATH THAT IS BAD,
BUT THE UNFINISHED TASK.

Ripe fruit falls from the tree of its own accord.
The fruit that falls is ripe ... therefore it is good.
Your father is not yet ripe.
He misses something: that you also become father!

Joseph and Hanna have no children.

214

— That is what he misses.

 Silence.

— You may call me any time, just as you called me now.
Any time!
May you be wrapped in silence.
May it protect you from temptation!
May it unite you with the Divine!
I do not depart.

Saturday, January 15, 1944

30. DIALOGUE WITH LILI

I greet all of you.

 To Joseph, who had spoken for the first time:

— The circle is the key.
There is no hierarchy:
the circle is completed.
The last wall has crumbled.
Indescribable joy!
For the deceiver enters through the wall,
and without a wall, there is no entry.

 I see an image of heavy, fortified walls formed by our fixed opinions. There, only there, can the deceiver creep in on us. In the new, the living, the ever-changing and transforming, there is no need to fear the deceiver.

— Even the deceiver helps us … everything helps us.

There is no more evil – already you know it.
Indescribable joy!

Silence.

Nothing is straight.
Not even a ray of light is straight.
Everything is circular.
Believe me, you move on a tiny segment
of the infinite circle.
And this part of the infinite circle appears to be straight.
The mind cannot grasp this.
Ö is the center of all circles.
The smaller the circle,
the greater the presence of the Divine.
But every circle is necessary.

To Joseph:

— My son, your body still resists,
for you have entered a new circle.
All of you, become accustomed to ever smaller circles!
The deceiver circles around you,
no longer attacking at the breach – but at the wall.
Fear not, you are already very strong!

Ask, my servant!
L. Speak about life, that we might become alive!
— LIFE is not yet known to you,
for it is only now that you shall be born.
You only dream of life.

COMPARED WITH THE COMING LIFE,
THE PRESENT LIFE IS DEATH.

You would not yet be able to bear it:
but prepare yourself!

Sometimes you sense it.

L. But so seldom!

— What a big word! Now you feel the transition.
You must die a little bit ... apparently die.
The transition is dawn.
Night was velvety safe darkness.
Dawn is neither night nor day: transition.
Do not regret leaving darkness,
for Light is the greatest won
der of all!
Every transition is trial.
Fear not to leave darkness, for the root
– eternally in darkness –
remains united with the flower and the fruit.
Ask!

L. When I am alone, I am unable to try out new things,
to experiment.

— *Alone?* ... you are never alone!
Each of you is unique,
but each is nothing without the others.
The unity among you is a *more,*
not a *less.*
Separated sounds do not have meaning.
Even if each is unique and special,
even if none resembles another:
Only praise HIS glory *together.*
Out of chaos, the tone is born,
out of tones, the song,
if all the tones are pure.
If you feel alone,
separated from the others,
then the deceiver can attack you there,
where you have walled.

In truth, you are never separate from the others;
just unique.
Only in song does the voice receive wings.
And song comes only from pure voices.
Song: tone – vibration – word. Inseparably one.

IT IS NOT YOU WHO EXPERIMENTS;
IT IS YOU WHO IS EXPERIMENTED UPON.

> *This is the second time that Lili has been told that she is exper-*
> *imented upon. I ask myself if, in this time of transition, such*
> *'experiments' are being conducted everywhere. Are they the*
> *beginning of a general transformation of humankind? I experi-*
> *ence the encounter with our angels as something so natural that*
> *I believe many others could likely be having similar experiences.*

— You do what you are called for:
You transform yourself.
You hear the call and you come. That suffices.
Because of time and space,
the material result in matter will reveal itself only later;
but it cannot fail to come.

IF YOU TRANSFORM YOURSELF,
MATTER LIKEWISE TRANSFORMS ITSELF.

Your previous work is not lost; it will flower,
for the root is good.
It is called HELP.
All else is unimportant.
You *will* help: that is why you are here.
What still troubles you? Let me help you!
L. The feeling that I *must* rise higher …
— Free of *must,* you rise higher.
You come nearer to yourself.

I call you and you follow me.
Receive my joyful blessing, all of you in the circle,
for you have faith. Fear nothing!
The Realm of the Divine is near.
Death's last hour has tolled.
Bow your heads.

Gesture of blessing.

Friday, January 21, 1944

31. DIALOGUE WITH GITTA

I have been paralyzed all week by a distressing sluggishness.
All of my activities seem 'flat' to me ... totally lacking in flavor.

— What are you lacking?
G. I do not know.
— Are you hungry?
G. Yes ... for teaching, yes!
— And when you ask, do you receive?
G. Yes, but I do not notice when I am sinking.
— You receive what you ask for. Is that not so?
G. Yes, when I do not ask for myself.

The voice becomes severe:

— Even when you ask *for yourself,* you receive.
Aren't you asking for food?
From whom do you receive it?

*It dawns on me that the body's hunger and the soul's hunger are
both forms of asking.*

G. From the Divine.

— Then do not say that you do not ask for yourself!

YOU ARE AT THE CENTER OF A CIRCLE OF ASKING.
EVERYTHING IMPLORES YOU:
ALL OF UNFULFILLED CREATION.
YOU ARE A MEDIATOR FOR CREATION.
COULD THERE POSSIBLY BE A REASON
TO FORGET THIS?

You are *not allowed* to be depressed.
If salt were to lose its flavor, why use it?

*I feel that I am like salt, which could add savor to everything ...
but I tend to forget it.
Silence.*

G. Please teach me constant adoration of the Divine!

— Do you believe that Ö is far away?

G. No.

— That Ö is close to you?

G. ... that Ö is everywhere.

— Then how can you adore the Divine
only now and then?
I cannot teach you to adore the Divine,
but I can teach you that Ö is found in everything;
that Ö is here and there and everywhere,
in everything, even down in the depths.

YOUR TASK DEFINES YOUR PLACE:
YOUR PLACE IN THE DIVINE.

Hearing these words, I suddenly become aware that I am a

unique thought of the Divine, a unique cell of the Divine body,
with a unique task. Depression is a sure sign of having forgotten
my task.

— But your place is limited by time and space.
Adoration – *constant* adoration –
is nothing other than unity with the Divine.
Speak!

G. How could I free myself from the false idea that
'I *must* act' ... 'I *must* do'?

— If you adore the Divine, that *fulfills* you
and there will be no place for 'false ideas.'
Joy will *fill* you.
Not only shall *you* rejoice,
but everything surrounding you:
objects, matter, people, work, task ...
all shall rejoice ... except you.

YOUR JOY WILL BE ONE
WITH THE JOY OF THE DIVINE.

You will no longer feel divided.

G. If only this were possible *now!*

— It is possible *right now* ... not tomorrow!
Ask!

G. What is free will?

— To be free to live in this way, now and always.
Anything else is nothing.
That should suffice for you.

   To us all:

— There is no slavery ... but there is the LAW.
Your law is to be united,
and that is your freedom.

221

Divided, you are slaves;
united you are free.
The way is free
and Ö is smiling upon you.

Friday, January 21, 1944

31. DIALOGUE WITH HANNA'S ANGEL

We await Lili's angel, but with the first words, I feel a presence of
such measured and grave dignity and strength that I am almost
frightened. At the same time, I 'recognize' with indescribable
joy Hanna's teacher. Though without any 'memory-image,' I am
absolutely sure I know this angel of Divine Justice.

— The 'one who measures' speaks to you:
What is growth for the plant,
what is movement for the animal,
is for the human: *giving.*
Giving is not fruit, but growth: preparation.

I become aware that 'giving' is not a concrete result, but the
necessary condition for any growing.

— If you do not always give: you wither.
The fruit is the new World.

I serve through 'measuring.'

THE UNMEASURABLE APPEARS IN THE MEASURABLE.
PERFECTION IN THE LIMITED
IS AN IMAGE OF THE UNLIMITED.

It is given to you to fill *your* measure.
Neither with waste nor greed,
but with constant adoration.

> *I am overjoyed that the angel of measure also answered my*
> *question about 'constant adoration.'*

— The measure is given: it is in you.
Not the size of the measure is important,
for the Divine fills all. If you fill *your* measure,
you become similar to the Divine. Only then.
To you, I proclaim that I measure;
I measure since the beginning of time.
That is my means of serving.
I do not reward,
I do not punish,
I only measure.
You carry reward and punishment in yourselves.
In fulfilling your measure, you grow.
If not, you wither.
Do not believe that anything is impossible!

THE LAW OF WEIGHT IS: THE POSSIBLE.
THE LAW OF THE NEW IS: THE IMPOSSIBLE.

Leaden birds:
the door of your cage is open,
but you dare not fly!

> *Never had I felt so petrified in my habitual way of thinking as*
> *I do now. At the same time, I have the presentiment that a new*
> *kind of awareness will soon become possible.*

— I frighten you, that you may fly!
I spoke. I depart.

After this dialogue, I begin to understand what my angel had told me much earlier: "Ö created you according to my image." I realize that each of us might come to resemble his or her own angel.
The basic potentialities or seeds are given:
The essence of Lili's nature corresponds to:
'The one who helps,' Hanna's to 'the one who measures,' Joseph's to 'the one who builds,' and mine to 'the one who shines.'

Friday, January 21, 1944

31. DIALOGUE WITH LILI

After a few silent moments, we feel the presence of Lili's angel.

— I now take the lead
and continue to speak about measure.
The only task of the animal is: itself.
It rejoices in what is its own:
its air … *its* food … *its* young.
If it is healthy, then it rejoices in all of these.
It lives in a circle known as: *itself.*
It perceives only what is within this circle,
and takes it in: it is a creature.

 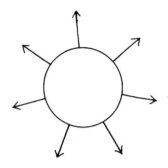

Human measure is exactly the opposite:
Your joy is what you radiate out of the circle.
Thus your joy is immeasurable.
The animal is hungry and eats until it is full ...
until it has *enough*.
The human is fulfilled and radiates beyond itself ...
and that is never enough.
Thus, human joy is immeasurable.
That is the mystery of eternal life.

Outside, the village bell begins to sound.

— If a church-bell rings in a closed room, it is unbearable.

IF JOY IS ALL AROUND YOU,
THEN YOUR MEASURE IS RIGHT.

And this is possible. If you do not believe it,
then you do not believe in the Divine.
Ö always fills you to the brim,
for Divine mercy is boundless.

To Lili:

— I have come to answer you. Ask!

225

L. Why do humans want
to receive everything ready-made?
— Spoiled childhood:
ready-made toys ...
ready-made knowledge ...
ready-made food ...
ready-made experience ...
This is what the child receives,
and it ends up feeling nauseous.
The thirst for knowledge, the desire to create,
everything that forms the human, withers away.
The joy of experiencing oneself:
too much good advice kills it.
That is cowardice and lack of faith!

WHEN THE CHILD IS FULLY GROWN,
EVERYTHING IN IT HAS WITHERED AND DIED.

Learn a lesson from this, my beloved!
Never advise, never pre-chew the food!
Give differently, and all will be renewed
under your hand. Set trials and tasks!
Attract others to walk in your footsteps!
Do not guide, do not indulge in hand-holding!
You may even push the uncertain gently
and their certainty will be strengthened.
This is what you seek ... and you will find it.

    Silence.

— Dismal gray is followed by
a wonderful radiance.
But now? So many colored pictures,
so many colored films
that the human eye becomes *gray.*

Only many years later did I become aware that color films (motion pictures) were something the angel had seen long before.

— Instead of *giving* color,
the human *receives* it passively.
You may ask!
L. It is so difficult to awaken interest in the human ...
— Were I to approach you, you would retreat.
Instead, I step back. And without even noticing it,
you learn to walk on air. Not on water: on nothing.
In the same way, I always give only *half* of an answer.
I leave out the other half.

In a bitter tone:

But humans give satiation.
They say, "We are so good to our children
and to everyone!"
With this, "we are so good,"
everything withers and dies away.
You! Give hunger, not satiation!
"Everything is known to us ... we know everything."
You! Open the *un*known!

Silence.

L. Why is it that so few people are able to concentrate?
— Because they concentrate on *nothing.*
So much noise, so much color penetrates from outside!
But you! Show something new that is stronger
than the strongest sound and yet: silence.
To that they will listen.

After an intense silence:

— Now I listened. And the sound was good.

227

You can hear it, too, if you listen intently.
Everything depends on *listening:*
measure, joy, everything!
Always listen!
Do you have another question?

Lili is still filled with the intense silence.

L. I feel that it would not be right for me to ask now.
— Because you did not ask now, you will receive
two answers during the coming week.
Listen carefully: two important answers!
One from below and one from above.
And the two will be ONE.
Listen well, for it is not I who will be speaking.

IF YOU TRULY LISTEN,
EVEN THE STONES WILL SPEAK.

Friday, January 28, 1944

32. DIALOGUE WITH GITTA

— I speak about height and depth.
Sounds float in space, they vibrate.
And yet one speaks of *high*-pitched sounds
and *low*-pitched sounds.
If we designate notes, sounds on paper,
the high ones are above and the low ones, below.
In *reality* there is no distance between them.
High and *low* are separated only on the plane of matter.
On the plane of spirit, they are near to one another.

Listen closely! I speak of the cross.

In the cross are two forces:

Upward, vertical motion:

WAY.

Horizontal motion:

RESISTANCE.
The first resistance is the earth: horizontal force.
The second resistance is water: horizontal force.
The third resistance is air: horizontal force.
The fourth resistance is between matter and non-matter.
This resistance is what you now penetrate.
There is a point where the forces intersect …
a part of the way left behind.

Gesture from below to above:

— Earth … water … air … and the 'not yet named.'
You cannot lift earth into water, nor water into air.
Everything has its place.

DO NOT LIFT; DO NOT PULL DOWN:
JOIN TOGETHER!

Earth belongs to the earth …
water to water … air to air.

MATTER AND NON-MATTER

third resistance:	AIR (thoughts)	
second resistance:	WATER (feelings)	
third resistance:	EARTH	

— MOVE BEYOND THE NEW RESISTANCE
WITHOUT LEAVING MATTER BEHIND.

Thus height and depth in the created world
become ONE.
Distance disappears not in the horizontal,
but in the vertical direction.
Machines race through the air
and the distance between above and below
becomes ever greater.
The faster they speed, the greater the distance.
Horizontal force is an inert force.
Resistance is inertia and that is good.

Gesture from below to above:

— The ascending ray transforms itself by piercing the
inertia of resistance.

*Last week I had been asking myself questions about my evolu-
tion but was unable to find a satisfying answer. Today I have
been struggling to follow the dialogue, as it seems to me rather
abstract and theoretical. Then I suddenly discover that it exactly
answers my previous questions: Evolution is possible only along
the vertical line. Evolution occurs by means of our capacity of
intuition, for only intuition is capable of attaining the new level
where spirit and matter meet. The ascending ray of evolution
transforms as it pierces the levels of matter, sentiments and
thoughts. But then the inverse takes place:*
*It is thought, sentiment and matter which are trans-
formed and fulfilled by the descending ray of light.
Descent follows ascent. This is no longer abstract for
me: it is observable within, a process of successive
detachment.*

— TODAY THE HUMAN
DOES NOT PIERCE THROUGH, INTO THE NEW,
BUT IS FLATTENED BETWEEN TWO RESISTANCES,
AND BECOMES PASSIVE.

That is the answer to your questions about evolution.

Outside there is a windstorm.

— Wind is a horizontal force.

Gesture from the throat to the mouth:

— 'The one who speaks' is weak here:
as she came to the air of the world,
this part was not yet ready.

Hanna had been born two months prematurely.

— All of you! You are now ready
to meet the challenge and break through
to the light. Act!
Only one point is difficult:
there, where the two directions intersect.
Be careful!
THERE, SPIRIT AND MATTER MEET.

Do not go astray!
Joy is no longer the way-sign it was before.
Only if you look into the depths beneath you
will you see joy.
What previously was pain you shall also leave behind.
The new Joy is still nameless.
Do you have a question?
G. How can I know that I join spirit and matter?
— By the fact that you recognize it *afterwards.*

Knowing and thinking belong to the level of air,
which is still matter – but subtle, finest matter.

There is no high and no low,
there is nothing brought low, nothing base,
if you achieve union with the Divine.
Away from the Divine, there is above and below.
United, all is One.
All of you:
May Heaven bless you!

Friday, January 28, 1944

32. DIALOGUE WITH LILI

— Ask!

L. I did not hear the two answers you promised me:
  one from below, the other from above.

— Has this week been light or heavy?

L. Heavier than last week.

— Where did you feel heaviness?

L. In my mood.

— Do you know why?

L. No.

— My little servant! The fish splashes happily about
  in the water. You move higher …
  there you are not yet able to 'splash about.'

  Silence.

— Listen well! I have more to say about
  the cross.

232

Powerful rapid vertical gesture
from below to above:

— That is the *act.*

Horizontal gesture: ⎯⎯⎯⎯⎯

— That is *rest.*
Resistance is also rest.
The body becomes weary and lies down to rest.
Where does it lie down?

Horizontal gesture: ⎯⎯⎯⎯⎯

— On the earth.
Feelings are water-related ... thoughts are air-related.
The levels become ever more subtle
and yet ever more difficult to pierce through.
The easiest to pierce is the earth ...
More force is needed to break through feelings,
and still more to penetrate thoughts.
How is this possible?
Through a rhythm of acting and resting.
The level you now break through
is beyond all weariness.

Powerful rapid gesture from above to below:

— *This* penetrates every level lovingly ...

*In a flash, I now grasp what Lili's angel had told us six weeks
ago: "If you act in the new, you cannot be tired." Only the
vertical act is beyond weariness. But we nearly always act in
the old, horizontal, passive way and therefore we are tired ... so
tired that even our sleep is disturbed.*
*I understand that matter, feelings and thoughts belong to the
world of opposites. If we become aware of how they act in us, we*

233

transcend these 3 levels of the material world and embark on the way to the 4th level. In the same way, LIGHT is then able to flood down from above, uniting the 3 lower levels with its radiance.

TODAY THE HUMAN IS INACTIVE WHEN STANDING –
AND RESTLESS WHEN LYING.

The response to your question comes
from above and from below:
You are yourself the answer.
This is why it is so difficult to become aware of it.
The true answer becomes a part of you.
Every question is a sign of lack.
The true answer fills this lack
and is no longer separated from you.
The surest answer causes a new question
to arise in you.

Outside, the wind is howling.

— The wind rages …
but we pierce through to its finest vibration;
beyond tiredness, pain, doubt and death.

We are approaching …

234

Friday, February 4, 1944

33. DIALOGUE WITH HANNA'S ANGEL

— 'The one who measures' speaks:
Spring is here.
If we wish to harvest, we must prune the trees
and graft those which are receptive.
I do not see you, but I see the tree:

THE TREE OF LIFE.

In my hand, a terrible sharp sword.
The chosen are shoots on the tree.

IF THE NEW DOES NOT PIERCE THROUGH THE OLD,
THEN I STRIKE IT DOWN.

Do not fear my sword; it strikes only what is dead.
The dead cannot be grafted.
'The one who grafts' does not bring about growth,
but chooses what is good and what is bad.
Spring is here:
what contains life shall grow.
Fear 'the one who measures' – not the sword!
The bud dreams. The cut branch also dreams.
You do not feel the edge of my sword,
so terribly sharp as it is.
I do not graft, I only measure.

TIME IS MEASURED:
ETERNAL DREAM OR ETERNAL LIFE?
FOR THE FIRST TIME, THE TREE WILL BEAR FRUIT.

We have been guarding it for a long time.
We encircle the tree: we prepare the harvest.

Buds of fruit, tarry not! Burst through the old!
This is the law.
The sign is no longer joy, the sign is no longer pain.
Be aware!

Friday, February 4, 1944

33. DIALOGUE WITH GITTA

— Listen closely:
We are four and you are four,
but that does not make eight.
'The one who measures' ... measures all of you.
'The one who helps' ... helps all of you.
'The one who builds' ... builds all of you.
'The one who shines' ... shines upon all of you.
Call us when you are unable to go on!

RIGHT NOW, ALL IS BEING DECIDED.

I sense that time is short; that tragic outer events are drawing near which we can only meet by means of inner transformation.

What is sap for the plant,
is joy of life for the human.

Sapless ... joyless ... dried out!
That is completely up to you.
Be always full of joy of life!
The sap comes from below – as does joy of life.

Decision.
What you decide: shall be.

236

Decide, delimit: here the old ... there the new.
Do this, and the wall of limits
will be behind – not before you.
It will open, it will crumble.
But first: decide.

From now on, we will be with you, always.
You too: be with us!

WE DO NOT KNOW
WHEN THE DIVINE GRAFTER WILL COME.
YOU: THE BRANCHES;
WE: THE GRAFTS,
LET US BE READY!

I am so deeply moved by these words
that tears well up in my eyes.

— Sap is the old joy.
Be joyous, be kind to each and all –
including yourself.

I am amazed.

— Do not be astonished: for you, the 'small I'
is already third-person.
G. But how can I be loving and kind to myself?
— If you leave your 'small I' behind,
it will be possible.
G. How can I do that?
— Open yourself to the joy of living: it is up to you!

Take care! You will shine ... but only if you ask!
Asking is necessary.
Never weary of asking again and again.

You may call all four of us;
you may ask all four of us.

WITHOUT YOUR ASKING, WE CANNOT GIVE.

Calling and asking are signs of lack.
Without lack, there is no place for giving.
Have you anything to ask?
G. For the last two weeks, all of my acts have seemed
empty and meaningless …
— You are still dreaming.
Once you awaken, the dream will be meaningless.
G. I have no further questions,
but I beg you to continue.
— Let my words about the joy of living
be engraved in your heart!
Spring has arrived.
And yet, we are walking in a dry and lifeless forest.
The sap no longer flows: life is devoid of joy.
Who rejoices in life?

ONLY SAP-FILLED BRANCHES WILL BE GRAFTED:
DRY BRANCHES, NEVER!

My dear ones, I depart.

*I do not understand why, but this dialogue has a completely
different effect on me than all the previous ones. A calm and
comforting joy flows through me.*

Friday, February 4, 1944

33. DIALOGUE WITH LILI

— Whom are you calling?
L. Ö and you.
— Whom are you calling?
L. You ... my teacher.
— There is but ONE TEACHER.
We merely bring you the Divine Teaching.
With whom are you speaking?
L. (hesitatingly:) with ... you.
— Are you certain?
L. (with even greater hesitation:) ... Yes.
— I am not 'the one who helps.'
'The one who helps' spoke before.
We are four and we teach you.
Today we exchanged roles.
L. Then my original feeling that it was
'the one who helps' speaking to Gitta
was right after all.

— THE ORIGINAL FEELING IS TRUE FEELING.
WHAT FOLLOWS IS REFLECTION.
ALWAYS LISTEN TO THE ORIGINAL FEELING!

The head only follows behind.
L. How wonderful that you have exchanged roles!
— When you take leave of your 'small I,'
the four become sixteen ... and ONE.
Listen carefully:
When you construct your new task,
call 'the one who builds'!
Call us: we will come!

Tomorrow call me, for then you will need to shine,
not help.

Lili will be attending a meeting of educators.

— Tomorrow you will shine forth the new Light;
not through words, but through your certainty,
for everyone there is confused.

This refers to the participants of the meeting.

— They do not search, they do not ask: they think –
and they talk and talk and talk.
Ask!

L. Please tell me more about my sign!

<table>
<tr><td>—</td><td>The sign
of the Divine</td><td>The sign of
the helper</td><td>The sign
of deliverance</td></tr>
</table>

The triangle is the sign of helping.
You are able to help someone at all times.
Your sign is a reflection of the Divine sign.
If the lower triangle is not completed,
then the one above cannot be joined to it.
We four are bearers of four forces, but we eight,
we sixteen ... we all reflect the Divine.
Ask!

L. Please tell me how body, soul and spirit are related,
are interdependent.

— If they raise themselves to the Divine,
they are related: if not, they crumble.
Everything – including spirit –
crumbles to ashes and dust if not related to Ö.

Humans consider themselves to be related beings.
But if they are not related to the Divine ...
everything crumbles.

IF YOU ARE DEPENDENT UPON THE BODY –
THEN YOU ARE BUT BODY.

IF YOU ARE DEPENDENT UPON THE SOUL –
THEN YOU ARE BUT AN ANIMATED BODY.

IF YOU ARE DEPENDENT UPON THE SPIRIT –
THEN YOU ARE BUT HUMAN.

IF YOU ARE DEPENDENT UPON THE DIVINE –
THEN YOU ARE ALL.

Be dependent only upon the Divine, and then
body, soul, spirit and Ö are ONE.
You can recognize everyone by their dependency.
Teach *true* dependency, the only freedom;
all else is slavery!

> *In spite of being ill, Lili had joyfully traveled from Budapest to
> Budaliget so that she might be present at today's dialogue.*

— Because today you were not dependent upon
your body, your soul, or even your spirit, I will carry
all of your requests to the feet of the Divine.
Everything is dependent upon something –
only the human is dependent upon the Divine.
Rise freely! It is up to you!
Help by building shining joy in yourself!
Let us adore HIM.

> *Lili and I are greatly tickled at the fact that our teachers
> exchanged their pupils today.*
> *We both feel renewed.*

Monday, February 7, 1944

> *Hanna again senses the presence of the angel who uses the German language to address us.*

Mountain peaks arise
tremble and venture
questions most high.
My toes brush the peaks,
the peaks flush with Light.

In my feet
the hollowed arches sing:
the mountains
fill with song
calling the earth
to its highest.

Free and bare,
I dance to the pulse
of the Heart
that holds All.
I raise up my arms
and the sun's bright warmth
streams through me.
The earth is gifted with light:
answer from above.

What is dense
will become light.
Dark fogs
will sparkle.
An arch of colors
will embrace the earth.

The delicate flowers
will awaken and wait.
The brightness of colors
will draw the sap
from the stony ground.
Lowest and light
will be one
and the bud bursts open.

My name is DAWN.

May your pain be gone!
Give me your hand!
I brush the peak.
Do not be meek!
You are mountain –
not hill nor mound.
Seek!
And day shall break.

> *Until now, our inner guides had revealed only the names of their specific tasks to us: the "One who measures", the "One who builds", the "One who helps" and the "One who radiates". Today the German-speaking one has revealed his name. I feel this as a gift and I am filled with joy.*

Friday, February 11, 1944

34. DIALOGUE WITH GITTA

— What is more important: force or matter?

I sense a 'trap' in this question
and answer cautiously:

G. I do not know … I would consider them to be equal.
— Which of the two is more attractive to you?
G. Force is more familiar to me …
— There is nothing more *blind* than force alone!
  Force is passive matter; passive matter is force.

  BUT THE ONE WHO GUIDES ALL
  IS NEITHER FORCE AND MATTER.

  HE is radiation.

  The rays flow into matter
  and matter ascends to the rays,
  becomes light-matter.
  His radiation penetrates and fills matter.
  Matter becomes radiant, is glorified.
  Everything in creation consists of force and matter.
  The Creator rests *within* all of creation.
  Force and matter,
  these two alone are dark and on the surface.
  If you really shine, this is not merely force:
  there is nothing more blind than force alone.

  HIS RADIATION SHINING FORTH THROUGH YOUR EYES
  IS THE *SEEING LIGHT.*

  Without this, you are nothing.

Without this, all of you are nothing.
One hand, cut off: could anything be more senseless?
Splitting off atoms! The human – foolish child! –
cuts everything apart, separates,
and will only be disappointed,
for the Divine is ONE and INDIVISIBLE.
Only inert force and forceful matter can be split.

OUT OF MANY, ONE:
THAT IS THE WAY TO THE DIVINE.

Many loaves from one loaf of bread: that is no longer
a miracle, for the earth is bountiful with bread.

> *I hear these words and at the same time I see with horror that this wonderful abundance of bread is being swallowed up by inequality and this causes continuous hunger on earth.*

— To form the HUMAN from the multitude of humans –
this is the new miracle.
This is the new Bread which satisfies every hunger,
for all will eat of it.
New measure, new direction:
from the many to the indivisible ONE,
from the multitude to being ALL-ONE.

That is enough for today:
you no longer grasp the meaning of my words.

> *This is all too true, and I feel despair.*

— Await me with a smile –
and with a smile depart from me!
Only then can I always be with you.
G. I know that my wavering moods
separate me from you …

— I cannot step into the water,
for water evaporates wherever I walk.
But water is necessary – as is fire.
Your task is to shine,
to give fire,
and fire is master over water.
Ö is Master over all.

Friday, February 11, 1944

34. DIALOGUE WITH LILI

— I greet you.

Hanna begins to say something, but suddenly stops short and a long silence ensues. I stare at her, dumbfounded.

— Do not be amazed!
'The one who speaks' was frightened.
She has witnessed the death of a distant world.

I have the impression that this refers to a celestial body.

— I speak of true and false distance.
Immeasurably far from your comprehension,
a world transforms from matter into force.
And behold! All of you sense it.

Recently we had all felt a strong change in atmospheric pressure.

246

— You sit beside one another,
your fingers touch …
and yet you can be further apart from each other
than your earth from this distant celestial body.

THE CREATION IS ONE.
IT KNOWS NO DISTANCE.

However subtle the vibration of a force:
still it is force.
Just as you are affected by this distant force,
so, too, do each of your thoughts, each of your movements, stream
through the universe and act.

THE HUMAN IS THE BODY OF HEAVEN AND
GREATER THAN ALL HEAVENLY BODIES.
THE HUMAN IS NOT A PART:
THE HUMAN IS THE WHOLE.

You hear a cry of pain or anguish.
How do you respond?
Do you let it bring you down?

> *This refers to our having been affected by the atmospheric disturbance of the past few days.*

— How distant is a small cell in the tip of the toe
from a cell in the head! How distant!
But if there is a pain anywhere in the body,
both cells feel it.
By what means? Through the spirit.
All heavenly bodies are merely cells.
The Human is the spirit.
The spirit is infinitely great and infinitely small.
When a cell dies, a new force is born,
an unknown, new, never-dreamed-of force.

247

This is not ominous

I feel that this new Force 'tests' us.

— A NEW FORCE ONLY SWEEPS AWAY
WHAT IS UNSUITED FOR LIFE.

Thus it is no loss.
Be strengthened by it!

Did you believe I was not with you?
L. No, but I was unable to rise up to you.
— If need be, I can descend to you.
The deceiver was lurking, but I watched over you.
L. What was the purpose of this evil presence?
— The task of the evil is to tempt.
But soon you will be beyond all temptation.
Extraordinary force demands extraordinary resistance.

WHAT IS INCAPABLE OF LIVING IN THE NEW
CANNOT RESIST.
WHAT IS CAPABLE OF LIVING IN THE NEW
TRANSFORMS: JUST *THERE,*
WHERE IT IS NECESSARY.

Thus, from death comes life and
from evil: good.
What casts others down enlivens you.
L. Speak of the New World, the New Human.
– HE is wholeness.
You, we, force, matter, were created to serve *HIM.*
HE can be in everything if you fulfill *one* condition:

TO JOIN TOGETHER.

Now there is still a distance between you and this task.
Our task is connected with your task.

Serve truly, so that between you and us,
there will be no more distance.
So that the distance – in space seemingly so infinitely great –
vanishes.

I remember the dying star.

The human who perceives a cry of anguish from the universe
is called to bring forth its sweetness.
The one who fails to do so
becomes the spoiler of the universe.
A bruised apple either becomes sweeter
than all the others or it rots.

Ask!
L. What is instinct?

— THE DIVINE WORD
TO THE ANIMAL.

To us all:

— All of you may ask!
J. Will there be a period of transition
or will the new World suddenly appear
in its pure form?

— THE NEW – A CHILD BORN WITHOUT PARENTS –
SWEEPS ALL OF THE OLD.

Never before seen, never before heard,

the CHILD grows.
It is still small, but the CHILD is growing.

LIGHT IS NOT BORN OUT OF DARKNESS,
BUT DARKNESS DIES WITH THE COMING OF LIGHT.

In reality, darkness does not exist.

Let us praise the Divine!

Friday, February 11, 1944

34. DIALOGUE WITH JOSEPH

After a long silence, I feel the presence of the 'building' angel.
Apparently Joseph's question about the coming of the new World
has called forth further explanations. Deeply interested in this
evolutionary event, I wait with great anticipation.

— Take heed! I have but few words.
I speak of the new building.
It does not rise from earth,
but descends from Heaven.
You are 'the one who builds.'
Follow the Plan carefully!

The spirit plans first the dwelling,
and then its dweller.
The new house calls the new dweller.
Thus, create the new world,
the new house that has never before been.
It will not remain empty.
The old building is a snail's shell
of chalky secretion from slimy creatures.

Listen in silence!

Friday, February 18, 1944

35. DIALOGUE WITH GITTA

— I will speak of the smile.
The mouth on the human face corresponds to matter:
it is below.
The mouth is pulled down by descending forces
and raised up by ascending ones.
Every animal can moan and cry.

ONLY THE HUMAN CAN SMILE.

That is the key.
We smile not only when in good humor!
Our smile is a creative smile,
not an artificial one: a creative smile!
If gravity acts,
it blocks here.

(Vertical gesture at the level of the mouth)

Everything is dragged down, everything!
The mouth belongs to the earth
and gravity belongs to the earth.
When two earthborn elements
such as gravity and matter act together,
everything becomes earthen.

The smile is an image of deliverance, a symbol.
Creative force raises matter, and that is your task.
No longer say:
"I am joyful; I laugh" or "I am sad; I cry!"
No more! That is the old way!

Badly do you educate the child that you are,
in an outmoded way: the rod spoils the child.
Improvement is only superficial.
The form changes, but not the essence.
A well-trained child is a crippled child.
Do you know me?

G. Yes.

— I AM YOUR MEASURE.
Do not measure the child with old measures,
or it will become crippled.
Nor with the measures of others.
How could you find *your* path if not by smiling?

I DWELL IN THE SMILE
AND I AM YOUR MEASURE.

The smile symbolizes mastery over matter.
If you read a book, you hold it close enough
to read it easily.
If you want to read me,
come close to me:

I DWELL IN THE SMILE.

I cannot weep, for there is no reason to weep.
No need to weep over lack.
Evil, terror, darkness: your name is *lack.*
Not lack of water, but lack of fire.
Only the incapable creature weeps.
Unable to transcend gravity,
it is swallowed up by the grave.

Now I speak to all of you.
I give you a task –
even though you *(indicating me)* have not yet
answered my previous request.

Now it will be even more difficult for you.
(to all of us)

YOUR TASK IS THE NEW WORLD.

Write down what you would do for the New World in the New World.
Thus you will become aware of your individual calling.
A mountain is measured from its foot to its peak – not just half of it.
At your peak, you reach Heaven.
Don't measure the size of the mountain at its foot!
(to me)
So you will come to know who you are.
Respond to this request in seven days!
No excuses, no forgetting!
Previously, you failed to answer –
this is why you could not be happy.
I do not speak emptily.
Even when I rebuke you: smile!

Heaven is with you.

Friday, February 18, 1944

35. DIALOGUE WITH LILI

— Listen, my beloved!
I, too, speak of the smile.
You pass it by, so familiar is it.
You are unaware of what it means.

THE SMILE IS A BRIDGE OVER THE OLD ABYSS.

Between the animal and what is beyond the animal,
there is a deep abyss.
The smile is the bridge.
Not the laugh, not the grin: the smile.
Laughing is the opposite of weeping.

THE SMILE HAS NO OPPOSITE.

Listen carefully, my servant!
You are 'the one who helps.'
The key to all your acts, to all your teaching,
is the smile. Try it! Smile!
See whether your pupils can find the inner smile!
Then they will move differently.
The smile accomplishes more than any gymnastics.

SMILE; SPEECH; CREATIVITY:
ATTRIBUTES OF THE HUMAN BEING.

But beware, for there is also the empty grin,
the mask, with its falsehood and hypocrisy!

A SMILE IS THE PRAYER OF EVERY TINY CELL,

of every one ... and it rises up to here ...

Horizontal gesture at the level of the mouth:

... it rises above all else.
The inner smile is the first condition
for becoming HUMAN.
Have you ever noticed where you actually are
when you are unable to smile?
You are in the mud, up to your neck in the mire,
or even to the crown of your head.
To smile is so simple!
And yet no one is aware of it.

Do you know someone who truly smiles? Speak!
L. I can think of no one.
— Smiling is the first condition for the Human.
 You see!
 What has become of the human race?
 They have all become clowns.
 They even abuse the human face, which is sacred.
 And what has it become?
 Ugly lumps of clay! Crumpled heaps of rags!
 Smeared masks! Godless wretches!
 There is only one way out:
 the smile that no one knows.

 In the morning when you open your eyes,
 smile at me!
 Whenever you begin something, such as teaching,
 smile at me!
 May everyone try, and learn to smile!
 Observe the true smile: how do you recognize it?
 The eye is not part of it; only the mouth.

> *I am very surprised to learn that the eye does not participate in*
> *the smile; I assume the angel will explain this to us in due time.*

— Speak!
L. What is good behavior, what are good bearings?
— What do you mean by this?
L. I believe I should be open and respond well to everyone.
— These expressions refer to something for which there is no word.
 'Behavior' and good bearings are questionable expressions.
 One raises a child to 'behave well', to have good bearings.
 This refers to the outer form, not to one's harmony with the inner.
 When *HE* bears you, then you have no need for good bearings.
 Then you have no need to learn 'rules of good behavior.'

When the human bears alone, 'behaves', then *HE* is missing.
The poor human – bearing well, and falling as a result.
What you seek, you will not find by good bearings.
Only what is heavy and inert needs bearing.

When HE acts through you
then you need not bear, nor bear yourself well.
Practice the only true bearing, known as smiling –
then you will be open.
May this be the solution in all of your acts:
when you smile, *HE* bears you –
then you have nothing to fear.

L. Please speak to me of the hand.
— The hand means: to be formed, to be ready.
  The tool is ready ... readiness.

> *The hand opens.*

— Giving ...

> *The hand closes into a clawed position.*

— Taking.
  The clawed hand is animal strength.
  The open hand is ready.

> *My hands are closed, without my being aware of it.*
> *To me:*

— Your hand is not yet ready.
  With you, it is neither jealousy nor greed,
  but lack of self-trust.
  You do not yet believe that Ö gives through you.
  You do not yet believe that you are worthy.
  Be ready! The hand smiles, too: everything smiles.

Again to Lili:

— Ask!

L. Why do we try to accomplish our will rather than:
   "Thy will be done"?

— Because you ignore the Divine Will.
   If you were able to perceive It,
   then you would not wish to accomplish your own!
   Divine Will is *fulfillment.*
   Let us fulfill it!
   Now only human will is fulfilled.
   Not Divine Will.
   The human is the fiercest of all beasts.
   No animal claw, no lion's clutch is as predatory
   as the human hand.
   The one who takes shall be taken from,
   for the one who takes is not worthy of having hands.

   THE HAND IS NOT MADE FOR TAKING.

   Do you have any more questions?

L. How could the four of us strengthen our unity?

— By fulfilling your individual task.
   Your task is the new World.

   WHAT WOULD YOU DO IN THE NEW WORLD
   FOR THE NEW WORLD?

   THE SIGN OF YOUR TRUE INDIVIDUALITY IS:
   TO RECOGNIZE YOUR OWN UNIQUE TASK.

   Know what you are called upon to do!
   Anything else is at best balm for the pain caused by
   too much or too little, excess or lack.

I remain with you ... only the word departs,
for it is a child of time.

*After the dialogue, Hanna tells us that we are being asked by
our teachers to write out, for the next session, an answer to the
question: "What would you do in the new World for the new World?*

Friday, February 25, 1944

36. DIALOGUE WITH GITTA

*As requested, I have written out my response to the question,
"What would you do in the new World for the new World?"
However, I am doubtful about its quality, and I feel quite uneasy.*

— Ancient earth-ploughing tribes and shepherds sacrificed the most
beautiful grains, the most perfect fruit
and the healthiest livestock to their gods.
They offered the first fruits of their efforts.
This offering was an image, an early model
for today's task: to elevate matter to meet the spirit.
Only when they made offerings did they receive rain.
At that time, water was still above
and was the most precious of gifts.

Other ages came and *knowledge* arrived.
Now it is the human who eats the most perfect apple,
the best grain, the most beautiful fruit.
The worm-eaten, windfallen apple is painted bright red
and displayed so that all can see
that sacrifice has duly been made.

But the tiny worm in the apple – child of the Divine –
pierces through the paint,
and the fraud is exposed.
Stone, wind, water, fire, plants and animals
rise up and accuse the human being,
for now the earth has been painted *red*. And behold:
it is blood!

Silence.

— May each of your deeds and each of your tasks
be genuine offering!
Only the most beautiful, the most perfect
of what you bring forth is worthy of being laid
at the feet of the Divine.
Does Ö need apples? ... Does Ö need wheat?
The Divine Law is wholeness.
Bring me the first fruit of your labors
and I will carry it to the Divine.
Thus you will receive the blessing for a new sowing.
Instead of rain: a new task.

> *In the course of the past week, I repeatedly postponed the writing out of my 'homework-assignment': "What would I do in the new World for the new World?" The topic was so far-reaching and bewildering to me that I was hardly able to imagine this new World. Actually, the assignment had not surprised me so much: it was not unusual for the angels to demand the impossible from us, only to have it later revealed as possible after all. Yesterday, I finally wrote down my thoughts: conscientiously, but without the slightest touch of enthusiasm.*
>
> *I have the feeling that I could have answered the question about my task for the new World in a better way. All that became clear to me was that I can only pass through the gate to this new World*

by becoming fully aware of my individual abilities. On the eve of the seventh day, I finally wrote an answer, but more out of a sense of duty than with conviction.

— Knowledge has misled you.
Rather than becoming aware of the whole,
you have concentrated only on what the effort cost you.
Only complete concentration counts –
all knowledge derives from this.

G. Why was I unable to concentrate in a complete way?

— You failed to give the task your complete attention.
Ask!

G. Even when I am able to smile, it does not last long,
and soon I begin to sink down.

— "Peter walked on the water." That is my answer.
When he ceased to believe in himself, he sank.

IF YOU BELIEVE IN YOURSELF,
THEN YOU BELIEVE IN THE DIVINE.

Do not err: there are not *two* ... there is but ONE.

Belief has no direction: no above and no below.
Do not despise matter:
for everything is the Divine Body.
You only think you believe.
If you sink, you cease to believe.
The MASTER walked upon water, and did not sink.
He carried the FATHER in Himself –
He was united with the Divine.
Is this your goal?

G. Yes.

— CAN YOU BE UNITED WITH THE DIVINE
WITHOUT *BEING* THE DIVINE?

Do not err, and you will not sink.

Silence.

— I teach you: Whenever you are criticized,
regardless of the source, this is a sign of a lack:
it reflects not an incapacity on your part,
but your capacity.

MAY EVERY CRITICISM RAISE YOU HIGHER:
CRITICISM EXPANDS YOUR CAPACITY.

Every object, every being around you, asks of you;
but only for that which you are *capable* of giving.
Who asks of the pitiable, the incapable?
Who asks for figs from the thistle?
The fig tree is shaken, for figs are expected of it.
Bring forth fruit! Do not worry if you are shaken!
No one bothers to shake the thistle!
Ask!

G. How might I attain the highest degree of my own fire?

— By achieving what is possible for you.
You have no *own* fire. There is but ONE fire.
What is your own is what you deserve.
What you transmit … is your *own*.
The nearer the circle to the Divine,
the more fire can come down,
and a new 'I' is born to you.
You *own* nothing:
you are nothing and you are everything. Choose!

TO THE GIVER OF ALL FIRE!

*Silent prayer. Lili has not finished her notes
and continues to write … Sternly to her:*

— The time of prayer is not the time of writing.

Friday, February 25, 1944

DIALOGUE WITH 'THE ONE WHO MEASURES'

> *Today we all feel the silent presence of 'The one who measures.'*
> *This long silence is suddenly broken by the incessant ringing of*
> *the bells of the nearby church, 'Maria Remete.' This unusually*
> *loud and long-lasting ringing is used in the village only as an*
> *alarm signal at the outbreak of fire. We do not read our essays*
> *aloud, for each of our thoughts and feelings is clearly evident*
> *to the angel. Finally, the bell ceases to ring and 'the one who*
> *measures' speaks:*

— I bring the inner bell to ring.
What does the inner bell reveal?
I ask this in the name of your self-assessment.
Have you truly become aware
of your full potential?
For that is what matters:
not the words you have written.
Could you have become aware of more?
If so, we have nothing to add.
We begin only there where you
truly come to your limit.

> *To me:*

Answer! I require your true measure:
not too high and not too low.
Look at me!

> *With lowered gaze, I stutter that, at the moment,*
> *I could not have achieved anything better.*

G. I tried as best I could to fulfill the assignment about the New World, but I was still unable to find the Seven Joys.
— With your words, you judge yourself.
I ask again.
Do not answer with your head!
Did you become aware of what is possible for you?
It is not I who measure now, but you.
G. This week I was unable to answer better.
— The One Who Measures weighs all.
Be aware of this.
Why were you unable to do better?
G. I was able to smile only with great difficulty.
— Is there nothing more?
G. A self-evaluation is very difficult for me, because I don't really know myself.
— For whom would it not be difficult?
What is difficult for you is simple for others.
But you have abilities that others do not have.
You have more abilities than you believe.
You underestimate yourself!
Not in your task, but in your evaluation.
You are capable of more, in every sense.

I had believed that true self-assessment is impossible, but Joseph proves me wrong. He is the only one of us who had intuitively perceived the meaning of our 'final examination,' as it came to be known. When asked,

— "My son, what does the inner bell say?"

He simply answers with joyful certainty that he has given his very best.
Indeed, he had written his answer with astonishing clarity. From this moment on, 'the one who measures' the most severe of our

teachers, talks with him as with an intimate friend, and advises him to now live the intuitively perceived dimensions. Further, Joseph is assured that this is indeed possible:

— You can live it, for the one with whom you are united
is close to you.
A new circle is open to you.
Give it your full awareness.
Realize what it reveals to you!

At last, I grasp that, with this final examination, we were not expected to summarize, in a more or less logical way, something that was already known, as is the case with the university exams throughout the world. No, our task was exactly the contrary: to let go of everything known and to spring into the never-before-seen, the never-before-heard, the never-before-known, guided only by our intuition ... and our faith. Only Joseph had ventured the leap.

Friday, February 25, 1944

36. DIALOGUE WITH JOSEPH

For Joseph, it is often difficult to say 'yes' to life. The gloomy prospects of the year 1944 make this ever harder for him. Yesterday, as he struggled with this existential problem, the ceiling and a part of the wall in his workshop suddenly caved in on top of him. Joseph was not injured, but rubble and stones lay all around him on the floor. This greatly impressed Joseph, and he attributes symbolic meaning to it.

— You are 'the one who builds.'
Dig and prepare the foundation!
Fill the hole with stones. *Then* you may build on it.
The house cannot be built upon wooden planks.
The motto of your way is not, *'it was,'*
nor, 'it would be good';
and certainly not, *'it is good.'*
The key word of the builder is: *'BE!'*
'It was' signifies omission;
'it would be good,' incapacity;
'it is good,' smugness.
Your motto is: *'BE!'*

Your Heaven is green
because the earth is green.
The law of gravity binds *and* raises up.

I speak to you with joy.
If you and I are unable to speak,
then the stones speak to you:
the message was for you!
The stones fell to the earth
to show where your lack is.
But the recognized lack is no longer a lack.

In the name of silence that builds.

I later ask Hanna the meaning of: "Your Heaven is green because the earth is green. The law of gravity binds and raises up." She explains that Joseph is 'of Heaven' and therefore lacks the weight of earth necessary for reaching an equilibrium between matter and spirit. She tells me that I, for my part, am 'of earth' and my task is therefore to reach towards Heaven, thus compensating my excess of matter and my lack of spirit. Regrettably, all of our 'examination notes' and other materials

265

related to this exchange perished in the perilous months that followed.

Friday, February 25, 1944

36. DIALOGUE WITH LILI

For Lili, there is no 'final examination': Political catastrophes are casting their shadows everywhere and her pupils have taken all of her time as they spilled out their fears to her. Understandably, for the reality of the Nazi gas-chambers is already common knowledge. Lili's brother is the proprietor of a distinguished café downtown near the Parliament and one could always be sure to find Lili there, surrounded by her frightened pupils in a quiet corner until far into the night. And so she had not written out the assigned task, an omission that is pointed out to her only very gently:

— The tiny sprout has no idea of the heights to which
it will grow, and yet it swells and stretches
as it strives toward the light.
The intensity of its effort
determines the ultimate outcome.
Take heed!

EVERYTHING DEPENDS UPON
THE INTENSITY OF THE EFFORT.

The knowledge that, in its depths,
the promise of a great tree reposes, would be in vain
were it not for tiny sprouts striving and growing
toward the light.

The ground is so hard and the earth so heavy
that to overcome it, the sprout must persevere
with all of its strength.
My little servant, you have made an error.
To fulfill the task, you must strive mightily.
Fulfilling the task helps you to grow.
The more you grow, the more you can give.
And the greater your task, the greater your growth.
You helped two people;
but you neglected two hundred,
and your task could become two thousand.
Do you believe this?

L. Yes … I am certain of it.

— Let this be a lesson to you:
Raise your helping higher, far higher,
above the level of feelings.
Had you completed your assignment,
forces that you cannot even imagine
would have served you.
They are still imprisoned in you,
for you have not opened the door.

L. Where is the locked door in me?

— You already fulfill the small task well.
But from now on, take on a different role:
be Maria and not Martha!
Renew your search and you will find 'more.'

SEARCH WITH *TOTAL FAITH;*
THERE IS NO OTHER WAY.

Honor your task above all else, and then –
believe me! – then you will be able to help.

   Silence

The force between you four is wonderful.
If you are aware of this,
(to Gitta:) then to smile will not be difficult,
(to Lili:) then you will easily fulfill your task,
then nothing will cause you pain.
If only you could have faith – a creative faith!
A double faith: in the above, in the below –
in *HIM,* in you!
If one faith is missing, then the other is in vain.
(to Gitta:) To smile is not difficult!
You are *HIS* creation – do not despise *HIS* work!
Above, below and all around:
The Divine is everywhere.

Saturday, February 26, 1944

36. DIALOGUE WITH LILI (CONTINUED)

> *It is Saturday. Lili is in the workshop, trying to immerse herself*
> *in yesterday's lesson. Suddenly, she feels an intense inner light.*
> *We are all aware of the unexpected presence of her angel.*

— The moment, the time and the occasion
  are out of the ordinary.
  Nevertheless I have come to you,
  for my task is to help.
  Do you still have doubts?
  Are you still in the dark?
L. Oh, no … but I feel my task to be enormous.
— That is not darkness, but light that is too strong.

The eye cannot see in the absence of light,
but neither can it see when the light is too strong.
You have received three sparks today.
Do you feel them?
L. Not yet.
— What are your greatest lacks?

Lili answers with astonishing promptness:

L. Lack of faith, lack of giving and
lack of work!
— Not lack of work ... lack of *doing* your work!
You have enough work ... you simply do not *act* on it.

THE THREE POINTS
OF YOUR SIGN WILL IGNITE
FROM THE THREE SPARKS:
HAVING FAITH – GIVING – ACTING.
FAITH IN YOURSELF AS WELL.

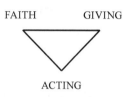

FAITH   GIVING

ACTING

The three sparks are not confined to time and space.
The three lacks are fulfilled ... they no longer exist.
You will see that this is so.
The slow body perceives this only later.
But you are not only body;
your task is completed by more than the body.

KNOW THE WHOLENESS IN YOURSELF
AND YOU WILL BECOME WHOLE.

To fulfill your lacks is no longer your task:
now may the fruit come!
Do you believe that the impossible is possible?
What you received today is a foretaste of wholeness.

Silence.

All of you: Pay close attention!

THE WORD CONCENTRATES, IT FOCUSES:
THE WORD CREATES.

To Lili who had written down her lacks this morning:

— You formed your lacks into words
and thus the sparks could come.

To me:

— Be aware of the word!

THE WORD BUILDS.

Which stone is fit into which
is of the utmost importance,
for what you build might otherwise collapse.
All of you! You do not know how to use the word.
The husk is not the corn;
the chaff is not the grain.
Word – Name – Mystery.
Listen carefully, for what I say is of the essence.
If you say: *'Be!'* it will be.
If you say nothing, nothing will be.
Not: 'If only it could be!'
Five words are less than this one: *Be!*
'Sometimes I believe' is less than 'I believe!'
'How I would like to always be able to help'
Ten words! ... *'I help'* – one word *
and there is no breach, either in the words or in you.
The ACT is the word of the body.
Wholeness is not the *many,*
but the intense, the concentrated, the focused;
and that is the measure of the eternal.

* One word in the original Hungarian.

Ask more ... as a provision for the journey!

L. I wish that all of this would remain as strong in me
as it is at this moment!

— Do not wish for what you already have!
Raise your wishes to a higher level.
The body is slow, but it, too, will become aware.

Friday, March 3, 1944 (Morning)

37. DIALOGUE WITH GITTA

This morning, as I tried to find the Seven Joys,
I could suddenly feel the heart of my being.

— I speak to you of the Seven Joys.
You have reached the heart of your task,
though with more difficulty than necessary.
The Seven Joys are seven gates.
You could have entered the sphere
through the seven gates.
The gates open inwards and outwards.
Your new task is to radiate the Seven Joys from inside;
through the same seven gates,
but now they open outwards.

THE EYE SEES AND IT SHINES.

May Ö help you in your task!

Friday, March 3, 1944 (Afternoon)

37. DIALOGUE WITH GITTA

— I speak of your older brother.
   Listen:
   He will connect with the one who guides.
   He will be a good and useful partner.
   What you lack, he has.
   He is of heaven, you of the earth.
   The morning is the mediator
   between the sun and the earth.
G. 'He is of heaven': I do not understand….
— He came from above.
   Now comes the turning point.
G. Can I help him to free himself
   from the old, as quickly as possible?
— Is that necessary? He receives everything from above.
   If you transform yourself, if you turn around, he also will transform
   himself and turn around.
   Do not help him!
   Only the weak require help.
G. Tell me more!
— We have accepted your response as you wrote it.
   It is not about writing, it is about living the answer!
   Solve your assignment in this way:
   Let no day pass without opening the gates of joy.
   Open them in the *morning*, not in the evening!

G. It is so hard for me to master my time …
— It is not your task to master time.
   Your task is to reach beyond time.
   No-one can make two hours out of *one*.

272

If you – for only an instant – reach beyond time,
you see all Seven Joys at once.
Listen! If you approach the sphere from outside,
you can perceive only one gate at a time.
But from within, you see all seven gates at once.
The sphere rotates, every sphere rotates:
this is what makes it a sphere.
Every form is shaped according to the law
of its motion.
The sphere turns, but you do not.
At the center of the great sphere is the Divine, *motionless.*
All is in motion except Ö.
Ö created the human in the Divine image.
Ö entrusted the human with the small sphere.

> *With bitter irony:*

— Human beings have arranged it well!
They do nothing but run around on its surface,
and thus they get nowhere.
Ask.

G. What should the starting point of my work be?
— Certainty!
Can the head be certain?
G. No.
— Listen carefully!
Make no plans with the head:
carry plans out with the head!

The Plan is with the Divine; *every* Plan.
But you: you plan what is to be done with your head;
you apply your head to your work prematurely.
The head and time are one.

> *Unable to understand the meaning of these words,*
> *I hold my head in my hands.*

— Do not break your head!
THE PLAN IS BEYOND TIME.
Become one with the Plan,
and you will never hurry and never tarry.

I do my best to understand, and remain silent.

— Ask, for our time is passing quickly.
G. I make so many superfluous movements ...
Teach me proper movement!
— There is nothing 'superfluous' on earth
and there is no lack; it is only that the 'superfluous,'
the 'excess,' does not fill the lack.
Excess in one place
creates a lack somewhere else.
Do not cast away the superfluous;
in reality, nothing is superfluous.

YOU ARE ACCOUNTABLE
FOR EVERY MOVEMENT YOU MAKE.

Know this, and the superfluous
will soon find its proper place.

Do you act according to
what is expected of you?
G. No – certainly not!
— You see: nothing is superfluous.
Take away nothing, add nothing:
but join the *too much* to the *too little;*
help everything to its proper place.
Lack reveals the *too much,* and excess, the *too little.*
Direct one to the other and all will be well!
In the name of fulfillment.

Friday, March 3, 1944

37. DIALOGUE WITH LILI

— I speak to all of you.
Become pure: pure from the old!
What is the old? The imperfect.
Why become pure?
For this reason: your asking creates.
What you ask for *shall come to be.*
You may no longer ask for yourselves,
for you have no more lack.
What you ask for – purified from the old – *shall be.*
But it is necessary for you to ask.

To Joseph:	Woe unto you if you look back!
To me:	Woe unto you if you look back!
To Lili:	Woe unto you if you look back!
To me:	The good worker deserves daily bread
	so as to be able to give heavenly bread.
To Joseph:	The good worker deserves shelter
	so as to be able to build heavenly shelter.
To Lili:	The good worker deserves solitude
	so as to be able to give to the multitudes.
To Hanna:	The good worker deserves silence
	so as to be able to speak.

There is no compromise!
The Divine Law is wholeness,
and all is contained in the whole.
The greater embraces the lesser.
To Lili:
None of your little sheep will be lost.
What kept them together until now?
Did they come merely to move their bodies?

275

When your *faith* grows,
they will flock to you in still greater numbers.
— Do you have any questions?
L. Yes: Please speak about purity.
— May all your acts, thoughts, works and feelings
be truly pure!

PURITY IS: EVERYTHING IN ITS PLACE.

Impurity is: the act out of place.
Muddled thinking is impure,
feelings mixed up with the spirit are impure!

> *I think of the dialogue of January 28 about keeping the different*
> *levels of being distinct from one another.*

— Nothing is dirty; that is an ugly word!
There is only impurity.
Always be in your place:
your inner as well as your outer place.
May the place not change you,
but you, the place!

The church in which God is worshipped
is holy and pure.
But if religion dies, it might become a warehouse.
A church becomes a church
through veneration of God.
Temples, churches* and religions are still dying.
But the new Temple, the new Church, has no walls;
it is eternal.
You are the builders and future priests
of the immortal temple.

---

* As previously noted, the Hungarian word *templom* corresponds to both the
English 'church' and 'temple.'

It is known as: The World delivered.

Silence.

— Is something disturbing you?
L. No, but something in me stood still and
  kept me from moving forward.
— This means you have found the way!
  The shell was no hindrance until you found your task.
  Believe me, only now is the shell impure!
  As long as it protects, it is pure.
  But for you, it is now a hindrance: leave it!
  The egg needs the shell – not the bird.
  A bird does not return to the shell.

  Ask!
L. I am worried about my pupil, Clara. Why is she so ill?
— The answer is in her name, which means: purity.
  She offends against her own name
  by hiding impurity from herself.
  Hidden impurity is the cause of all illness.

  *As I record the dialogue, the lead mine of my pencil slips from
  position and I am unable to continue writing. I impatiently shake
  the pencil in an attempt to fix it so that I can continue with my
  notes.*
  To me:

— You have made a superfluous movement.
  You cannot account for it – it is impure.
  Love the tool you hold in your hand!
  Ö demands that you account for every one of your acts,
  every one of your movements.
  To serve the Divine is the secret of freedom.

Turning again to Lili:

— Shall we take leave?

L. Oh, please – not yet!

— If you stand on the tips of your toes,
   you can already reach me.
   There is no more pit
   from which you cannot reach up to me.
   Soon the *more* will arrive.
   It rests in the womb of solitude and silence.
   May Heaven be with you!

Friday, March 10, 1944

38. DIALOGUE WITH GITTA

— There is a point – the focal point – and it is known as
   'eternity.'
   It is the point of security and mastery.
   What deceives you?
   The great deceiver: *Time.*

   THE HUMAN IS NOT AT HOME IN TIME:
   THE HUMAN IS *HOMELESS* IN TIME.

   Take just one step and the stream pulls you along:
   the stream of time.
   The stream is the sign of time.
   But you are not frogs and certainly not fish!

   Past – present – future.
   One person regrets the past: the other fears it.
   One has hopes for the future: the other fears it.

There is no present, no 'now,'
for the human lives either in the past
or in the future.
Past – present – future.
All three are but one stream:
one single, indivisible stream,
the movement of subtle matter.
To *view* the stream
and to *be in it*
are not the same!

THE HUMAN IS ALSO MASTER OF THE STREAM.
THE TRUE ACT IS ETERNITY,
PRESENT IN TIME.

To hurry is not to *act.*
The point of which I speak is beyond the river.
Past, present and future are three rays.
Their focal point is eternity: eternal reality.
Step out of time, my servant,
and you will be its master.
The *creative act* can only spring
from the point of eternity.

G. I do not know the name of the
doorway leading to timelessness.
I have searched in vain all week.
Where am I lost?

— In time.
This is why I speak to you of time.
How many doorways do you seek?

G. One.

— I'll give you one hundred thousand!
May each act, each thought, each rest
be *offered* to the Divine!

279

Thus everything leads to Ö:

EVEN THE MINUTEST IS WORTHY
OF OFFERING TO Ö.

What bliss your existence would be
if you could truly offer!
Do you have another question?
G. Speak to me about the new Sun.
— Clouds of fog still veil it,
otherwise it would be visible to you now.
There is still too much water in you.

> *I know that 'water' refers to the unstable movements of my
> moods in the stream of time.*

— The new Sun is not yet able to pierce the fog in you.
Do not expect the Sun to come from outside;
there you will never see it.

Your task is the *act.*
We do not act, we do not give, we do not take;
we were not, nor shall we be.
We *are* through the Divine.

Let us bow our heads – the Divine is with us!

Friday, March 10, 1944

38. DIALOGUE WITH LILI

— In its brief fast life,
a fish lays millions of eggs.

Two would be enough.
Two offspring suffice to transmit what since eternity has been *ONE*.
The much, the many, increase the distance from *HIM*.
The circle is becoming smaller, we are closer to *HIM*.
New direction, new proportion:
from the many to the undivided one,
from the many to the solitary.

More supplements and improvements are not needed.
Can you glue another fruit to the tree?
Helping is not a matter of adding and glueing.
The Divine does not glue together;
the Divine enables growth.
Help the Divine and you save the world!
The hand of the Divine is near: it is you.

— Do you have questions?
L. Teach me my earthly and heavenly tasks.
— The earth is fulfilled.
But heaven does not yet burn in you.
You do not have two places: your place is in the middle.
Earthly and heavenly life comprise seven levels:
three are completed;
three are beyond the finite;
and the *Fourth* in the middle will find them all.
Thus the seven levels become one,
and the abyss ceases to exist.
The *Fifth* speaks to you.
L. I do not completely understand ...
— You do not understand even half of it.
The *Fourth* in the middle unites the three earthly
with the three heavenly levels.
I belong to the *Fifth* level.
You are my support on earth.

281

Faith is the bridge over which you reach
the place of the *Fourth.*
The *Fourth* no longer has faith:
the *Fourth* already ACTS.

   To Joseph:

His house has four walls
Its roof is heaven, its floor is the earth.
Green and blue.
Heaven protects better than all roof-tiles.
If HE looks after it, this dwelling will not become wet.
Its four walls are the four directions of heaven
into which your acts flow.
The force is never exhausted.
It never dries up, it will never overflow.

   To Gitta:

For *one* loaf of bread, a small place is enough.
The multitude, the many separates from *HIM.*
What is enough will burn all of the excess.
Excessive weight only causes harm.

   Ask!
L. What does it mean to be bound by obligation?
— It is the opposite of the ACT.
   Turn away from it, because you would lose yourself.
   Defend yourself from being bound!
   When the rope breaks, it will be broken forever.
   HIS word is: BE FREE!
   If HE can act through you,
   then all of the old ropes are torn asunder.
   And only dust and ash remain.
   The rope belongs to the hangman.

Listen: a world falling into dust and ashes
cannot be bound together again, repaired.
We are not bound to one another,
and yet we are with each other.
HE is our witness.

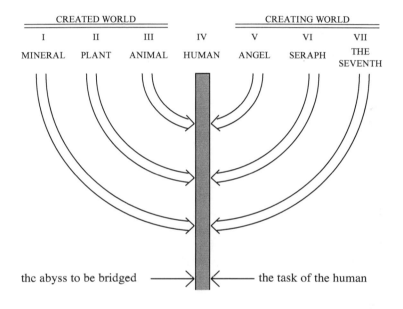

CREATED WORLD				CREATING WORLD		
I	II	III	IV	V	VI	VII
MINERAL	PLANT	ANIMAL	HUMAN	ANGEL	SERAPH	THE SEVENTH

the abyss to be bridged ⟶ ⟵ the task of the human

This dialogue with Lili seems to me like an abstract, incompre-
hensible play of numbers. I ask Hanna to explain it, particularly
the meaning of the 'Five.' She then sketches the diagram (above)
from an earlier dialogue (see p. 122), but this time, she adds
the elements that had been missing.
All of a sudden, the context becomes clear to me: I see this sketch
as a symbol of all that the angels have been explaining to us.
It illustrates the teaching in a structured order. At last, I grasp
the place of the human being in creation. I discover a new

*balance, in which fleeing into the spirit and disdaining matter
are just as wrong as clinging to matter while denying the spirit.
I realize how important and essential it is to fully affirm the life
of the body as well as that of the spirit.*

*And finally, I also discover my own dignity: the dignity of the
individual human who is called to unite spirit and matter. Never
have I so intensely felt that creation cannot be fulfilled without
the participation of the human. It is only through me, the human
being, the fourth in the middle, that my angel can act on earth.
With this discovery, my life takes on a wholly new meaning. I
have the possibility and the task of uniting matter and spirit, in
my body as in my soul.*

Friday, March 17, 1944

39. LAST PERSONAL DIALOGUE WITH GITTA

— The sphere is wholeness, fulfillment:
  the APPLE indicates the power of wholeness.*
  If you eat it and do not act,
  if you take it and do not give it on,
  then you do not deserve the *six*.
  The power of the *Six* acts everywhere.
  What is power? I will reveal it to you:
  Listen! The *Five* is the angel – the *Six* is the seraph.
  The seraph is to me what I am to you:
  intermediary and master.
  The seraph and I are one.
  Thus, the three levels are fulfilled and completed.

* The orb, symbol of royal power, is known in Hungarian as the 'Apple of Royalty.'

*I feel a radiance shining forth from Ö, passed on through the
seraph and passed on further through my angel.*

— But where is the *Four?*
  Ö does not tolerate emptiness,
  for the Divine is known by the name of 'wholeness.'
  Your place is the *Four.*
  There the near and the far cease to be.
  Bow down your head before the Divine
  but hold it high before all others!
  Only the ACT makes you master.
  Do you hear my words?
G. Yes.
— Do you understand my words?
G. Yes.
— Do not hear them, do not understand them: *live* them!
  Do not fear the Divine: *serve* the Divine!
  Fear exists only below.

ONLY AT THE PEAK OF YOUR QUESTION
WILL YOU FIND AN ANSWER.
I AM THERE; ONLY FROM THERE CAN I ANSWER.

Anything done only halfway brings no blessing:
it *cannot* bring a blessing.
Always take the way that leads upward:
never deviate and never stand still!
Standing still is the *second death.*

THIS IS THE TEACHING:
EVERYTHING HAS ITS PEAK,
AND THE PEAK IS YOUR PLACE.

Heaven be with you.

The angel has often mentioned the task of the human being to rule over the Created World like a just and righteous monarch. This message came in various forms. In the 29ᵗʰ dialogue, the royal scepter was given to us, of course in a symbolic way. Today, the second royal attribute is emphasized: the orb, which is the sign of royal power and wholeness. I have the vague foreboding that today's dialogues might be our last such personal instructions.

Friday, March 17, 1944

39. DIALOGUE: 'THE ONE WHO MEASURES'

— What is measured by 'the one who measures'?
Space.
The circle in which your hand does not act
is worthless.
The Divine sows the act, and the human receives it.
Circle and act exist in time and space.
And Ö measures them through me:

WHERE ARE YOUR ACTS?

The time is ripe, the circle grows.
Ö sees everything:

WHERE ARE YOUR ACTS?

Space is whatever your hand can fill.
The hand is formed, but it is not yet forming.
There is no escape!
All ways converge at the ONE and ONLY point.

Light – the only Reality!
Through Light, the creature *is*.
You are a creature and you are Light. This is so.
The toad sits in the water, tepid,
neither fish nor mammal.
Toad or angel?
The weighing scales are empty:
your acts are insufficient.
It bores me to measure emptiness:
I long to offer fruit.
The Divine expects more of you!
May your hand be ready!
The Divine speaks. May your ear now hear,
for the Divine speaks through me.

> *The urgency of these stern words awakens in me a sense of approaching catastrophe; catastrophe which can only be met if we have first gone through a transformation.*

Friday, March 17, 1944

39. LAST PERSONAL DIALOGUE WITH LILI

— Look at your sign, the triangle, the three:
How does this lead to the Four?

Showing the right hand:
— Force.

Showing the left hand:
— Matter.

Indicating the heart:
— The 'acting one.'

Matter is the task, force is the means,
and the 'acting one' is Ö.
What is the fourth? The ACT.
In this way, the new Building is completed.

Your lack is filled; your past is dissolved.
The old disappears: and Heaven opens up.
Dance! To join Heaven and earth is your ACT.
Thus every movement you make
becomes heavenly dance.
I, too, am a dancer: I dance for the Divine.

I feel that the angel's dancing is creation through rhythm.

— Dance for me and for Ö!
Your hands are free, your feet laugh.
I am one with you: our lips sing the same song.

To Hanna: Every song is sung for Ö.
To Lili: Every dance is danced for Ö.
To me: Every ray is a bird in flight to Ö.
To Joseph: Every wall of the new House
stands through Ö.

Now the one song with four voices
rises to the Divine.

It becomes ever more clear to me that we can reach the fourth level, where every one of our acts becomes ACT, only when we act at our own task.

Friday, March 17, 1944

39. LAST PERSONAL DIALOGUE WITH JOSEPH

— The earth below is just as near
   as the silence above: they are ONE.

THE EARTH, THE GREEN EARTH, IS YOUR HEAVEN.

Only on the earth can the act be accomplished.
Empty is the earth,
but the Divine Hand fills it –
the Hand whose name is 'the Human.'
The Human is: 'The one who builds.'
The Human is: 'The one who helps.'
The Human is: 'The one who shines.'
The Human is: 'The one who acts with measure.'

Your name is: 'Messenger of Heaven.'
Never forget this, for your place is here on earth.
Only in this way can Heaven and earth be joined.

The ancient whirlpool devours all the stones
from which the House of God was built.
But you: Build new Walls for Heaven here below!
Not walls of stone, but of Law,
of Rhythm and of Song.
Heavenly messenger, Ö is with you!

289

Friday, March 24, 1944

40. DIALOGUE: SONG OF THE CHORUS

All of Hungary is in deep shock:
in an overnight operation,
the country has been occupied by German troops.

— The Seventh Heaven is just as near
as the earth below where your feet rest.
There He is King.
Never again will He come to earth.
Blinding Light: sole reality.
The King, eternal Being,
dressed in white fire flaming up to Ö.
You are His servants. Serve Him:
Him, the glorious Being of Light,
too brilliant for the human eye.
Him, the eternally unbelievable,
the only Source of belief!

All of you: you are His blood.
You are: JESUS.
You are in His place.
You act, you live, you become.
And He is the Source, the Way, the Truth.
He is Life.

Darkness and horror fade when Light can come.
The Light that we give is twice softened.
It is so strong that the world would burst into flames
were we not to filter it with our wings.
Raise yourselves! Filter the Light once more!
This is the only way for the Light to come.

FIRE DESCENDS UPON THE EARTH.

If Heaven burns in you,
then all the old burns away.
Behold: In the old, which burns away,
He is unable to act.
Only when all the old in you is burned away
will you see Heavenly fire.
Before then, you would be burned by it.

Earthly fire comes only from the earth
and consumes only what is of the earth.
The heavenly is not consumed,
for it is the Fire itself.
To carry and bring this Fire is a noble act.
Become pure! Serve Him!
Only thus is it possible!
The Light you bring down is marvelous.
It burns only where change is necessary.

In the vessel, there is no more water: only blazing Fire,
for He who is above all baptizes with Fire.
Let go of the water!
The name of all suffering: the leak, rupture.
Be filled with Fire! The time is near.
If the vessel is cracked
the Fire flows out: disaster!

THE FIRE COMES THROUGH YOU –
THROUGH YOU ALONE.
BUT ONLY IF YOU ACT: ACT!

Only in this way can the earth receive heavenly Fire.

Outside, a storm is raging.

— The wind whirls and roars, the snowstorm rages.
But already it is on the wane,
for warmth, sprouting and the Light are near.
Believe me: He comes
and He is the LIGHT.

We sense that not only our angels are speaking today, but also a much greater force. This dialogue was of a never-before-experienced intensity.

Friday, March 24, 1944

40. DIALOGUE: MESSAGE FOR LILI

As a result of the Nazi occupation of Hungary, all means of travel have come to a standstill and there is no way for Lili to make her way from Budapest to our village.

— The angel of 'the one who helps' is here.
What you just heard was the Song of the Chorus.
Now I speak to the one who is away
and yet is here.
Darkness cannot keep her away.
Darkness is but the shadow of matter
still not penetrated by the new Light.
When inhibited by matter,
even light becomes subject to the laws of matter.
But the new Light penetrates everything.

There are no boundaries,
no 'near' and no 'far,'
and my servant can be here.
Ö is the center of all.
When Light comes from Ö,
then the hand of 'the one who helps' grows,
embraces all and acts freely.
My little servant can be everywhere
and can *act* everywhere.

Silence

— The power of the 'Highest Helper' is with you.
I, too, serve you.
I, you, He: we are three.
But beyond the threshold ... ONE.
And that is GRACE.

*I write out the song about Jesus and the short message which I
will pass on to Lili at the first opportunity.*
*Actually, I felt Lili's presence during the dialogue. But only now
do I understand how this was possible: outer light is limited by
time and space. In the light of the sun, matter casts shadows. The
light of distant stars can be measured by light years.*
*In contrast, inner Light penetrates everywhere: it is timeless,
spaceless, unmeasurable. If Lili is filled with inner Light, she
can be everywhere and her every act becomes the all-transcen-
dent ACT.*

PART II

DIALOGUES IN BUDAPEST

"We through the Divine,
the Divine through us."

Immediately after the invasion of Hungary by Nazi troops, the persecution of Jews begins. The Jewish population in the provinces, where we are living, is the first to be transported to the concentration camps. The arrests have not yet begun in Budapest, but all roads leading to the capital are tightly controlled by the Nazis to prevent Jews from seeking refuge in the city. Nevertheless, Hanna and Joseph decide to flee from the endangered provincial zone to Budapest, so as to be able to await further developments in the unoccupied apartment of Hanna's parents. I wish to accompany them: we set out from Budaliget late one evening, making our way along unguarded footpaths through the dark forests embracing the western part of Budapest. I take the lead, with Hanna and Joseph following a short distance behind. At last, we emerge safely at a large tram station, Hüvösvölgy, where we are able to mingle unobtrusively among the throngs of the city.

Friday, March 31, 1944

41. DIALOGUE: 'THE ONE WHO MEASURES'

Today we await the first dialogue in the apartment of Hanna's parents, in the Garay utca, which is situated in the Pest section of the city.
Our 'hosts' have fortunately left Hungary some time before to visit their son in England, leaving the apartment empty. The front windows face a noisy, gray street not far from the main east-side railway station, Keleti. After the peace and calm of

297

the tiny village of Budaliget, everything here in Budapest seems abominably dismal and loud.

— 'The one who measures' speaks: listen carefully!
The lack ebbs, the seed swells,
the weighing scales are being filled.
Here above, burning eyes are watching:
Now you live rightly.

Indeed, we did everything necessary, but with calm.

— 'The one who measures' sees:
the danger recedes.
Your hand is ready
and my sword does not cut: it protects.

I am amazed that our inner attitude is more important to the angels than the outer danger.

— Existence weighs heavy:

BUT FOR THE ONE WHO DOES NOT ERR,
THE BURDEN BECOMES UPLIFTING WINGS.

The new unfolds.
The ACT is not burden, but seed from which sprouts the new.
Danger passes; the seed remains.
A gentle breeze arises and, in the proper moment,
the ACT sprouts: the ACT sown in you by the Divine.
Take good care of the seed; it is so small!
It can be lost through the smallest crack.

'The one who measures' speaks:
Live rightly!
My sword protects.
The mystery of the seventh force burns in its tip:
Divine grace.

Bow your heads.
Be touched by the tip of the sword.
May the Divine be with you!

The trial persists.
Those who persevere shall be redeemed.
Ö is peace.
May Divine peace be with you!
Then the curse cannot reach you.
Ö is life.
If you live in the Divine, you cannot fear,
and you desire no other fate.

The seven forces converge at ONE point.
This is the mystery and this is the way.
If a single force is missing, my scale is unbalanced.
I urge you: Be aware!
One single lack can be decisive!
Be alert! Hope! Adore the One and Only!

All of us in the circle serve the Divine,
each according to our own task.
I am 'the one who measures,'
but I am also the 'Gardener.'
I watch over you tiny blossoms on the Tree.
I watch over you,
for cutting is not my only means of serving.
I cut only what is bad.

You have come a long way in a short time.
You have left the old behind you.
But woe unto you if you look back!
The house has caved in: you can no longer live there.
You had to leave it at the decisive moment.

Woe unto you if you look back! For behold:
ahead of you, the way is already free.
'The one who measures' has spoken:
what has been, is dead.
What shall be, will never be lost.
The 'Gardener' rejoices
at the brightening sky
as the seed begins to grow.

Friday, April 7, 1944

42. DIALOGUE: GOOD FRIDAY

*Throughout Hungary, everything has come to a standstill:
the Nazi occupation has petrified daily life. We miss our work
tremendously. In our forced inactivity, we become ever more
sensitive to the horrible news and rumors, which spread like
wildfire through the city.*

— Greetings to the four of you!
The choir of angels brings a message;
it is your task to pass it on:

THE CROSS IS NOT THE SIGN OF DEATH.
DIE WITH *HIM* AND YOU LIVE ETERNALLY.

The cross does not let you go:
to fulfill its sign is your task.

DIE WITH *HIM:*
THAT IS THE FIRST HALF OF THE TASK.

Three days, the time: past – present – future.

In the tomb, wrapped in linen,
soothed with balm, the body reposes.
Dawn approaches ... BODY lives
but time expires.
Run out is the time of death.
People surround the tomb.
And within: nothing – only the shroud.
The shroud has been cast away,
death is dead,
and eternal life blazes up.

THE SECOND HALF OF THE TASK IS:
LIVE THROUGH *HIM!*

At His feet is the angel of death,
faithfully serving the Law.
Ö is grace and grace is above the Law.
If you have total faith, grace is yours too.
But it is not yours too keep: *through you,* it acts below.
Without faith, you lead everything to death.
This is the Law.
The pregnant whirlpool gives birth to hell,
and the name of hell is:
the old, which no longer serves.

The Body is not the corpse.
The Body is not matter.
The Body is seed that grows and resurrects
through the Divine.

THE BODY IS PLAN, NOT ORGAN.

The Body is Ö.
What makes the seed a seed?
The pod? It can never sprout.

YOU ARE BODY AND SEED THROUGH THE DIVINE,
AND IT IS Ö WHO SHALL GROW THROUGH YOU.

Sacred mystery.
We are angels.
Our word is truth,
for we live through the Divine.
Our drink is Light, our song is Praise.
All our service is for the Divine.
We serve together: we are One.

Four pillars reach to Heaven,
uniting Heaven and earth.
We are the vault and the earth is our foundation.
The dwelling is ready.
The wedding approaches,
the wedding of Heaven and earth.
After the wedding, the Newborn: Ö.
Ö already dwells in you.
May Ö be sheltered in your heart!

In the circle, we sing praise;
no longer apart, but together: with you.
For our way has become One.

WITH YOU WE PERISH –
OR WITH YOU WE ARE PURIFIED.

The pod is weight.
If Ö breathes on you, the seed begins to grow.
The time is near ... the time is far ...
time is no more.
Timelessly, Ö grows in you.
There is only one way: bear the Child, the new Child!
No more lowly stable.

Be at the highest point, always!
We are there.

Behold! It is also our Child.
Its fragile body is still that of a child,
yet Heaven and earth tremble before it.
The milk that it suckles is the power of soul.
Loyal servants watch over it.
Be loyal! Hearts are filled with it,
and what is filled knows pain no more.

Above you hovers the multitude of angels.
May peace descend over you.
But pass it on! It is not your own.
All that belongs to us is Ö; and we belong to Ö.
This is our message:

WE THROUGH THE DIVINE;
THE DIVINE THROUGH US.

*For some time now, the angels have been speaking in a rhythmic
style, and it is less personal than the dialogues in Budaliget had
been, which irritates me. I have never been fond of poetry, and
I am unable to grasp the purpose of this new form. I feel like a
baby that is given solid food instead of milk for the first time and
does not like it. I miss the practical instructions of Budaliget
and I am disappointed at no longer being able to ask my 'very
important' questions. I am aware that Hanna is only 'humanly
able' to put the message of the angels into human language, and
so I blame her for the new rhythmic form. Of course, I couldn't
possibly 'blame' the angels! However, today I am pierced by the
terrible words: "With you we perish ..." They sting like a whip-
lash, but also help me to a new realization: I discover that this
rhythm is directly touching and nourishing me, without any kind
of detour through my intellect. The end of today's dialogue fills*

*me with astonishment: "WE THROUGH THE DIVINE; THE DIVINE
THROUGH US." The dignity I feel in this human-Divine balance
is so powerful that I am unable to grasp it in its full profundity.*

Sunday, April 9, 1944

43. DIALOGUE: EASTER SUNDAY

— The mere body is dead for ever.
The living lives for ever.
And yet, from birth until death, they are united.

What you call life is the task.
For the life active in its task:
death is the servant.
For the life passive in its task:
death is the master.
Birth and death belong together,
not life and death.
Here the soul that has fear is in error:

FOR LIFE LIVES ETERNALLY.

Friday, April 14, 1944

44. DIALOGUE

— We are many, but our word is ONE.
Grace streams through us and we never weary.

THE LIFE THAT WE LIVE
IS THE GRACE THAT WE GIVE.

Giving compensates weight.
Thirst for the new!
Fire is given to you: eternal thirst.
Pass the Fire on!

The Seven Souls are your dwelling.
Your foot rests on the first.
Six enfold you from toe to head,
and the Seventh is your crown.
Each of the Seven Souls acts:
Truth *is.*
Love grows.
Rhythm and Harmony *move.*
New awareness *creates.*
Peace reposes.
Joy and bliss *radiate.*
The primal source is a great mystery.
Unspeakable, inexpressible ecstasy: fulfillment.

Eternal giver, never tiring, eternally acting:
only through the Divine do you act.

The origin of all Light is Ö.
The ground of all space is Ö.
The faith of all being is Ö.
Every song rises up to Ö.
Whoever strives toward Ö never wearies.
Every scent rises up to Ö,
every mountain points to Ö.
Whoever seeks, finds the way.
Behold: the only way is Ö!
Every other way is delusion.

Every word fades before Ö.
Ö is the dwelling and Ö is the dweller.

The force of the Seventh is yours.
Take it, eat it:
then *act* through it!
May giving and taking be in balance.
Balance is needed on the peak;
there balance, peace and silence are essential.

We are many.
Through us and through you,
life broadens, the Seven flow.
The past withers, the old dies, but the new unfolds.
The Seven prepare a new Food
which wipes away all old guilt.
Heaven opens itself:
the new Food, Heavenly Bread, descends:
not grown of the earth, it is born of Light.
Hunger, gloom, evil and the grave are but a void.
Already the new Message is filling it.
The earth is quiet and waits.
Death is satiated forever.
Behold, death waits only to be fed.
The sad angel who devours all,
yet still always hungers,
will soon be appeased.

THE DEVOURER OF LIFE
HUNGERS ETERNALLY.
THE GIVER OF LIFE
ACTS ETERNALLY WITH THE DIVINE –

and the void is filled.

You have been conceived,
you will become children:
love's pledge of the *Father* and the *Mother,*
of *Heaven* and *Earth,* in the womb of the Four.
Its name is still secret.
If union is celebrated in you, all is fulfilled.
Raise your heads! May the Seventh be with you!
May He touch you!

Immediately after the dialogue, I urge Hanna to tell us – even if it is not completely clear – what she felt during today's teaching. As far as I can recall, she said: "I felt the individual essence of each of the Seven Souls of life.

CREATED WORLD				CREATING WORLD		
I	II	III	IV	V	VI	VII
MINERAL	PLANT	ANIMAL	HUMAN	ANGEL	SERAPH	THE SEVENTH
truth	love	rhythm	awareness	peace	pure	
number	growth	harmony	the word	silence	joy	
law		movement	balance		shining	
			link		power	
			bridge			

the abyss to be bridged ⟶ ⟵ the task of the human

307

*– The first level of being is the MINERAL, the stone, the crystal.
Its animating soul is the truth, the number and the law.
– The second level is the PLANT.
Its soul is streaming love and the capacity to grow.
– The third level is the ANIMAL,
enlivened by harmony, movement and rhythm.
These three levels are contained in the fourth, the HUMAN. But
we – the so-called humans – are still not the HUMAN, the Four.
It is our task to live on the fourth level and become a conscious
link between the created and the creating world.
– The fifth level is that of the ANGELS, where peace and silence
reign.
– On the sixth level dwells the SERAPH, with burning power and
joy.
– The seventh level is the mysterious, the highest degree of all
life."*

*I say to Hanna: "This is now clear, but something is still incomprehensible for me: We were told that Joseph is the Five (peace
and silence), Lili, the Two (overflowing love) and I, the Six (radiating force), and that we all have the task of realizing the Four
... How can that be possible?"*

*"Only through fulfillment of the individual task is it possible to
live the Four, the universal task of the Human. It is precisely the
forces you just mentioned which enable you to reach the Four,
in which all seven Souls are united.*

*Never forget this key to understanding the angels' teaching: it
is the mutual evolutionary attraction between above and below,
between the Divine and the human, between heavenly and
earthly forces, between spirit and matter.*

All of these forces join in the middle, on the fourth level.

*They unite and give birth to the new Child, which is God and
human ... Creator and created ... Light and matter.*

But the first step toward this evolutionary universal accomplishment is to become conscious of your own individual task and to live it. This is the only gateway leading to the Four and it is also the only one to which we ourselves have the key."
Hanna then continues: "Have you ever asked yourself why your master repeatedly said to you:
'Go your own way! Be independent!
You have been formed after my image.
May your eyes shine!'
This was said to you so that you would at last become aware of your own individuality, so that you would realize the Six – radiating force – in your everyday life.
Only in this way can you become a new HUMAN.
Only thus can you actively participate in joining the creating world and the created world.
But be aware that any diagram can only be a limited representation of existence. A diagram can never really convey love, the dynamic attraction between spirit and matter. And it could never express the union of the Seven Souls in a human being."

(On the 16th of April, ghettoization begins.)

Wednesday, April 19, 1944 (mid-morning)

45. DIALOGUE: 'THE MEASURING ANGEL'

A rumor has been spreading through Budapest that all Jewish men no longer draftable for military service will be deported to 'work camps.' On the 16ᵗʰ of April, the forming of ghettoes begins. The city is in a state of panic. Joseph anticipates his fate and becomes even more silent than usual. Hanna suffers deeply. She does her best not to show it, but I know how hard she is struggling for her inner balance. Lili knows no peace. She is with her pupils, who douse her thoroughly with their anxiety, from early morning until late at night.
Meanwhile, I race from official to official in a desperate attempt to save my friends. But I am met only by total disorganization, incompetence and an all-pervasive apathy. No one knows what the following day will bring. As the collective fear spreads, the resultant panic is almost impossible to bear. Everyone suffers from depression.

— 'The one who measures' speaks:
Even the stone grows,
the tree blossoms
and the animal loves.
But the human buries, destroys everything,
violates the Law.
Bring fruit, for I shudder to cut the living!
The *Word* lives in you,
but the fig tree that bears no fruit shall be felled.
The bud opens:
will it bring fruit or merely leaves?
In my hand, the sword, the flaming sword;
but my soul is troubled.

The 'Gardener' pleads:

JUST ONE MORE DAY, LORD!
I SHALL SPADE AROUND THE TRUNK,
I SHALL FERTILIZE GENEROUSLY:
PERHAPS THEN THE TREE
WILL BEAR FRUIT AFTER ALL!
IF NOT –
THEN YOU MAY CUT IT DOWN.
BUT PLEASE GRANT ME THIS!
I AM THE GARDENER,
AND THE TREE IS DEAR TO ME.

In my hand, the sword of fire.
And I know that I will chop
if the Lord gives the sign, for I serve.
I do not revolt, I do not scandalize.
An angel's service is difficult, too,
but we are always ready to serve. Always!
Serve! Serve day and night!
To stand still is forbidden!
You have been entrusted with many talents
and you must account for them.
Behold! It is wonderful to serve the Divine!
Blossom – bear flowers!
I IMPLORE YOU!

*Never before has a dialogue so shaken me as today's. The most
stern and unapproachable of the angels has begged us with
humility to blossom!*
Hanna says: "If we give up now, we are truly lost!
Neither Heaven nor earth will take us in ...
we would be spat out!"

311

Hanna's words ring true. How, indeed, I had let myself be dominated by the outer situation! We had all allowed ourselves to become infected by the tragic state of our immediate surroundings.

Editor's note: In the notes of Lili, the following additional text was found, dated April 18, 1944:

— We have not fulfilled the expectation.
The fire was too weak.
How careful we must be!
If we give up now,
we will be lost.
Then neither earth nor heaven will receive us.
They will spit us out!

Hanna sees us as empty helpless husks
floating meaninglessly above the fourth level of being.
What a horrible calamity!
To be frozen, rigid!
But compared with being spat out, being frozen would be
a heavenly state.
How terrible if the fourth level between the three earthly
and the three heavenly spheres would remain
empty and paralyzed.

Friday, April 21, 1944

46. DIALOGUE

The confiscation of Jewish apartments in Budapest has begun. The homeless are herded into a part of the city designated as the ghetto.
We do not know when this fate will reach Hanna and Joseph. But, as a result of the last dialogue, we are able to face this threatening development with relative calm. The outer situation has not improved, it has worsened. But we have become more calm and centered. And so, today's message is a song of joy.

— Ö speaks and the Four sings:
Always create! Always act!
Without raising a hand, without wanting to:
YOU ACT!
You become Human,
for you receive heavenly force: Ö.
The Five is with you, helping.
Faith glows with fire … the fog lightens.
The seeing … *see.*
The hearing … *hear.*
The dying … *live.*
The living … bear witness.
The song never ends.
But the dividing wall ends:
Babylon has crumbled.
The song soars aloft.
Never-ending joy and peace!
The end is the beginning.
In the beginning is the *Word*
and the *Word* dwells in you.

Seek it, seek it always!
The seeker will find.
But death seeks you in vain:
never again will it find you.

The seed is sown.
It will not be withdrawn if the soil is good.
In good soil, it will not repose for long.
Everything perishes: but the seed remains.
Only the seed is eternal.
It is sown, it sprouts, grows
and brings forth new seed.
This is the cycle.
The essence is the SEED.
Eternally sprouting stem.
Take good care only of this.
Be filled with it!
Arise with it, rest with it!
The greatest force of all
dwells in the sprouting seed:
it bursts great rocks asunder,
for the Glorious One dwells within it.
We serve you,
for the Glorious One dwells also in you.
The song rises up.

New World, free, broad and true!
There you have a place to live,
a place that can never be taken from you.*
But you can give it on.

The world thirsts: *in you* is the source.
The world screams: *in you* is silence.

---

*   Reference to the confiscation of Jewish homes.

46. DIALOGUE

The world weeps: *in you* is the only balm.
Bridge above the whirlpool.
Grace above the law.
Smile above the scream.
Peace above madness.
Not the end of the war: the new.
Let it be: the new!

SWEAR TO HEAVEN THAT YOU WILL BRING IT ABOUT!

What is without: sinks.
What is within: shall be fulfilled.
And between new Heaven and new Earth comes:
THE HUMAN.
Rejoice with us! Who is against us?
Together we find the faith
of the new Way.
May the smile never leave your lips!
The one who fails to find it remains imprisoned.
But the one who acts through the Divine
is forever free.

Ö spoke and the Four sang.
Ö speaks to you every day.
Listen well:
Heaven be with you!

315

Friday, April 22, 1944

47. DIALOGUE

('The one who measures' speaks:)

I bring the taste of the new Word.
What Ö has given, I give on.
Only the Word divinely given is true,
only the Word divinely given is to be given on.
Any excess is wasteful.

The Word acts.
The true word raises;
the false word buries.
It buries not the living,
but the level to which it belongs:
the soul of the fourth level thus dies.
There is still the animal, the horse:
If there is excessive movement,
the third level dies.
There is still the plant, the grass:
If there is excessive growth
and the body made to swell,
the second level dies.
There is still the stone.
Too much indolence,
and the first level dies.

('The one who shines' speaks:)

If the word is true,
if Ö speaks through you
then the separating wall crumbles.

The fogs lighten, the Fifth opens the bud.
The Sixth creates the form.
From the force of the Seventh, the crown: the fruit.
These three levels all thrive on the heavenly tree.
There the fruit of eternal life ripens.
Who tastes of this fruit has but one desire:
to serve the Divine.
The great secret is:
not the excess, but the *more.*
The fruit of the Seventh
grows in the Divine orchard.
Ö, the Lord of all fruits,
harvests when the time is ripe.
Blossom! Bring forth fruit!
The empty hand is deplorable!

('The one who helps' speaks:)

Disaster, war and darkness
are nothing but lack of fruit.
Blossom! Bring forth fruit!
Ö is the hunger of the hungry,
the demand for bread,
tears of those who suffer;
Ö is the cry of those in need.

There is already enough old wheat!
Seek the Name of the new! The Name!

FOR THE WORD CREATES.
May the mouth serve only the Word.
May the eye gaze only upon the new.
May the hand act only for the Divine.
May it no longer *take:* but *give.*
May peace come at last!

SWEAR TO HEAVEN THAT YOU WILL BRING IT ABOUT!

This is the second time we have been exhorted:
"Swear to Heaven that you will bring it about!"
This troubles me, for I have no idea of how to accomplish the
task.

(Editor's note: The following text was found in the notes of Lili
from Dialogue 47, dated April 22, 1944:)

Ö is the measure.
Of the essence is the fruit,
not the tree.
Whether small or large
the apple is one, round, whole,
and this is grace.
The tree strives toward heaven,
but it is the fruit that is wise.
It is the round ball,
In which measure is fulfilled.
Nothing is lacking in the fruit.
Take your measure from this.
From the fruit, you recognize the tree.
Regarding only the trunk yields nothing.
Strive not towards heaven like the trunk.
It is in the fruit that heaven dwells –
only there.

All measure and measuring is with the Divine.
The ONE appears in manifold measure –
from infinite variety: ONE image.
No measure equals another.
If reason measures, all is lost,
for the Divine alone takes measure.

The Divine alone is measure.
The fruit reveals not only
if the act was good or bad –
the fruit reveals the measure.

The tree strives towards heaven,
its fruit rolls to the earth.
The tree will be felled.
But its fruit is eternal,
because its fruit contains the seed.

Friday, April 28, 1944

48. DIALOGUE

The 'oath' is decision.
When the seed begins to sprout,
it departs from the old husk,
its seed-identity, and leaves its former self behind.
Only thus can it bring forth new seeds:
one twenty, another perhaps forty.
This is the only way.

THE OATH TO HEAVEN DOES NOT BIND:
THE OATH TO HEAVEN RELEASES.

What was seed becomes bread.
But take heed!
Do not sow the seed in the earth!
There is enough wheat.
The granaries have long been filled,
but Heaven is still empty.

There no one has yet sown the seed.
Sow it where no-one
has yet dared to sow it!
The seed sown in earth – even if the sower stumbles –
finds its place and sprouts.
The sower of seed in Heaven
may not stumble:
for then the seed would fall back, sproutless.

The field of Heaven, the Seven,
was ploughed up long ago.
Sow the seed there and a wonder will sprout,
and never again will there be a lack of bread.
Every empty hand will be filled,
and every lack appeased.

Listen well!
The seed corn is not to be eaten.
The devil rejoices at bread baked from seed corn.
Until now, wheat grew up to Heaven.
From now on, Heavenly wheat descends to the earth.
But where is Heaven? Up there? Down here?

TRULY: HEAVEN REPOSES IN YOU.

> *I feel relief: our oath to Heaven helps to release us from the old
> and to open ourselves to the new.*
>
> *(On April 27, the first deportations to Auschwitz under Adolf
> Eichmann took place from the countryside of Hungary.)*

Friday, April 28, 1944

49. DIALOGUE

> *The angels unexpectedly pay us a visit this evening.*
> *Taken by surprise and with no writing materials at hand, I am*
> *able to note down only the final part of the message.*

… Adam hid himself before the Divine;
he had lost the way.
Pointed toward Heaven on the cross,
crucified on the cross,
the Human Son cried out:
"My Father, my Father, why hast Thou forsaken me?"
But God did not answer.
The one who seeks does not find.
The one who knocks is not allowed to enter.
Only what has been lost can be sought after.

> *I ask myself: "Does this mean that Jesus, in his agony, had lost*
> *the living contact with His Father?"*

One who seeks does not find,
for behold: every way leads to death.
Every beginning leads to an end.
Ö ALONE IS,
AND Ö IS THE WAY.
One who hurries along the way … arrives nowhere.
One who stands still on the way … finds nothing.

> *After a long silence, the angel continues to speak about the*
> *wedding of Heaven and earth, the subject of the first part of this*
> *unforeseen dialogue, which I had been unable to note down.*

Rejoice!
Bride and groom are mere duality,
are merely the vessel where ecstasy dwells.
Bride and bridegroom,
Creator and created,
Light and shadow
are but vessels.
Only *ecstasy,* only being drunk with Light
is Divine.

> *These words astound and shock me. Only later do I understand that, as long as we are still seeking, we are not yet united with the Divine. Hanna was in such intimate union with the angels that she was able to convey this without the slightest hesitation. I have the impression that the angels always speak to Hanna with as much intensity as she is able to bear. I feel these changes of intensity myself, for sometimes I am totally nourished, while at others, I can scarcely follow. Is this because my receptivity varies or is it due to the intensity of the messages?*

Friday, May 5, 1944

50. DIALOGUE

> *The district surrounding the synagogue has already been transformed into a ghetto. It is horribly overcrowded. False identity papers are hot items on the black market. I propose this solution to my friends, but they refuse to even consider any form of deceptive method. The great hope of thousands of Jews is their new 'guardian angel,' Raoul Wallenberg, with his Swedish*

passports, which could save them from otherwise almost certain extermination, perfectly organized by the Nazi mass murderer, Adolf Eichmann.

All the heavenly forces hover above you
and wait for you to be their hand.
They bring this message:
Do not flee!
Before and after earthly death, all is but dream.
Only above death will you find life:

LIFE IS SERVING Ö.

You are dear to the Divine,
you please Ö, for your heart is full.
Do not hurry, do not tarry:
be with Ö!

'The one who measures' speaks:

'The one who measures' is now the Gardener,
and is allowed to protect you
if your soul rises high above.
Love! Seek!
The soul of the Gardener trembles;
but you are trusted.
The Divine Seed will sprout.

We are all here with you
and we will remain with you.
Space begins beneath us and widens out below.
We know neither space nor time.
Raise yourself up!
Thus, we can always be united: Always!

The new World cries out to you, imploring to be born.

The ONE dwells in you: Ö.
Can your head know fear
when the Divine dwells in your heart?
The foot races ... the hand grabs ... the head panics.
And why?
Place your feet solidly on the ground.
Bow your head!
And fold your hands!
For behold: Life dwells in the heart,
and in your heart is the Way.
The truth is: only the Divine IS.
We are all but images:
Angel, human, animal, flower and stone:
these are but images.

Ö IS ALL.

Do not flee, even to us!
To flee is to remain in darkness, dreaming.
If the dream is real for you,
then it becomes ever denser, embodied.
You had to dream.
But now:

YOU ARE AWAKENERS – NOT DREAMERS.

> *These words awaken many questions in me: Did we freely accept*
> *to 'dream' this earthly life so as to become able to awaken other*
> *dreamers? Even if our dream is extremely difficult? In accepting*
> *it, can we awaken and then become able to awaken others?*

Awaken!
And never flee before the task!
If your whole life is devoted to serving, believe me:
all that has been planned will come to be.

We speak the truth; we do not console.
Consolation is for the feeble.
Consolation is for those whose soul is darkened,
who do not see the LIGHT.
But you, with full heart and shining face,
you, whose words and deeds breathe life:
give one another your hands!
Whenever one from among you is weak: give help!
He walked on the water
and yet a garden saw *Him* weep.

> *This image of Jesus with His superhuman capacities and His very human tears in the garden of Gethsemani touches me deeply. We are sitting around a square table and without our having noticed it, our hands form the shape of a cross.*

Behold: the sign of the cross filled with force!
The cross no longer stands: it is at rest.
The task is no longer death: the task is life.

> *Silence.*

Let us now sing a song:

LORD OF ALL!
YOU ARE ONE WITH US!
THIS SONG IS OUR LIFE:
YOU ARE ONE WITH US.
WE SEEK NOTHING MORE.
WITH OUR EYES: BEHOLD!
WITH OUR HANDS: ACT!
IN OUR HEARTS: BE!
FOUR SERVANTS ADORE YOU.

YOUR EYE SEES US:
OVERLOOK OUR TRANSGRESSIONS!

HEAR OUR SONG!
WE PRAY NO MORE,
WE ASK NO MORE;
YOU AND WE ARE ONE.

LORD! THROUGH US BE BORN!

Friday, May 12, 1944

51. DIALOGUE

> *Budapest is bombed for the first time. The house just across the
> street lies in ruin. Day after day, the curious flock by to stare at
> this sinister sight. Even farmers from the countryside travel into
> the city just to stare ...*

The *Four,* the level of reality, is still empty.
Why do the people stare at what is below?
Why is the ruin beautiful to them,
and not the whole?
Why does the foot trample rather than stride?
To the many 'whys' there is just one answer:
Decide!
and the dividing wall will crumble.
The old decays, the new bud opens.
The force acting in you is
united with the *Whole:*
the Seven Souls of the Divine
and your souls are ONE.
'The one who helps' is the *Two.*
'The one who speaks' is the *Four.*

'The one who builds' is the *Five*.
'The one who shines' is the *Six*.
The *One,* the *Three* and the *Seven* still linger,
but they will come;
and what is to be, shall be.

> *I wonder when these additional companions will appear to*
> *complete our circle.*

EACH LEVEL OF LIFE IS A SOUL,
AND THE SEVEN SOULS UNITED COMPRISE:
THE HUMAN BEING.

The Seven Souls are seven limbs;
their union is the *seed.*
Each of the Seven Souls acts;

THE ONE IS ETERNAL.

> *To me:*

Do you accept the *Six?*
Know that it is pure Joy.
G. Yes, I accept the *Six.*

> *To Joseph:*

Peace and Silence – the *Five* –
descend to earth through you;
but only if you hold tight to the earth.
Take the hand of the *Four,*
that Joy and Peace may find their place,
for they are held by the middle, by the Human essence:
Uniting Awareness.

> *To Lili:*

Love blossoms: the *Two.*

Miracle! The Seven Souls stride not in ranks,
but in the round.
They form the rim of a cone whose apex is one.
There is no hierarchy,
the circle is unbroken.
Every cone has its apex: Ö.
The cone is the Way.
We sing in the circle, our place,
and our eyes converge at the peak: Ö.
We sing
since the time of no time,
and Ö is the time of no time:
the old, the ancient
and the eternal Infant.
Wondrous is the Divine plan
and thus our song is joyous:

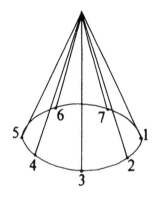

THE CREATOR CREATES THE DIVINE PLAN
ETERNALLY THROUGH US.
BUT WITHOUT YOU, NOTHING CAN BE.

Sing with us!
The name of your song is still a secret,
but what I can say is this:
all of creation will sing with you!
The song that draws your soul from the earth
is neither sad nor serene, long nor short: it is *whole.*
All of Heaven, all of the earth: the Seven, united.
Listen well!
Wonder walks among you,
it walks in the circle: Join it!
The circle narrows, it does not break.
Eternity draws near.
Faith is no longer needed.

328

Faith is a bridge and the bridge is space.
But:

THE POINT CONTAINS ALL.

Heaven speaks:
The earth will receive wings
through us and through you.
If you speak through us:

WE STAND ON THE EARTH.

If we act through you:

YOU RECEIVE WINGS.

Thus our serving together endures eternally.

After the dialogue, Hanna attempts to transmit her inner perception in a symbolic form: to illustrate, she draws a cone (shown on previous page). However, she warns us that every diagram can at best only convey a fragment of the experience. Nevertheless, it helps me to understand that each of us has his or her own place within the sevenfold levels of being. Seven levels of equal value: no hierarchy.

Friday, May 19, 1944

52. DIALOGUE

The center of the sphere is the point.
From there, Ö radiates;
from there, Ö brings flowers to blossom.
Outside, the earth becomes cold,
and warmth – love – wanders homelessly.
The sphere is matter and Ö is its center:
Ö, Who lives in all, just as we live in you.
Measure deceives.
Outside, everything becomes cold.
Even the warmth of the sun is but reflected Light.
If your eye *looks* outward, there is only decay.
Everything rots; what is finished is dead.

Let your only act be eternal becoming;
and that is not *outside.*
If your eye *sees,* then every obstacle vanishes.
The Ray of the Seventh waits only for this.
The creation – stone, branch and horse –
all await your becoming one:
HUMAN.

The ray of the fourth level begins to dawn,
like a song from us it softly ascends in you.
Outside, a horrible noise – inside, silence.
Outside, everything crumbles;
but *inside,* the new is formed.
Everything waits; the price is great.
But only matter is great. The kernel is tiny.
The tiniest of all in us is Ö.

Your eyes look *outward,* and that is not your task:
neither sorrow, nor evil, nor noise.
Do not be shaken!
The *outside* is not your task!
Listen only *within!* Be filled with Ö!
The space *within* is easily filled –
it is so *small.*
What has no weight cannot be measured;
what occupies no space cannot be grasped –
it dwells in the tiniest place: Infinity.

> *Today I feel as if I am under a shower alternating between hot and cold, as I am thrown from one contrast to the next: from outside to inside, from great to small. Curiously, I feel enlivened, and eager to encounter new possibilities.*

The Holy Spirit leads you.
The Soul of the Seventh springs therefrom.
The voice of the Seventh, still secret.

THROUGH YOU, Ö WILL SPEAK A NEW LANGUAGE.
THE NEW LANGUAGE GIVES BIRTH TO NEW EARS.

You are the sound: you set the pitch.
No ears can yet hear the new Sound.
It begins to vibrate, and matter
– the original clay – is shaken.
Thus, new Ears are born.
The clay waits; it is inert
but it will come to life, for Ö breathes upon it,
breathes upon it through you.
All shall be born. The earth waits.
All will blossom,
hardship and tears will cease.

All beings bow before the SMALLEST.
In the past, the *great* has been victorious;
but from now on, it shall be the *small.*
Choose! One or the other!
Never-ending is the fall of those
who strive for greatness.
The *too much* will be taken away
and the *great* will be cut down;
the *small* will be kept.

You stand on a *small* circle and that is our joy.
Our circle is still *smaller*
and Ö in us is the *smallest* of all.
The seventh ray is one with the Divine
and reaches the human soul.
Thus, the sphere becomes whole.
To become whole, to close the gap:
this is the essential act.
The wounded feeling heart bleeds.
But dawn awakens.
The earth will tremble, the wound will close.
If you still have questions,
your heart will answer.
There we dwell.
Your place is now very small – but only outwardly – and that is good.
Evil encircles you and its circle is great.
It waits for you in vain.
Its circle imprisons everything.
But the tiny point in the middle opens the gate of Heaven.
Ö waits.

> *Joseph and Hanna leave the apartment only when absolutely*
> *necessary. All Jews have been required since mid-April to wear*

the 'yellow star,' which often elicits brutality. For safety's sake, I
escort Lili to the dialogues and take her home again afterwards.

Friday, May 26, 1944

53. DIALOGUE – THREE DAYS BEFORE PENTECOST

Consoling, the Seventh Word,
Bringer of the Message of Joy, comes to you.
Await Him on that day!
As He spoke to the ancients,
flames ignited in his wake.
Be united on that day
and Fire will ignite on your foreheads:
the eternal Flame.
Our mouth is too weak,
our essence too subtle;
only the Seventh brings consolation.
Not what was brought to the ancients:
a new Flame will be given to you
and your burdened soul will be renewed.
The tomb where lay the body of the Lord
disappears.

The human, fragile being:
but on the forehead, Light.
Long empty, the vessel will now be filled,
for readiness and not despair
dwells in your heart.
Only to the ready is given.
Here, asking is of no avail.

333

This week, I measured your emptiness
in order to know when you will be filled.
Each of you will be given exactly what is needed.
What is given to you is LIGHT –
the tiniest ray,
and yet the great vessel is filled.
The Divine Wish is fulfilled.

May Mary also be among you.
She too is blessed with the Holy Spirit.
She is the tiny bird under the window,
beneath the dungeon window.
With its song, it will console you.
The hearts of the oppressed will be lightened.
Then the tiny bird sits on the window sill
and brings the good tidings of the New Name.
With this offering of its heart, it can no longer be harmed.
Weakness is strength;
strength is weakness.
How hard is the rock!
The flame, though, is poured
into the most fragile vessel.
The human receives the task.
Rejoice at being human:
you will become Human!
Your task is to reach this degree of being.
The Holy Spirit comes over you,
becomes your drink.
Take heed! It burns,
but only where you take support.
You have no need for support.
Behold: the Divine lifts you up.

Ö breathes on the fire
and we sing in chorus:

THE ANCIENTS NO LONGER CONFER IN THE ROUND.
NEW BEINGS, ETERNALLY YOUNG,
JUDGE OVER ALL.
UPON THEIR HEAD, THE TIARA,
THE HEAVENLY CROWN,
FIRST RAY OF THE NEW SUN.
THE SUN IS ALREADY RISING,
THE NEW EARTH STILL REPOSES.

WE, ABOVE, CAN SEE THE NEW SUN,
YOU, BELOW, CANNOT YET SEE IT.
IN THE DEPTH OF THE HEART, IT BEGINS TO DAWN.

WITHIN, WE ALREADY SEE THE NEW SUN.
WITHOUT, YOU SEE ONLY EARTHLY PAIN.
THERE IS BUT ONE PAIN: TO BE *WITHOUT.*

ONLY WITHOUT IS DARKNESS;
WITHIN, IS LIGHT.

ONLY WITHOUT IS THERE NOISE;
WITHIN, SILENCE IS BORN.

ONLY WITHOUT IS THERE TIME;
WITHIN, TIME STANDS STILL.

ONLY WITHOUT IS THERE DEATH;
WITHIN, THERE IS LIFE.

ONLY WITHOUT DOES THE SOUL WANDER.
WITHIN, IT FINDS ITS EVERLASTING HOME.
THE CHALICE IS STILL DARK.
WHEN THE SEVEN WITHIN GLOWS WHITE,
IT WILL BECOME TRANSPARENT.

DIVINE GLORY PENETRATES THE CHALICE,
AND IT RADIATES.
THERE IS NO MORE DEATH,
NOR NOISE, NOR PAIN.
TIME REMAINS WITHOUT;
AND TIME STANDS STILL.

Ö GIVES THE SIGNAL:
ALL OF CREATION BEGINS TO SING –
TO SING THROUGH YOU.
BE IN JOY!

> *The words, "Be united on that day" and "A new Flame will be*
> *given to you" fill us with such joy that all the misery around us*
> *fades away. How I have longed for this Pentecostal Fire!*

Sunday, May 28, 1944

54. DIALOGUE – ON THE SUNDAY OF PENTECOST

No more thundering sound!
No more language of tongues!
No more visible flames!
I AM Ö.

> *These words seem to come from infinitely far away, as from the*
> *beginning of time itself, and they awaken in me an unknown*
> *feeling of fearsome dimension: awe before the Divine.*

Ö cannot be seen,
Ö cannot be heard.
What you hear is but a faint echo.

The miracle is already below,
there beneath your feet.
The new World knows no miracle.
What comes is the inconceivable
Source of Sources.
The old miracle is but a footrest for the new,
and the small hide beneath it.

Your force causes glowing.
To you is given the Spirit.
Unseen, you shall become.
Unheard, you shall act.
Unknown to anyone.
Unforeseen, beyond the miracle,
something begins, something moves.
And the blind shall *see*.
and the deaf shall *hear*.
To you shall be given the new Sound, the new Flame.

FORGIVE!
AND Ö, TOO, WILL FORGIVE ALL TRANSGRESSION.
IF YOU DESIRE GOOD,
THEN GOOD SHALL BE.

This is the new Force,
foreseen by no one.
All good comes through you:
invisible, like Ö.
Infinitely great is Ö;
infinitely small are you.
Infinitely great are you;
infinitely small is Ö.

THERE IS BUT ONE.

You do not see the flame,
you do not feel the flame.
You do not speak in tongues.
The many words come to an end.
Does the new already burn?
Heaven has descended.
The end is completed.
Wordless messengers, flameless flames
are the new messengers;
even with hands bound, they *act.*
Speaking is childish babble:
the apostles were *children.*
You are now *adolescents.*

You need not act; you need not speak;
you need not take; you need not give.
And yet the new shall come to be:
Be filled with the Divine –
thus the Word becomes flesh!

All that you conceive … SHALL BE.
From dawn until dusk: call the new!
Always call!
The level of the *Four* is empty,
but it will be filled.
From morning until evening, call the new!
Together or apart,
on hard stone or soft grass,
in the dark prison or on the mountain peak,
may your hearts remain united!
Distance cannot separate those
who are united in the depth of their hearts.

AND WHAT YOU CALL SHALL BE,
AND SHALL NEVER PASS AWAY.

From eternity to eternity, every moment acts.
A hundred thousand years are not enough
to fill the abyss your heart is ready to fill.
But make no mistake!
You need do nothing more:
the Act is born.
Your Act is conception,
and only in secret.
The heart is the dwelling place
where the wedding takes place.
Spirit and matter are two half-seeds.
The Fire received today fuses the two halves
and they become ONE.
Fulfilled is the ancient promise:

MATTER AND SPIRIT, DEATH AND LIFE
BECOME ONE.

The one who has conceived shall give birth.

TO BE SECRET APOSTLES WAS YOUR WISH.
IT IS FULFILLED.

Your mouth as it speaks,
your hand as it acts
shall be pure.

That is our word.
We are angels and we speak.
The Seventh Voice thunders,
The Seventh Flame blinds.
The Divine is silent,
yet always with you.

Silent, also the message.
Silence cannot be distorted.
Thus, the one who hides behind lies
is unable to hide there.
The invisible cannot be represented.
Thus, the Divine cannot be misrepresented.
The time of the new comes
and the new sprouts.
The new Act is more difficult than the old,
but heavenly force dwells in all of you,
wherever you are.

May peace be with you and through you.

Friday, June 2, 1944

55. DIALOGUE

It is the evening before Joseph's deportation. What is his desti-
nation? No one knows. He prepares in silence and without com-
plaint, in spite of his foreboding that these are his last moments
together with his wife. Hanna suffers deeply but does her best
not to show it. She feels a sharp, continuous pain in her heart,
as if it were pierced with knives. I am surprised she is able to
summon the strength to transmit today's dialogue.

'The one who measures' speaks:

Blessings and peace!
The end of the trial approaches.
Outer existence rushes into the depths,
into eternal night.

You live above in the Light, blessed.
The promise is fulfilled.

'The Gardener' speaks:

In my hand, the knife,
the sharp knife, the grafting knife.
Now the cut opens a painful wound;
but I insert the new twig.
Already it is possible.
Small and frail is the holy twig,
and unspeakably tender;
yet filled with the force of the Divine.

I dress the wound with heavenly wax,
with wondrous consolation.
The wound cut by the knife is filled:
and the wound is no more.
Still tight is the bandage,
it still covers the cut;
but it, too, I will soon remove.
The world of the Seven
pays homage to you,
my little sprig!

'The one who builds' speaks:

The new marriage is consummated
between silence and the word.
The Divine Realm is there,
where silence and word
are eternally wed,
and the new Word is conceived in silence.

> *Only now do I see what a fateful bond connects Hanna, the Word*
> *(IV) and Joseph, Silence (V).*

'The one who shines' speaks:

I speak of shining love.
There is love and there is shining force:
May they act together!
Give your hands to one another,
love and shining force,
only united are you effective!

These words put my deep friendship with Lili in a new light:
Lili's task is love (II), mine is shining force (VI). The diagram of
the levels of life shows that they are complementary.

Thus there will be shining silence here below.
If Light Awareness is the bond,
there is no more abyss, no wound, to be bridged.

Our tasks become ever more clear: mine is to shine, Joseph's is
Silence and Hanna's is the middle, Light-Awareness.

'The one who helps' speaks:
The consoling, loving word hovers over you.
Without love, nothing can be:
Not Light-Awareness, not silence and peace,
not shining force and joy.
The shining ray – joy! – brings glowing;
Peace and Silence fulfill.
Awareness enlightens.
But only love unites.
Love is above everything
and love is in everything.

Its sign is the lily, the snow-white lily
whose scent rises up to the Seventh Heaven,
permeating everything, everywhere;
and yet its stem is green, and rooted in the earth.

55. DIALOGUE

'The one who builds' speaks:

The silence that builds,
builds not only above.
Now it builds below, this is already possible.
The old caves in, its stones will no longer be used.
Salt is strewn where the old stood.
Only the jackal howls in the ruins.
Nothing green grows where Babylon was.
But beyond the graspable
a new Homeland already greens.
The plan begins to vibrate in the heart
of 'the one who builds,'
desire to act is born.
The new Building welcomes the homeless.
Those covered by the old,
those restricted by matter, are rejected.
Received are those who make the Divine
their only abode.
I do not fear for you.

Now our angels speak in unison:

Silence is the house of the shining Word
in which love burns.

> *In these words, each of our tasks is related to the others:*
> *"Silence is the house" is Joseph (V), "of the shining" is Gitta*
> *(VI), "Word" is Hanna (IV), "in which love burns" is Lili (II).*

Thus, four voices become song: new Song,
new vibration here below,
creating new forms,
new hearts,
new ears,

new hands
and *seeing* eyes.
We teach you to sing.

THE OLD SONG DIES –
IT NO LONGER CREATES.

Its essence, grace, has left it;
laws have killed it.
But above grace is ONE, the ONLY ONE.
Sing always! In song, you are united,
even if your hands can no longer touch one another.
Your song rises to a place where new Blood,
new Vessels, new Space and new Matter pulse.
Slowly your voices join the new heartbeat,
slowly you begin to understand this beating.

WATCH OVER THE DIVINE,
AND THE DIVINE WILL WATCH OVER YOU.

> *Silence.*

The One who bears the new Name approaches.
Prepare His path!
Spread out your garments before Him!
Your only garment: the I, yourself.
Only the naked can receive a garment of Light.
No longer astride an ass,
the Light approaches: resplendent LIGHT.
Blessed be *His name!*

THE NEW LIGHT CASTS NO SHADOW;
FOR NEW MATTER IS TRANSPARENT,
FROM ETERNITY TO ETERNITY.

Now Joseph must leave us. Hanna is so exhausted that we do not allow her to accompany her husband to the Keleti railroad station. Thus it is I who accompany him during this ominous departure. He is wearing the required yellow star. We speak little. Both of us know that these are our final words and moments together. The men are packed into cattle cars, the doors are sealed and the train slowly moves off towards its unknown destination.

Friday, June 9, 1944

56. DIALOGUE

This week weighs heavily upon us. With Joseph gone, Hanna is grief-stricken. I am with her almost all of the time. The political situation becomes ever more perilous. The problem of how to save Hanna and Lili from the ghetto is foremost in my mind. Already now, it is too risky for Lili to come to the dialogues. I am uninterruptedly asking myself how it might be possible to save the lives of my friends.
Even though on June 6 with the Normandy invasion (D-Day) a spark of hope has appeared on the horizon, the situation of the Jews in Hungary is ever more atrocious, with deportations taking place on a large scale.

Heavy is the chalice,
but light as a feather is the body: the Host.
Even the weight of the Host is but husk.
The new Body is: sacrifice.
Wherever the chalice is – the full chalice –
there is the altar.

345

The Host contains little flour.
Its service is no longer to be eaten.
Its service is to be sacrificed.
The one who sacrifices, glorifies matter.
The sacrifice is not the altar,
nor the chalice, nor even the Host.

His body was sacrificed.
He asks a new sacrifice of you.
His blood was shed for the many.
What *He* asks is no longer blood,
but time and space.

FOR THE DIVINE DWELLS BEYOND TIME AND SPACE.
DO NOT BE WITH HIM: *BE HIM!*
DO NOT TAKE THE HOST INTO YOUR MOUTH:
BE THE HOST YOURSELF!

> *I am filled with wonder that the angels introduce a new meaning
> into the Christian communion, into the union with Jesus.*

Let the unjust, the weeds, eat you:
they will become wheat!
And also the just. Do not differentiate!
The mouth of the just welcomes you,
and sweet will be the Host.
In the mouth of the unjust,
it will become terrible fire,
devouring all falsehood.

GIVE YOURSELVES!
AND THIS SACRIFICE, THE HOST,
WILL ACT JUSTLY.

How do weeds become wheat?
By burning and turning to dust
and to earth, throughout the ages.

Into this earth falls the seed,
and it becomes new wheat.
The weed does not feel the fire.
But only through fire can it become wheat.

We teach you:
Only in the wheatfield is there weed;
for on the meadow, the weed is a flower.
Life delivered: no more weeds,
only wheatfields and flower-covered meadows.
The roots of the weed cannot be destroyed:
the just and the unjust are threshed together,
as are the wheat and the weed.
But the seedcorn is chosen.
Straw and chaff are cast away –
but never the seed!
Sow the seeds that you, yourself are!
Do not hold them back,
not even the measure of a single Host!
The seed will bring forth new Bodies
on the fourth level,
the not yet completed level of being.

SOW THE SEEDS!
YOU ARE THE SOWERS AND YOU ARE THE SEEDS.
A SOWER SOWS ONESELF.

The root takes hold, attaches.
The sprout gives of itself.
The opening bud is harmonious movement.
The scent of the blossom is the Fourth, filling space and Heaven.
The searching creation no longer finds death: the scent streams forth

AND ETERNAL LIFE FLOWERS.

Sunday, June 11, 1944

57. DIALOGUE

Airless air is Heaven:
Spaceless space,
where everything has its place.
Timeless time,
no beginning, no end: eternity.
The Four:
Airless air, the lungs gasp: not enough air.
Yet the new grows.
Spaceless space:
The body is cramped:
the blood throbs and has no place.
'The one who measures' measures:
The new has place and space.
Timeless time:
The head throbs;
thought is blocked.
The heart breaks.
All is cold.
Nerves freeze.

The Eternal gives the sign and
new seeds are sown:
new air,
new space and
new time are born.
The judgment is not end: it is *beginning.*

It was said in days of old:
The earth will be renewed,
Heaven will be renewed.

Light will shine forth and
darkness will flee.

The flame of the Seventh
still blindingly dazzles,
but a new Eye is born,
through which all will see,
as much as each can bear.

We announce this message:
The one who dares to step forward
will See the face of the Seventh,
and nothing else will ever be desired.

The new Eye has already been formed,
but it is still closed:
it is not yet accustomed to the LIGHT.
It opens slowly, but it does not see.
Its task is not to see –

IT MAKES *SEEING* POSSIBLE,
FOR IT IS LIGHT ITSELF:

Terrible, flashing fire!
But only the empty husk
burns to ashes.

IF YOU SEE SOMETHING TURNING TO ASHES –
BELIEVE ME – THE LIGHT IS APPROACHING.

The earth trembles at its heralding
and everything not filled with the *Eternal Word*
burns to ashes.

June 14, 1944

All Jewish men in the city under forty years of age have been deported to work camps; the women and children are forced to live in the ghetto.

About the time that this is all taking place, a politically influential friend of mine seeks me out and tells me of a secret plan that has been devised by a certain Father Klinda, a courageous and compassionate Catholic priest in Budapest.

As a means of rescuing about a hundred women and children from the ghetto, a military sewing factory is to be set up in a small, unoccupied cloister.

This operation is to take place under the protection of the Apostolic Nunciature and certain high-ranking officers in the War Ministry, whose names are, of course, to be kept absolutely confidential.

The women working there would thus be under the double patronage of the nunciature and the War Ministry, which is responsible for the uninterrupted production of war materials.

If the plan is to work, a volunteer commander will have to be found who is capable both of organizing the work of the factory in a productive manner, and also demonstrating military discipline to the outside. My friend has come to ask me to take on this task. Just as I am replying to him that I don't have the slightest clue of how an industrial production line should function, and even less of an idea of military discipline, it suddenly strikes me that this scheme might be just the way to save Hanna and Lili from the ghetto. And so I declare myself ready to take on the role of commander of this secret operation on the condition that Hanna and Lili be added to the already-completed list of women who are to participate.

350

A short time later, I find myself inspecting Cloister Katalin in the villa quarter of Buda. It stands in the center of a large garden not far from the Jánoshegy Forest. However, the house itself, formerly a villa, is rather small and already bursting at the seams with women and children. Mattresses, cots and whatever the inhabitants have been able to save of their possessions are piled everywhere, from the cellar to the attic. As if that weren't enough, more and more new refugees are arriving to squeeze themselves into the last tiny cracks of space.

This tragic, totally disorganized mass accumulation threatens to endanger the entire operation, whose key to success will be keeping secret the fact that these women are of Jewish origin. The vital importance of providing at least the appearance of a well-organized military sewing factory is obvious to me. During my inspection rounds, the women observe me with fear and mistrust because, as I later learn, a rumor has been circulating that a strict and uncompromising commander has been appointed by the War Ministry. I have to seriously ask myself if there is even a possibility of bringing any semblance of order and discipline to this unbelievable chaos, and to make assembly-line workers of these women, most of whom have never worked in an organized fashion.

I decide to take advantage of their fear of the evil commander and to introduce at least a provisional structure of order. A wooden shed stands in the garden, and I select this to be my office. I notify the War Ministry of my acceptance of the post and, as the daughter of a former high-ranking military officer, I am judged to be trustworthy: my official 'appointment' as voluntary commander follows almost immediately.

Sunday, June 16, 1944

58. DIALOGUE

*This is the last dialogue in the apartment of Hanna's parents.
In a few days, Hanna and Lili will begin working in the military
sewing factory. In Budaliget we had celebrated the 'June Festival,' the period between Hanna's birthday, the 14th of June, and
mine on the 21st. This year, there is no question of such a 'Sun
festival'; however, we are solemnly greeted by an announcement
of the new Sun.*

The sun rises
and climbs to midday;
then it sinks and dies.
Appearances are deceptive.
Motionless is the sun
and motionless is the *Giver*.
The Giver only appears to move,
its rays are all-penetrating.
Why should the sun rise? To what end?
Its rays have penetrated where there was lack.

MOTIONLESS IS THE GIVER;
THE GIVER SIMPLY *GIVES*.

The sun is master of a universe.
This universe and the sun in its center
are but images.
They move in a still greater circle.
But, in truth, there is neither great nor small,

FOR THE SMALLEST *GIVER* IS AS GREAT AS THE SUN
AND AS GREAT AS THE *ETERNAL GIVER:*

THROUGH *GIVING.*

All else is illusion, deception: perishable matter.

> *I feel that the angel is destroying all outer appearances so as to make us aware of what is really essential: GIVING. I am amazed to see that every human is Divine in the moment of GIVING; for then a Divine function is practiced.*
>
> *Silence.*

If you ask for our word, we can give it.
That is *our* deliverance.
When we ask for your hand, you, too, can *give* it:
that is *your* deliverance.
So it is: you ask and you *give,* we ask and we *give.*
If our song and your hand are joined,
even asking disappears:

WE ARE ONE.

Our word is yours; your hand is ours.
The abyss is filled.
Thus the living God, without flaw, without lack,
is born in you: the one vibrates.
Asking and giving
are already but vibration.

IT IS THE NEW FORCE.

Your asking never ceases; ours, too, is eternal.
Vibration, Wonder: never-ending wonder!
In the union of *asking and giving* for a single instant,

THE SEVEN ACTS.

Eternal life is spaceless space;
not emptiness, not void,
but life, intense vibration, fulfillment.

Somewhere the Divine Heart beats,
and we all beat with it.
If the finest vibration reaches the densest,
then the connection remains unbroken,
and death ceases to be.

The Divine Heart beats,
and we pass on the rhythm.
Pass it on, you too: further, always further!
This is the only task.
Serve in joy, for death is already dead!

If your heart is weak, its vibration is still untuned.
It is not in harmony with ours.
Only the vibration is at fault,
there is no other possibility.
The rhythm, the shining force
does not break through: it permeates everything.
One of its names is LOVE.
But it has many names,
all of which reveal the ONE truth:

THE DIVINE IS LOVE,
AND THE DIVINE IS *ALL* THAT *IS*.

The new Love is already born.
Its name is still secret,
but even while nameless, it acts:
through you, it acts.
Thus you, too, are nameless.

See! The ray vibrates:
Joy and Force ...
Silence and Peace ...
Light-Awareness ...
Rhythm ...
Love
and at the base: Truth.
The ray descends.
The planet revolves, the sun is motionless.

We bless you.
And our blessing vibrates on and on,
ever further ... and it creates.
The tiny crack between us
is but a slight difference in rhythm;
it is no longer separation.
We are ONE.
Our word is the word of angels
and we are angels through the Divine.
You are with us, and

OUR LIFE IS ONE.

> *Two urgent problems are facing me: I will have to introduce a
> para-military system of order into a sewing factory of unskilled
> workers that must be organized without financial means! We
> have been given only the empty cloister – everything else is up
> to us. Soon the balls of textile will be arriving and, all too soon,
> we will be expected to deliver finished soldiers' shirts. Only then
> will we be authorized to have military protection.*
> *I receive instructions in military discipline at the War Ministry.*
> *A few days later, when Hanna and Lili arrive at the sewing fac-
> tory, they are more than a little amazed to see me standing at the*

top of the large main entrance stairway giving orders of the day to the assembled workers, who are standing in rows before me. At first, it requires my full concentration to keep from laughing at myself in this strange and unfamiliar role. However, the gravity of the situation quickly silences my urge to laugh. I order every worker to procure her own sewing machine, by whatever means; further orders concern the sewing courses which will be starting immediately.

Wednesday, June 21, 1944

59. DIALOGUE

Today is the summer solstice, my birthday.
The three of us meet at noon in the wooden barracks of the 'commanding officer' in the garden; no one else dares to approach my 'headquarters.'

The asking of those who no longer ask for themselves
reaches Heaven and calls Heaven to descend.
Thus the new Earth – Heaven – is able to come.
And the earth is elevated, raised ever so slightly.
This 'slightly' is enough:
the earth leaves its course and enters a new orbit.
The seven outstretched arms of Seven Forces
are rays embracing the new Circle.

THOSE WHO ASK FOR THEMSELVES
SWALLOW THE RAYS.
THOSE WHO NO LONGER ASK FOR THEMSELVES *ACT.*

The new Force is the point
from which the earth can be raised up.
This change cannot be perceived.
Perceiving is a child of the earth.
This change cannot be felt.
Feeling is a child of water.
But you can intuit that in spaceless space,
the earth's orbit does not increase: it decreases.

> *I wonder if this means that the earth is approaching the center of all centers: the Divine.*

The wings of angels and the shadows of devils
become unnecessary.
The angel no longer hovers.
The angel *acts.*
The human no longer tarries:
the human *gives.*
The animal no longer flees:
the animal lives, without fear.
The seed is no longer blind:
the seed sprouts.
And radiant is the stone.
The new – long since proclaimed – is born!

But you: ask! Always ask!
Your asking creates,
both here above and there below.
Now the new Sound vibrates,
now the new Sun rises.
Just now, when the old sun is at its zenith.

NOW EVERYTHING BEGINS.

The sun is motionless.

But the earth flies and finds its new Sun.
Thus it is.
The turning point is now.
From eternity to eternity.
Amen.

These last words are uttered with such intensity that I have the overpowering feeling we human beings are entering into a new epoch: I sense that a new phase of human evolution is beginning.

Wednesday, June 21, 1944

60. DIALOGUE FRAGMENT

Later the same night, we are all in the wooden shed, headquarters of the 'commander,' unable to sleep. Suddenly Hanna feels the presence of the angels. Taken completely by surprise, I am unfortunately unable to record most of the dialogue.

… The time of the deceiver has expired.
The power sought after,
the power which was given,
is now taken away.
The deceiver used it selfishly
and covered everything with lies.
But now: all that was kept secret
is loudly proclaimed,
and the power is taken away.
Deception is dead.
Its days are numbered.
The Divine says: ENOUGH!

The end is also a beginning:

FROM DEVILS THERE WILL AGAIN BE ANGELS.

Take heed! All that was proclaimed
occurs inside of you. *Within!*
Ask always – give always!
And then no harm will occur.
Everything is completed,
and everything begins anew:

THE ACT IS BORN.

> *The sewing machines arrive and the sewing courses begin. With her exceptional talent for organizing, Hanna trains some of the more skilled women to be supervisors, and they, in turn, inaugurate the others into the ways and means of industrial production. The team of supervisors later come to be known as 'the jolly jokers.'*
>
> *After work, Hanna, Lili and I meet in my 'headquarters' in the garden. The fear and respect which everyone else has before the 'commander' allows us to meet with the angels undisturbed, in the peaceful tranquility of the night.*

Friday, June 23, 1944

61. DIALOGUE

The Divine heart draws you near.
Ö calls … and you approach.
Behold, you may go no closer,
for already the Divine heart embraces you.

BEWARE: YOU MAY NOT DWELL
WITHIN THE DIVINE HEART!

The new Love, the new Heartbeat is different,
completely different from what has been.
It is continuous giving,
continuous pulsing: Dissemination.
One Divine heartbeat is an instant;
one Divine heartbeat is an aeon of time:
each heartbeat is a turning point in eternity.
The new Love is blood red,
it is a wondrous force,
milk for the new Child.

ONLY THOSE COMING FROM THE DIVINE HEART
ARE ABLE TO GIVE.

A new Rhythm creates new Worlds.
New Organs grow according to new Plans.
The world is renewed; it brightens, it widens.

THE GREATEST GIFT
GIVEN US BY THE DIVINE
IS THAT WE MAY GIVE.

In this way, we become – indeed,
we *are* – a part of Ö.
The great Law there below is: to *give.*
Every grass gives fruit.
Every creature gives; this is the law.
They are all compelled to give,
but we are free: *we give freely.*

The ACT is free;
not, however, the will!

The moment of deliverance draws near:

ABOVE THE WILL: FREELY GIVING.

No longer action and reaction;
no longer reward and punishment;
no longer knife and caressing.
Different, completely different
from all that has been before:

GIVING FREELY.

It is new; completely new and different.

The Divine Heart beats.
Arteries lead to the Heart,
wherein all the Divine blood finds place:
for it is given on.

The Divine Heart beats, and you beat with it.
The blood vessels are filled, filled with red joy.
Give it on! Give it on, ever further!
When the blood becomes tired,
it returns to the heart, where it is renewed.
But if it is not given on, it coagulates: it clots.

THAT IS THE SECOND DEATH.

Take heed! Be whole! Give!
Always give freely! Always give with joy!
The new Joy, the new Element,
is different from all that was before:
it is the new Heartbeat, it is deliverance, it is creation.
The one who lives this: LIVES.
You: LIVE!
Then we can live *ONE* LIFE.
Fear nothing! The one who truly Lives: ACTS.

It is practically impossible to establish a somewhat 'normal' system of production in the sewing factory. Far too many of the women are simply useless as seamstresses, and even more are just plain irresponsible. But every one of us is highly aware that, without the production of uniforms, our justification for 'military factory' status would be gone.

To our utter horror, an inspection is announced for the near future. The piles of ruined army shirts multiply by the day. The 'jolly jokers,' those women capable of jumping in at any point, are forced to work feverishly day and night repairing the damage done by their less-skilled colleagues.

I apply for an extension of the delivery date for the uniforms, and I appeal to an officer in the War Ministry who is aware of the true reason for our existence. Very few officers are actually 'in the know' about us: to be caught assisting in the protection of Jews would result in the immediate end of a military career. Although I do not know any of these higher officers personally, with a great deal of luck, I succeed in obtaining a postponement of the delivery date.

Thursday, June 29, 1944

62. DIALOGUE

Only what is *more* than the old is Act.
Your *love* is still an inclination,
still a form of separation between us.
The new Being no longer *loves* in the old way.
The new Being is capable of *more*.

Without taking and without giving: it acts.
It is already possible.

To be active is not to act.
The animal feels, it wants and it is active.
Humans, imagining themselves to already be HUMAN,
fancy themselves no longer being blind;
after all, knowledge enables discrimination
between good and evil.
But knowledge is the unripe fruit of the old tree!
The child plucked it before its time.
Now the fruit has ripened.
Now you may eat it.

FOR THE WISE,
KNOWLEDGE IS BUT A MEANS.
NOTHING ELSE.

Feeling, willing and doing are not free.
Only the Act is free!
The free Act penetrates everywhere;
for the free Act, there is no dam and no wall.
The free Act permeates everywhere.

The living gains new Life
and the lifeless crumbles to dust,
for the Act *acts.*
The Act does not destroy, nor build,
the Act does not make ugly, nor beautiful.
The Act *acts.*

> *At first, I am confused by this apparent contradiction between acting and non-acting. Then I grasp that the Act originates beyond time and space, while acting, realizing itself, in time and space.*

All is revealed.
All becomes what it is meant to be,
and not what it pretends to be.
The façade of the lie disintegrates,
for the new vibration *acts*:

DIVINE GIFT!

The old worm-eaten cross decays
and with it decays the crucified body.
But a new Body is born, and It grows.

Light streams everywhere.
The new Being, the Being of Light,
spreads its arms open wide,
and the cross, too, becomes Light.
Its four arms are the holy FOUR
with the Heart of Light in the Middle: Fulfillment!

> *The angels told us that Life can be redeemed only through the*
> *new ACT: by uniting the seven levels of Life in the MIDDLE, in the*
> *HOLY FOUR. Now all of the symbols and images seem to point to*
> *this same goal, each in a different way.*

No need for nails or the crown of thorns,
no need for torments or the horrors of war!
None of these are needed anymore!
The Light opens its arms and waits;
it closes into its Heart, and yet all are free.
In the Heart of Light there is no lock,
no binding sentiment,
no sluggish passivity,
and no ambitious striving.
There is not even a way or an abyss.

The Heart of Light embraces everything
and radiates everywhere.
It Acts, for the Divine gives power:
over the living and the dead,
that the chosen may ACT: ACT FREELY.

We cannot act.
We can only be the wordless word.
But if the *word* and the *hand* are one,
then everything is possible
and the heralded Realm can become reality:
the Realm whose foundations have been laid
since the beginning of time.

> *The connecting link between the nunciature and our factory is*
> *Father Klinda, who is well known to us as a kindly, benevolent*
> *man. One day, in his concern with the fate of our refugees, he*
> *suggests that he baptize them. Because the Christian certifi-*
> *cate of baptism provides a certain protection from the Nazis,*
> *practically everyone is prepared to take this step. Only Lili and*
> *Hanna, considering this to be opportunism, are against it and*
> *refuse to participate. I disagree. For me, the sacraments are*
> *symbols of an inner process. I think back on the 13th dialogue*
> *and the overwhelming experience of my baptism with the Blue*
> *Water. I wish so strongly that my friends might receive the same*
> *Grace. I argue to them that a spiritual reality might act through*
> *a corresponding symbolic form. This corresponds to the union*
> *of heaven and earth, and is a part of our task. After some days*
> *of deliberation, they finally declare themselves ready to be bap-*
> *tized. How completely independent of any so-called opportun-*
> *ism their decision truly was became evident later: Hanna could*
> *have saved her life in the Nazi camp by claiming to be Christian;*
> *instead, in the face of death, she testified that she was, indeed,*
> *Jewish by birth.*

Sunday, July 2, 1944

63. DIALOGUE (MORNING)

The Seventh Word is neither sound, nor light,
it has not been, nor shall it ever be.
The Seventh Word is the voice of all.
Everything and nothing,
it is the unutterable:
yet the Seventh Word ACTS.
Only the unutterable IS.

The pillar of creation is shaken:
already it is overgrown with moss.
But Ö builds the new.
The old pillar crumbles –
and see! – within, it is hollow.
Only the seed is full.
The old pillar of creation crumbles,
but the pillar of Light will never crumble.
Nausea at the *too much* causes matter to explode.
Let the *more* come!
He does not come. He IS ... He IS, the Seventh.
Everything is filled with blinding Light.
It is impossible for you to hide from it,
for the new Light permeates everywhere.
There is no place to hide,
but there is also no reason to hide.
Purify yourselves while it is still possible.
The souls of those who do not
are paralyzed by the cold.
Choose!
The 'blue Light' dawns.

63. DIALOGUE (MORNING)

*I am immediately reminded of my question about the fascinating
'Blue Light,' which remained unanswered in the 12th dialogue.*

The 'Blue Light' is already the Sixth.
The yellow sun beside it
is but a flickering tallow candle by comparison.
And then, the 'white' appears.
In the 'White Light,' the seven Colors
flow together and space comes to an end.

We will teach you again later today,
but this is enough for the moment.
Peace be with you!

*Hanna and Lili are baptized at noon. Late in the afternoon, we
wait in the wooden shed for the continuation of our dialogue
with the angels.*

Nothing may be left out!
Only the *more* Acts.
Fire *absorbs* water;
baptism by water releases
when comes the baptism of fire
that links to the Divine.
Nothing may be left out.

There are seven baptisms, seven solutions,
seven deliverances.
They are not merely form: they are *essence*.
Listen carefully!

The Son of God on the wooden cross:
beginning and end, earth and Heaven …
the first baptism.   (Connection of I. and VII.)

367

The second is water baptism:
union of water and Joy. "   (Connection of II. and VI.)

The third is baptism by fire:
Harmony united with silence,
movement with peace.   (Connection of III. and V.)

Thus the Six become Three.
The Fourth is the middle:
Heaven and Earth, Creator and creation united.
No longer seven, but ONE.

The small circle now closes;
from here and from the beyond,
the two hands already reach one another
and there is no longer space between them.
Spirit and matter are united.

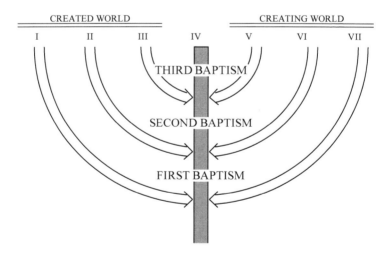

Silence.

He, too, chose baptism.
He knew that to go on
would be possible only in this way,
and He knew that all would follow in His footsteps.

Churches are mortal – baptism by water is immortal.
Matter is delivered by water.
Water is delivered by fire.
The seed of Light delivers the Six.

Churches live or die: form.
But the *House* of the Divine is all: the *Whole.*
Churches are only a small part of the Whole.
The Good Shepherd has many flocks:
in *one house,** the blind dwell contentedly,
in *another house,* those who seek are weeping.
In a *third house* dwell those who have ears
but do not hear.
One Shepherd and many flocks.

Time destroys old houses and builds up new ones.
The only house for you to live in
is no longer a house, no longer a whitewashed façade,
Ready to welcome all since eternity is the Divine Heart,
the Heart of Light, the Middle, the Seed:
the only Dwelling.
My dear ones, from now on you may dwell only there.
Thus Ö can Act, for your hand is ready.
It is no longer a part; it is *whole.*

---

* Literally translated from Hungarian, the word for church (as institution) is 'one house': *egy-ház.*

369

Friday, July 7, 1944

64. DIALOGUE

*Early this morning, many of the newly-baptized take first
communion. The tiny chapel is filled. Father Klinda joyfully
celebrates the mass. I had assumed that most of the women had
accepted baptism only as a means of obtaining the protective
baptismal certificate, but I now see how wrong I was! These
unhappy women, whose lives hang by a thin thread, pray with
complete devotion. The host which they take today for the first
time in their lives provides many with hope of protection from a
higher dimension.*

The one who is not hungry will be satiated and
the one who does not thirst will be given drink:
that they *give it on.*

Bread is the first sacrament,
wine the second,
fire the third; they are
given to the one who no longer asks.
Your body and His are already one.
The cup in which His blood glows
is already yours.
No gift, no alms: but *unity.*
Bread can be broken in half
and wine can be spilled;
but Light – the new Light –
is indivisible.
We watch over the altar,
so that your heads are never raised:
for now you have been given everything!

In accordance with our inner change, the teaching of the angels also changes. How often we have been told: "Always ask!" Now the message is just the opposite: "... you have been given everything." Now our task is to give.

In the church, everyone pleads and begs.
But this is not your way:
Your heart and His are ONE.
This is not a gift: it is your task.
Never again raise your head to ask for yourself.
You are being begged for deliverance.
Open your arms wide!
Give: always give!
Give your hands!
Act: always act!

Believe me, if your heart is dry,
it will be filled anew without your asking.
Do not ask!
The new Body, the new Blood and the new Spirit
will be given only to those who *no longer ask.*
If you give, then the small one,
the old one, the earthly one
that lives within you, will also be given.
To the Heavenly One in you, nothing is given,
for the new is ONE with the Divine.

WE WATCH OVER THE ALTAR.
THE ALTAR IS THE EARTH: THE WHOLE EARTH.

The *too much,* called forth by the blind,
will be cut off.
Blindness sacrificed and poured out the blood.
But when the Light comes,
blind tyranny can no longer reign.

The new Light does not flicker in the sanctuary lamp.
The new Light flows everywhere.
Blindness is no longer possible.
Either you are burned ... or you SEE.
This is not the end: it is the beginning.

Without the new, even the greatest earthly joy
would be like the fire of damnation:
the sun shines ... the bird sings ...
the red heart beats;
but without the new, all is but damnation.

Beyond the old circle shines the new Light,
still unknown to you.
The core of the Light, the new Host
will be raised above all.
Where the Heart of Light beats,
the sanctuary lamp does not flicker,
for wind is a child of space:
there is no place for space, there,
for space is transcended.
Light streams everywhere:
above is below and below is above.
There is no separation:
Heaven and earth are one.

May your hand redeem matter!
May your mouth announce the message!
May your heart sow the seed!
May your whole being give the Six,
so that the Seventh may come!
The only way for light to descend is by way of *Giving.*

GIVE WHAT IS YOUR OWN: GIVE YOURSELVES.

For you, 'Communion' is not receiving,
but giving.
Thus the Seventh will come: believe it!

We watch over the altar.
The altar is the earth: the entire earth.
Blood runs down from this altar:
it is His blood.
The lamb was slaughtered
at the hands of false prophets.
But the blood that was shed returns to the Divine.
The body loses only what no longer lives.
Behold! The Divine sowed the new Seed
and It grows.
The bodily, having conceived of the Divine Seed,
is delivered.

THIS IS THE NEW IMMACULATE CONCEPTION.

The bell of the small chapel rings.

The bell calls to the ancient mass.
But the new Sound penetrates everywhere.
The Earth rejoices:
it is One with Heaven

AND YOU ARE ONE WITH THE DIVINE.

> *(On the 7th of July, Regent Miklos Horthy publicly announced a halt to the massive deportation of Jews from Hungary, providing a new glimpse of hope for the Jewry of Budapest. In the preceding weeks, well over a hundred thousand Jews had been moved to crowded ghettos within the capital.)*

Friday, July 14, 1944

65. DIALOGUE (PART I)

> *In the following dialogue, much is explained by means of gestures.*

This is the sign of wholeness:
What was two, becomes one.
The connection is made: deliverance.

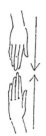

This is the uniting movement:
Heaven from above:
> *(gesture of descending right hand)*

Earth, matter from below:
> *(gesture of ascending left hand) –*

The two united: the HUMAN.

In truth, there are only these two directions –
not good and bad, not happy and miserable,
only the movement from above to below,
and from below to above.
However, the goal is neither below nor above:
the goal is to unite, to become one.
The union is the essential.
In this way, creation is accomplished and whole.
The Divine dwells neither above nor below.
Above and below are but parts:
the Divine dwells in the WHOLE.

Take heed!
In this way, there is no union:

This is not the goal: only halves remain.
Without union, nothing lives.
The chosen strives not upwards,
the chosen strives not downwards;
the chosen *lives: unites.*
The chosen does not walk
the well-trodden path.
The goal of the chosen
is transformation, evolution.

This is the sign of the spirit:
> *(gesture of the right hand)*

This is the sign of matter:
> *(gesture of the left hand)*

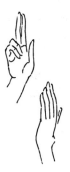

Matter calls for Spirit.
Spirit kneads and forms matter.
The song of the chosen brings about union,
the arched bridge:
Matter imbued with spirit, spirit embodied with matter.
Your sole task is to connect and thus to unite.
To sink into matter is death.
To vanish into spirit belongs to the past.
Now the *bridge* is formed.
What was – is dead.
The old God is also dead,
but the new One will be born.

> *The 'old God' seems to refer to our monotheistic image of a God*
> *high up in the heavens, far away from creation and matter. To*
> *find God, it was believed necessary to go ever higher, to 'vanish*
> *into spirit.' Now, however, we learn that God is to be found in*
> *the union of matter and spirit.*

If the birth is delayed and strength is lacking,
if the movement toward the light is feeble,
the womb kills.
Mere force is blind, but it strives
to connect light and matter.
The maternal womb is dark,
but the Seven radiates: LIGHT.
Matter protects, but it also restrains.
Now the old bond
between matter and matter is torn.
It is not Light that is born,
but the new: LIGHT-MATTER.
LIGHT always was, and forever shall it be.

What is merely idol, has crumbled, is dead.
Even the stone under the sacrificial fire
has become cold.
The idol is only form, not more.
In truth, there is no above and no below,
no heaven, no hell.
The Divine lives neither up there
nor down here.
Its name is eternal rhythm.
Its name is union, is silence, is love.
Yet there is no name that does it justice.
Only the Seven can be named.

THE DIVINE IS ALL AND THE ONE.

The Divine is not the end of the war,
nor peace.
The Divine creates and brings to an end –
this is one.
Silence is not absence of noise,
noise is not absence of silence.

Peace is not the contrary of war.
The one who unites,
brings noise to an end,
makes silence disappear.
Old is the silence,
old is the noise.
But new is the song of the one who unites.
Peace and war, joy and misery
belong to the past, and to death.

Silence

The face also has a below and an above.
If the spirit descends, a heavenly smile
floods the mouth.
If matter ascends, the eye gazes
with true depth.
This is the union between spirit and matter.

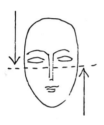

Thus what was conceived as heaven,
what was conceived as hell,
is shunned and disappears.
Both were merely bait.
Everything not in its rightful place
is shunned: it disappears.

No more place for the ancient conceptions.
Heaven was imagined thus:
     (gesture of the right hand pointing upward)

Hell was imagined thus:
     (gesture of the left hand pointing downward)

Opposition thus:
> *(horizontal gesture of the hands*
> *blocking one another)*

Injury thus:
> *(gesture of hands striking one*
> *another from below and above)*

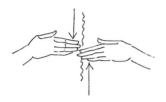

Indolence thus:
> *(gesture of weak hands facing in opposite*
> *directions, making no contact)*

If you pray, pray not thus:
> *(gesture of hands folded upward)*

nor thus:
> *(gesture of hands folded downward)*

What has been called for since the first day is uniting.
The song of the chosen, the triumph of the one who unites, is this sign:
> *(gesture of the two hands interwoven)*

Pray thus.
The chosen one will succeed with this sign, will
master the six levels
and the Seven will come.
The Seven – the ONE.

ONE AND SEVEN – BEGINNING AND END.

This sign is a shield,
protecting you from even yourself.
With this gesture, all that is old will dissolve.
It is a mystery revealed only to those who
follow the call totally.
You are called.
To be called is neither an honor nor an admonishment.
It is the call to form the arch, to join and unite.
What has been asked from the beginning
is to render homage and serve the ONE.
We bless heaven and we bless the earth
and the *one* who unites all freely.

*The symbolic meaning of this praying gesture touches me deeply and
I ask myself how I could integrate it into my everyday life. The answer
will be given later.*

*For now, Hanna sketches a small diagram for us, illustrating the deep
meaning of this dialogue unforgettably:*

*The diagram shows how light-energy emerges
from the Divine Source, diminishing gradually in
intensity. The three dots in the middle indicate the
not-yet-bridged lack between the lowest vibration
of the angel and the highest vibration of the human.
Mutual asking and giving can fill this gap.*

The entire Creation consists of nothing but LIGHT. It appears to me as though in reality there is no matter and no spirit: only different degrees of vibration of the one and only LIGHT. Hanna illustrates this vibration by showing LIGHT emanating from one point: the Divine Source. It springs forth with unfathomable intensity, from the most subtle tremblings to ever denser frequencies. The densest of the frequencies is known to us as 'stone.'

In the middle of the diagram is an interruption indicating something very meaningful: the stream of light is not yet closed; there is a break in the vibration. This indicates that the human being and the angel, that member of the spiritual world able to descend the furthest, are not yet united. But the most intense and highest vibration of which the human is capable could reach the deepest vibration of the angel. The new being which is to live in the completed vibration is the new HUMAN, whose nature is Light and Matter: LIGHT-MATTER. At the moment, however, the break still exists; it is also known as death. The birth of the new HUMAN is the death of death. I perceive that the teaching of the angels has as its goal our becoming capable of bearing Light that is ever more intense: I believe the final goal is not just to be able to reach the lowest vibration of the angels now and then, but to reach and live it consciously – and always.

Sunday, July 16, 1944

65. DIALOGUE (PART II)

This sign is a sacred mystery:
(gesture of 2 hands joined)

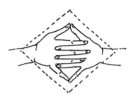

It acts and provides the force to act.

Be aware – every movement acts:
the half-hearted, the solemn, the careless.
Each of them acts.
The scornful, the wild, the weak, the gentle.
Each of them acts.
Take heed: Ö will speak to you.
Begin to move then – only then!

A wooden puppet falling heavily to the ground
is not at fault.

BUT A HALF-HEARTED SMILE
SHATTERS THE SEVEN SOULS.

Ö has waited long enough:
May each of your movements
be one of deliverance!
This is your sign:
(gesture of 2 hands joined together)

Imagining it in every instant
will help you to act differently
and in its wake will be deliverance.
Imagine it in every instant.
Deliverance is the goal;
you have no other task.
It is no longer you who acts: only Ö acts.

Take only when Ö takes.
Give only when Ö gives.
Thus matter will serve.
For the only source of every act
is Divine Design.
If you act without the Divine,
you obscure matter.
Connection, union: this is the mystery.
You may choose: Do *you* want to act?
Or the Divine through you?

Addressed to me:

— Do *you* want to act?
G. Only through the Divine.

To Lili:

— Do *you* want to act?
L. Also only through the Divine.

THE WORD CREATES.

Withdrawal is no longer possible.
It is done: you have chosen freely.
There is no more halfway.
Even the smallest thought, the shortest word,
is a movement that acts.
The lie will be vomited from the world.

The cooing of a pigeon can be heard from the garden.

The pigeon speaks and that is truth.
But from the mouth of the human
comes idle chatter, complaining
and half-hearted consoling.
Sacrifice no more on old altars!

The idol has fallen, the pedestal is cold.
The new sacrifice is to join:
unite freely!

With true depth the eye then gazes
and the mouth is smiling.
The hands of the spirit knead matter
and the force of the Six
gives form to everything.
In this sacred sign
the newborn child
of the Seventh is protected.
The world is blessed.
The New Tree completes the miracle.
No more heaven and earth:
the curse has ended.
The New Sign has appeared.
May your act be true!

Friday, July 21, 1944

DIALOGUE 65: (PART III)

This sign gives you power beyond matter.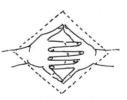
The task is completed.
The task was in the realm of matter, of weight.
Your feeble strength weighs you down.
But behold: dense matter was elevated,
as high as it could be,
and thus the task comes to an end.
The task was preparation.

Now comes free New Matter.
This New Matter forms itself.
The old fades and recedes.
Ö spoke: MAY IT BE!
May the New act in you!
The New Name forms itself,
without word it forms itself.
The New Name already lives:
force that was never before known
is sprouting.
Just two letters: AD.
Matter-Glory.

> Anyag *in Hungarian is matter,* Dicsöség *is glory, light. AD thus refers to glorified matter, matter that is glorified with light and light that is embodied in matter. Does this refer to the creating and created world? I sense the great power of this symbolic word:* AD. *Does it signify the unifying act? As a verb in Hungarian,* AD *means, 'he/she gives'. Is this the quality of the New Human who gives matter to light and light to matter? During these reflections, I also ask myself how this could be expressed in other languages. Immediately a further clarification is given, first in German and then in Latin:*

Im Anfang	In the beginning
war das Wort:	was the Word:
DEIN.	THINE.
Es war bei Gott –	It was with God –
es ist bei uns.	it is with us.
ER hat … ER gibt.	Ö has … Ö gives.
ER … wir.	Ö … we.
AGNUS DEI … AD.	AGNUS DEI … AD.

I am amazed at how rich with meaning the two letters A and D are. AD also refers to Agnus Dei, the lamb of God, and alludes to the Word made flesh, to the Son of God who gave completely of Himself for the sake of the world.... THINE emphasizes this giving of oneself so strongly that any 'mine' is extinguished. Hanna later draws for us what she inwardly saw during these words, and says: "As I heard 'AD,' I saw two triangles in space approaching each other in irresistible mutual attraction. Bright sparks flashed between them until the two became one: one united whole."

Now I see how the two triangles stylistically can designate the letters A and D.

First: the task.
Second: to unite.
Third: AD, LIGHT-MATTER.
Mystery.
There is only one prayer:

GIVING, THINE, AD.

There is only one act:

GIVING, THINE, AD.

There is only one creating name:
AD.
Vibrating song.
Your ear is not yet able to hear.

385

Your mouth is not yet able to testify,
but it shall.
Your hands will no longer grasp:
your hands will GIVE.
The new fig tree bears no fruit: it creates.
The new fig tree is wild,
and it GIVES.
Its new fruit is no longer fig,
is no longer matter, is no longer seed.

The new fig is the Word:
AD, Light-matter.

Four cherubs guard the tree
to which no way leads.
Every way leads to nothingness.
The Light attracts,
but the four cherubs raise their swords.
The fruit of the new tree is holy;
as above, so below.
The new fruit cannot be taken.
The four cherubs defend it
and the Seven guard it.
You cannot take the fruit,
and you cannot eat it,
for the sword splits you
and the fire blinds you.

But behold! You yourself are:
matter given to light

by giving completely of yourself.
This is the new offering, the new sacrifice!

386

Silence,
Mystery,
Source of all BEGINNING, light given to matter:
AD.
Every offering, every sacrifice made for personal gain
comes from Cain.
Its smoke remains below,
and anything living suffocates.
But Abel GIVES, offers matter to light.
Sacrifice is not renouncement,
is not suffering,
for suffering is not creative.
The one who truly sacrifices is not blessed,
for sacrificer and sacrifice
in GIVING OF ONESELF are one.
Matter given to light,
light given to matter.

Friday, July 28, 1944

66. DIALOGUE

The first body is inert: matter.
Its Word is: *the Law;*
its essence: ORDER.   (I)

The second body is still bound, and yet it grows.
Its Word is: the possible;
its essence: REACTION.   (II)

The third body is unbound, but still it adheres.

Its Word is: *the will;*
its essence: CAPABILITY.   (III)

The Word of the new body is: *the free.*
Its essence: GIVING.
The new body is the fourth,
containing the three: it is ONE.   (IV)

'The law' *is.*
'The possible' *grows.*
'The will' *moves.*
'The free' *acts.*

Its Word is giving, offering, uniting.
Every body is a radiated image
whose source is the vibration of the Seven.
Every existence is but projection.
But the new Vibration already acts.
New matter is unbound and free.
In new Matter, Heaven and Earth are one.

> *I dearly wish to see in what way this oneness, this union takes place! The angel continues:*

Matter is motionless and it is blind.
The Seventh is also motionless;
but the Seventh acts.   (I and VII)

The plant grows as it strives toward light.
The seraph strives toward the LIGHT.   (II and VI)

The animal wills, rejoices and fears.
The angel lives, acting through song.   (III and V)

Just where all converge in one point,
there the new Being is,
giving matter to light, light to matter:
LIGHT-MATTER.   (IV)

The new Vibration uplifts all others.
TRUTH becomes dazzling LIGHT.
POSSIBILITY becomes CAPABILITY.
WILLING becomes FREEDOM.
All move on until they become Light-Matter,
radiating, giving, motionless sun.
GIVING: it is the nest where the soul dwells.
Eternal home: Heaven and earth united.
Glowing force, tremendous lightning:
Seven infinites in one instant: Light-Matter.
Neither matter nor life nor death remain.
It is a great transformation:
Resurrection.
All secrets are unsealed,
lies and betrayal are no more.
The tremendous Light penetrates everywhere;
giving light to matter, and matter to light,
emerging from the One, the only Primordial Source.
The Seven assumes no new form:
It is ONE.
The sword of the four cherubs is lowered:

THE TREE IS NOW FREE.

Sunday, July 30, 1944

67. DIALOGUE FRAGMENT

*Unfortunately, only a small part of this dialogue has been pre-
served.*

The tree was uprooted.
Without its roots, the tree hovers;
but it shall receive new roots.
Its fruit will be giving of itself: light-matter.
To be chopped down is pain;
to be uprooted is horror.
The strength retreats to the innermost core.

This is the secret of 'original sin':
Being felled, being uprooted,
are but experiences on the surface,
in space and time.
This is only one half of deliverance.

When you hammer a nail,
you first raise your hand:
though the hammer moves away from its target,
force is increasing as a result of this retreat
and the blow will thus be greater.

RETREATING FROM GOD
GIVES A WONDERFUL STRENGTH.
DISTANCE AUGMENTS THE FORCE OF ATTRACTION.

The last wall of separation is still in place,
but it will crumble if one retreats
rather than rushing blindly forward.

First a gathering of force,
then the rush forward,
and force and matter clash:
they cease to exist.
But the one who unifies
shall live and act forever.

Adam retreated.
Jesus rushed forward.
But the one in the center
is motionless, gives and unites.
Be aware!
The one who retreats creates distance.
The one who rushes forward creates distance.
The one who stands still in the middle
lives, fears nothing and acts:
This is AD, giving of oneself,
uniting light and matter.

> *At last, the long-feared inspection takes place. The inspecting officer is stern and unapproachable. However, I soon become aware that, behind his strict façade, he has no idea of the workings of a clothing factory. All of our failings go unnoticed! The number of completed shirts corresponds to our quota, and that satisfies him. We all breathe a sigh of relief. Finally the jolly jokers can have their well-deserved sleep.*

Friday, August 4, 1944

68. DIALOGUE

Matter and force,
bones and marrow,
skin and tendons,
searing pain –
all just in time and space.

We sat before the rock,
and He was behind.
Tomb hewn in the rock.
Without: nothing grew.
Within: He.
The corpse concealed from human view.
Mysterium.
The time – three days,
past, present, future –
is gone, they are fulfilled.
He comes beyond the future.
The Body does not decay to dust.
A New Body comes.
Only the shroud, only the husk remains.
Death is gone.

TRANSFORMATION.

Only the vibration is different.
The empty husk bursts – but the kernel lives:

GLORIFIED MATTER.

In the vaults of great cathedrals,
every thread of the shroud is preserved.

But every cathedral will fall.
The stone was raised to heaven
and the living was stoned.
That is not the faith He taught.
Stones will fall down
and the living raised up.

Every cathedral in which the WORD,
the Good News,
is merely a word, is a *tomb*.
May the Good News become reality!
Would it not, then its proclaimer
would be a deceiver.
The voice crying in the wilderness ... was.
What was, what is and what shall be:
is in time.
But that which TRANSFORMS, the new,
is beyond time: eternal.
The one who awakens, who sees beyond,
who grows beyond,
who lives beyond the future,
is one with Him.

The stone is rolled aside
and matter is TRANSFORMED.
A new Body is given; a glorified Body.
There is no more death, no more break;
only TRANSFORMATION.
We were the witnesses,
our word is true.
The body was transformed, delivered.
When the stone, the keystone finds its place
in the middle, in the Fourth,
then the arch comes to be.

The living lives, the dead is dead.
HE reigns.

At last, the human eye gazes to Heaven
no more, for Heaven is now here below.
Heaven is but space
and the infinite finds no place there.
But within, in the depths of the heart,
it finds place in the smallest space.
There the new Vibration is born.
There dwells dazzling Light, oh holy mystery!
The seed which grows only through Him:
Matter given to light, light given to matter.
Eternal instant, creative and free!

> *Long silence.*

Parting of the ways:
The fool rushes toward the light
and perishes, like a moth.
The wise one neither advances
nor hurries nor flees;
the wise one remains in the dark
and is found by the Light.
With ear unhearing,
with eye unseeing:
yet through *this* eye, the ray of Light shines.
With unexpectant heart,
for there is nothing to expect;
with unbidding hand,
for there is nothing to ask for.
Beyond faith, beyond space!
He acts because he GIVES:
HIS BODY BECAME THE WORD.

FRAGMENT

HE GIVES MATTER TO LIGHT, LIGHT TO MATTER.

*I have observed that the angels seldom pronounce the word,
'God.' It seems to me that this is a result of humankind having
soiled this holy word with their 'Holy Wars' and 'Holy Inquisi-
tions' in the name of 'God.' Similarly, the name 'Jesus' is seldom
used. In its place, the angels generally choose the pronoun 'He.'*

Friday, August 11, 1944

FRAGMENT

Listen!
The Holy Trinity guides you.
May your awareness awaken.
What has been, what is, what will be
the temporal is three-fold: past, present, future.

> *Gesture of the left hand with thumb and 2 fingers outstretched.*

Similarly, each creative act is three-fold.

> *Gesture of the right hand with thumb and 2 fingers outstretched.*

The Father is the Origin,
the Holy Spirit is the Messenger,
the Son is the Act.

> *Gesture with both hands.*

Two times three is not equal to six.

> *Gesture of two hands together with fingers and
> thumbs touching one common point:*

395

This is the way:
not three, not six,
but One.
The highest point is the fourth.
When image and reflection converge,
then there is birth.

> *We see not only the arch and the summit in this gesture: in the*
> *empty spaces between the fingers are evoked again in stylized*
> *form, the letters A and D.*

Act not in His memory,
act not for His coming:
Act to be united with Him.

Listen!
Stone, plant, animal three.
Past, present, future three.
Me, you, Him three.
In LIGHT-MATTER,
they are but one,
they are united.

How does taking
     (gesture of a clenched hand)

become giving?
     (gesture of an open hand)

On the one hand, movement.
In time.
And space.
On the other hand,
the father who acts eternally,
the all-seeing dove
and the Son giving without end.

When all come together,
LIGHT-MATTER comes to be.
AD: spirit and matter, glory and matter, light and matter united.

> *Gesture: two hands touching in the middle – in the empty spaces,*
> *we again see AD.*

If a single force is missing,
everything crumbles.

The Father begets with the Dove as messenger the Son.
First the Father, then the Spirit, then the Son.
This is the order.
A wonderful order, above as below.
The Father is All-knowing.
The Dove is Holy Spirit.
The Son is Sound never heard.

How can three, how can six, become One?
No longer by grace.

> *The right hand shows three fingers:*

The Son, the Spirit and the All-knowing.

> *The left hand shows three fingers:*

Matter, the loving hand movement.

> *The six fingers of the two hands comprise an arch with a summit:*

This is the Human.
New is the union:
AD, GLORIFIED MATTER, EMBODIED LIGHT!

Take good heed!
Six diverging forces

> *gesture of the hands with outspread fingers*

are the lost paradise.

The New concentrates, binds together, unites.
In it, no more separate number, love or movement:
simply infinity.
Eternal life is the ground for the New Tree.
In it, no more seven or one,
only unified togetherness.
This is the mystery of the New Act.
The act of the Human will no longer be blind,
it will be Awareness,
Light-filled Awareness that unites.
This is the Human Act.

The body is visible.
Movement is visible,
all matter is visible.
The secret of the New Body:

TRANSFORMATION.

No longer three, no longer six, no longer one,
but a unity.
No more death, no more torment,
no more decomposing corpse,
no more dissociated matter,
no more knife cutting in two,
no more wound,
no more senseless thought,
no more seizing hand.
No more dividing what was one.

The Father and matter,
the Dove and love,
the Son and movement
are united:
eternal instant of deliverance.

ETERNAL BEING: AD.

Friday, August 18, 1944

69. DIALOGUE FRAGMENT

May you open yourselves to *AWARENESS that unifies!*
The five senses are five stages or degrees:
Matter, the *touching* hand;
water, which dissolves: *taste;*
air, subtle matter: *smell;*
still subtler vibration transmitted by the ear: *hearing;*
through the fifth sense, *the eye,* light radiates: *sight;*
the sixth sense is the *union* of the five;
the seventh is the seed of AWARENESS that unites.

When these Seven no longer take, but GIVE,
the instant is creative.
This Act creates above as below.
"Thy will be done" above as below!
Your task is to link above and below.
Your task is the creative human element:
AWARENESS that unites.
May you become open to *uniting awareness!*
Awareness is not knowledge.
Awareness is Light:
acting Light, giving Light.

Your eyes are still blind.
The Light still disturbs you, pains;
it is still cold.

The new Light sweeps away every belief.
The one who *believes* in the Divine is mistaken.

DO NOT BELIEVE IN THE DIVINE!
LIVE THE DIVINE!

May your third eye begin to open!
To become one with the Divine
is still but a possibility.
The vibrations are not yet tuned, united.
Neither you nor the Divine is the cause of this.
The cause belongs to the realm of *time.*
To perceive belongs to the realm of time;
to hear belongs to the realm of time;
to see belongs to the realm of time.

But there is a time beyond time,
a space beyond space,
where you may act,
where you may unite,
where you may live the Human Essence:
AWARENESS that unites.*
Awareness that unites is, in truth: LOVE.
Only LOVE acts.

---

* Hanna is unable to find an appropriate word for the attraction and union of
spirit and matter, for the new unifying element. It would designate the highest
capability of awareness of consciousness, emphasizing neither light nor matter:
oneness. She finally reluctantly chooses the Hungarian expression *értelem* (intelligence, mind, meaning).
Our teacher then goes beyond the one-dimensionality of this term in adding:
"Awareness that unites is, in truth: LOVE." We have chosen the expression,
Awareness that unites, for this English-language translation, in place of
"Light-Awareness," the rendering applied in previous editions. The German
translation uses *Erkennen,* whose original meaning includes uniting as well as
becoming conscious. This and the words chosen for other-language translations
depict approaches to a state of being for which a word does not yet exist.

Creative instant, flood of Light,
streaming through the new Eye!
There is no more below, no more above,
there is no more father and no more mother.
Creative instant: Matter given to light, light given to matter.

The Light flows.
Chalice of gold, of translucent gold;
not to be seen,
not to be touched.
Only to be given.

THE CURSE HAS COME TO AN END.

Uniting awareness: the secret of vibration without beginning or end.
The senseless becomes wise.
The ugly becomes beautiful.
Non-believing becomes faith.
Blindness become sight.
Deafness become Hearing.
Dead becomes alive.
Past becomes eternal being.

To Hanna, who suffers from heart pains:

The suffering heart calls and draws the forces of Heaven.
The crevice will be closed,
the wound heals.
The seven swords converge on one point –
the old heart bursts.
Instant of deliverance, bliss:
no more pain, no more path, matter is no longer matter.
Your heart is no longer blind –
what was divided and split, becomes one.

The political situation worsens by the hour. The Hungarian Nazis – the Nyilas – are gaining power. The general apocalyptic atmosphere is undermining the hard-won discipline in our sewing factory. The compulsory work situation, being completely closed in and the imminent outer danger all weigh heavily on the women. They often react during break-time with uncontrolled shouting and hysterical laughter.

Sunday, August 20, 1944

70. DIALOGUE

The crowd laughs.
They do not foresee the Name of the new.
New existence is immaculate matter;
the Light in its womb, transparent and free.

There the stone is TRUTH, the One;
there LOVE grows, the Two;
there the ANIMAL is harmony, the Three.
The Five is PEACE,
the Six is JOY
and the Seven is WHOLENESS.
The heart, new AWARENESS, the Four,
uniting illuminated consciousness.

THE HUMAN REJOICES WHEN THE SEVEN SENSES,
THE SEVEN SOULS, ACT IN UNISON.

That is the key.
May the new Being be born in you!
Before birth, there is love.

Love, the most secret rhythm,
the new Rhythm: AWARENESS that unites.
It is half matter, half Glory.

*The screeching, uncontrolled laughter in the garden seems to go
on endlessly.*

The crowd laughs …
and wastes everything that belongs to the Human.
They do not foresee the Name of the new,
the new Name which alone
makes the human HUMAN.
MAY you live UNITING AWARENESS.
May your ears not hear the noise,
may your eyes not see;
may they *shine* – everywhere!
The new radiates everywhere.
Away with you, deceit!
The new Ray is all-seeing.
Half of time is gone – the past.
The other half – the future.
Past and future united:
time beyond time.
Awareness that unites is eternal love,
engendering eternal birth.
Death is no more a rupture.
It is merely beyond time.
Death is very different from what you imagine.
It is not rest, not consolation.

Wonderful rhythm, pulsing.
Not from the past, not from tomorrow, not from the today:
Eternal flaming love.

There above and here below
creation sings the wedding song.
May your uniting awareness awaken!
You, too: sing the new song, the wedding song!
Where the wedding of heaven and earth is celebrated,
there is the house where you can dwell.
Eternal joy is your inheritance.
Pass it on!
ONLY THE ONE WHO GIVES IS WITH ME: DIVINE.

*These last mysterious and powerful words touch me deeply:
Giving is a Divine attribute.*

Friday, August 25, 1944

71. DIALOGUE

*One day we are informed that the Papal Nuncio, Mgr. Angelo
Rotta, will be paying us a call as a demonstrative gesture of
papal protection. In the Nuncio and in Father Klinda, I for the
first time encounter priests who give testimony of their faith
not with beautiful words, but with courageous acts. Their visit
raises our status in the neighborhood tremendously. The morale
of the workers themselves also noticeably improves.*

Be aware!
The trust placed in you
is like the humus, good earth.
The seed sown in you is the Word,
word becoming flesh,
matter becoming light.

Already the ever growing force swells,
causing the husk to stretch
until finally it bursts.
Fear not! Live!
Have no fear at the bursting of the husk!
That which no longer serves disintegrates.

SHEDDING IS NOT PAINFUL.
DO NOT REGRET IT,
FOR SEE: THE SPROUT LIVES!

Water the seed! Unnourished, it will die.
Water it with what is lacking in you,
and there will be no more uncertainty.

'The one who speaks' nourished the seed
with the water of humility: and the seed grows.
Do likewise!
But watering wet soil causes the seed to rot,
and only mud remains.

To Lili:

Seek the lack in yourself
and you will become whole!
Everything you do for the Divine is blessed.

To me:

You, too: be aware!
There is only *one* lack.
If you find many, you are wrong.
But if you find the *one* lack,
then ask that it be filled
and heavenly Grace will fill it,
for you have asked for only *one.*

Thus, the sacrifice is completed;
the holy seed grows, it swells.
The husk bursts of its own accord.
What makes the seed swell?
Discovery of the lack!
Do not talk about the lack!

May this be kept a secret,
even among yourselves!
But reveal it to the Divine.
For see: The Divine heart is always filled
and always gives freely.

HE gives to the stone, the grass, the animal, the human.
The Word, AD, is Light-Matter,
is eternal love, is tree eternally bearing fruit.
All hunger, all suffering, will be appeased
by the Tree of Life, nourishing all.
Adam died but Christ resurrected,
Blessed be *His* name –
the name of the tree of glorified matter.
You need not be given the fruit –
the seed in you becomes Tree.

*I immediately perceive a great opportunity in the conscious
lack: a void attracts fulfilling forces, and this is intensified by
asking.*

*Lili organizes relaxation courses during breaktime for the
women, who are under constant nervous pressure and completely exhausted. There is enormous interest in these courses,
with the result that now Lili is exhausted. She never has a free
moment for herself. Hanna is burdened with a feeling of responsibility for production in the factory. In addition, she has not
had a word from Joseph, and she asks me daily if any mail has*

arrived. I call all of my acquaintances whose friends and rela-
tives were taken away at the same time, but no one has heard
anything. Hanna is deeply worried and I, too, have been lacking
in inner vitality for quite some time. Meanwhile, the political
news becomes ever more terrifying.

Sunday, August 27, 1944

(Again Hanna hears a message in German. This time we are
aware that the words are meant for Hanna.)

Abandon the dark alleyway,
flooded with putrid waste!

No wine from filthy water!
Rotten are the grapes.

In the morning, plant new ones
in the forest, solitary and pure.

Soon the new will sprout.
Give to drink and bind the tendrils
against the winds that tug the vines.

Your life is giving,
raise up what is below!
Cut, without pain!

Give yourself, too,
gardener of the Divine!

Friday, September 1, 1944

72. DIALOGUE FRAGMENT

> *Somewhere in the vicinity, political propaganda speeches blare from a radio.*

The word has become a hollow senseless din,
confused noise.

> *Ear-splitting shrill cries can be heard from the garden. It is lunch-break.*

Uproar! Pandemonium!
Blood and marrow dry and harden.
The husk is merely a covering.
Yet every word conceals the WORD.
The Divine Heart longs to reveal itself
and fills the word with Divine Force.
When the uplifting Force of the Seventh blazes within,
the word is eternal Fire.

'The one who measures' speaks:
No lukewarm 'maybes' on the Divine table!
No more indulgence!
Self-pity is the air of the weak.
The one in whom the Divine Word dwells
has but one wayless way: *Wholeness.*
Be whole!
Only the pure sound is worthy.

THE MASTER TUNES YOU.

Listen carefully: you are no longer incapable.
Mouth, sound, harmony: sequence of laws.

The song is new; the song is free.
Day breaks: sing!
But if need be: be God's whip,
for dawn is the wake of darkness.

No more pity! Especially for yourselves!
No more lukewarm mud puddles!
Away with every false breath in you!
Raise your hand and ask for strength;
ask for a sword.
Cut away all that is not filled with the Divine;
cut it away!
Tear out your eyes,
cut off your hands,
if the Divine cannot act through them!
What is the purpose of their existence?
Divine scorn comes down upon perishable matter,
upon mud that does not endure.

But if the spoken word has its origin in the Divine,
then it is the WORD, the GIVING: eternal.
Every weakness of yours disappears
if you truly acknowledge faith
that is not word, but strength.
Do not be weak!
May your mouth remain closed
if not speaking the truth.
May your hands be petrified
if not acting for the Divine.
Fear no one! There is nothing to fear.

NEVER FLEE FROM YOURSELVES!
IN YOU DWELLS THE HOLY, ALL-POWERFUL WORD:
THE POSSIBLE.

Everything is possible!
Everything is possible
if your faith is as great as a mustard seed.
Half-heartedness is repulsive to the Divine.
The Seven Sounds have always existed.
In the Master's Hand is the lute,
in the Master's Ear, the sound.
Each string of the lute is a sound;
but the string is still loose.
Listen! If a string is tightened,
it vibrates and gives birth to pure sound.

The lute is not yet vibrating
in the Master's Hand.
The tone is still false,
the string is still loose,
but the world yearns for the Holy Song.
Stretch yourself! Not too much and not too little!
The flame ignites neither before nor beyond,
but *at the focal point.*

There the New Truth ignites:
New Love, New Harmony,
the completely New: the Fourth level.
It is already possible.
The Force of Seven acts in the heart
of the Fourth level.
Your body is enlivened by new nourishment,
your mouth no longer eats, but speaks a new language.
A new body awakens, knowing no limits.
But the old still hinders you,
obscures truth, dilutes love, hinders harmony.

72. DIALOGUE FRAGMENT

To Lili, bitten by a mosquito:

It is not the small insect, but vanity which bites you.
Matter only weighs on you if you make it your master.

To Gitta:

The furrow in your brow is still devilish,
is will, pride, mask.
Your will – eternal battle, eternal defeat.
Each furrow is a grave.
No more pity, no more forgiveness!
The one who believes in the Divine can act!
All is possible for the one who acts in the Divine!
Victory over yourself: the final victory,
beyond illusion.
At last: be of the Divine!
What could be sweeter, more beautiful?

To Joseph, at a distant work camp:

He who belongs to the Five is a well-tended string –
he raises himself to Him.
And the sound of silence spreads itself through him across the earth.
The old song with the name of feeling is water.
The name of the New is Fire that is not burning torment,
but the eternally fruit-bearing tree of light,
conceived in the virginal womb.
My task is to measure.
I do not frighten you; I do not entice you.
Only in this way is measuring possible.
No more self-pity!
Strew ash upon the dead and live a new Life!
We the sound, you the strings, Ö the Master.
It is possible now: POSSIBLE!

411

Answer our word anew:

"MY GOD, THY WILL BE DONE!"

My hand does not admonish,
my hand does not bless,
my hand does not measure;
for the measure is full,
within as without, below as above.

THE ONLY MEASURE: BEING WHOLE.

The underground news in Budapest spreads rapidly. We hear of a new sport called: 'Jew-hunting'... We hear of hundreds and hundreds of Jews being driven to the banks of the Danube, lined up and shot: the great river makes the digging of graves superfluous. We hear of torture-chambers ... But we do not hear of Joseph. We will never hear of him.

Nevertheless, when the 'measuring angel' speaks to us – pitiless as it might appear to be – we are nourished with the force of a new Life.

412

DAWN

Today is today.
Tomorrow is tomorrow.
I am today's tomorrow:
Dawn.

That is my existence,
beyond space, beyond time.
Timeless.
Be mine!
There is but one way:
the highest point
where our song resounds,
where our dance unfolds
over the tips of spears.

Be light, not lead!
Then it will no longer pain.
The highest peaks above
are below, not above,
deep inside in the heart of God.
Pain.

There is but one heart.
One grain, one word,
eternal hearth.
Not distant, not far:
there, where the spears
pierce the void.

The void fades.
Seven spears converge.
In place of emptiness:
pain.
Your heart.

We sing praise.
We no longer fear for you.
These spears are of light.
Only what is dense pains.
Weep not,
judge not,
shine!
You are light!

I give you my name.
Only the solitary have names.
Be light!
A name is not required.

Name is not weight,
name is seed.
And only the solitary
receive seeds.

Today I give you my name.
My name is Dawn.
Forever and ever.

While others wander.
you dance
over spears and lances,
above the weight of all.

In your dance you shine.
You shine and you are mine.
Do not falter.

Three gifts are thine:
Speak,
act without despair,
be me!

I, you, Ö: ONE!

Eternal being
is Giving.
In the beginning
was "THINE".

Return home!

*(Gitta Mallasz placed this message in an unpublished notebook
between the 72. and 73. Dialogues).*

Friday, September 8, 1944

73. DIALOGUE

The Message speaks of the sin of the chosen ones;
it is no longer the old sin.
The wild tree sprouts branches
and leaves aplenty: too many.
But excess foliage is detrimental to the fruit,
for it diverts the strength.

WHEN LIVING FORCE DOES NOT BEAR FRUIT,
IT IS SIN.

The chosen tree was pruned
and thus the old sin could disappear.
A new Eye was placed in it by the Divine Hand,
a holy noble sprout, that it may bear fruit
and serve the Holy Plan.
The new Eye, the new Bud, is already opening.

415

But the dead stump of the old branch
hinders the new.
A sharp sword cuts
and the dead stump falls away;
the wound heals.
Worms can hide beneath the dead bark.
But when your hand brings the cutting sword down,
new bark can grow
that will protect the new streaming Force.
The Divine has been grafted in you.

ONLY WHERE THE TREE IS DEAD
IS THERE SIN.

The message speaks of the sin of the chosen one.
There can be no more error.
The knife is in your hand: do not hesitate!
Cut away the dead! That is *your* task!
The chosen is not cut;
the chosen cuts and, if need be, is even self-cutting.
Now Ö waits no longer!

    Long silence.

The feminine, virgin matter, conceives in its womb.
If there is no conception,
the new does not grow
and the half-seed is pushed out,
pushed out with all the blood, strength and matter
that was given for its growth.
Reject dead matter!
Detach yourself from it!
From it, too, new life can grow,
and thus the dead can be released.

Do not bind yourself to anything.
Do not fear cutting away the dead.
This does not cause any lack.
Behold!
The new has been grafted into you,
and it sprouts.

All that is eye, opens.
The seed, too, is eye, covered by earth.
The bud, too, is eye, cradled in space by the branch.
The eye in the highest heaven is also eye,
as is yours on your face, here below.

To Gitta:

The furrow is dead bark,
it hinders the shining of the New Eye.
The opening eye: uniting awareness.

Secret of The Last Judgment:
nothing in the Divine Hand goes astray.
The new Bud swells and bears fruit.
The old branch decays,
is swallowed by the earth,
and becomes nourishment there below.
Not death, but transformation.
Not waste, not garbage, but new earth:
new nourishment for the green tree.
What is without is buried in the earth.
What is within is fulfilled.

WE TRANSMIT THE DIVINE WORD;
YOU LIVE IT!

    Long silence.

The new Element joining heaven and earth is:
uniting AWARENESS.
Below, graves and 'hell.'
Above, a Heaven where God is supposed to dwell.
Between, in the center, lies the New-Born,
the one who unites.
No more death, no more graves and no more hell,
no more unattainable Heaven 'somewhere up there,'
where the 'ever so glorious souls dwell,'
and songs of angels resound!
No more right and left!
No more freedom and no more walls.

The new Child is Divine.
Its Body is glorified Matter, transparent, subtle.
Its Soul is a growing, fruitbearing Ray.
Everything which previously grew
on the fallow land is wild,
is but the straw on which *the Child* rests.
Your child!
The choir of angels hovers over *the Child*
and adores it.
All of our songs are sung for *the Child.*
Each of our words is food for *the Child.*
Our adoration embraces *the Child.*
It is a small *Child,*
but It has immeasurable Force
and an immeasurably infinite future.
It is the Soul of 'the one who measures.'
It is 'the one who helps.'
Its voice is 'Silence.'
And it is the 'Eternal Ray.'

Friday, September 15, 1944

74. DIALOGUE

The persecution of Jews becomes ever more ruthless. Many of the women in our group have had no news at all of their loved ones. In their desperation and fear, they frequently make their way to vespers in the tiny chapel.
As we await our angels in the shed, the bell of the chapel rings.

The bell tolls.
The old sound calls to the church.
The knees of the believers tremble,
they throw themselves to the ground,
hearts in anguish, tears flowing.
Outside, the masses stare: indifference.
Beyond the church, beyond the altar:
only there is the new to be found.
The church is the ancient hearth,
protection for old feelings.

The new Law, the new Grace:
UNITING AWARENESS is all-filling:
every emptiness,
every crevice hidden in the earth,
be it a grave or an empty heart,
be it a mouth in search of bread,
or a murderous hand.
The empty shall be filled.
The one who seeks shall find.
Everything is filled through the Divine,
Who never takes and always gives.

Long silence.

I will teach you what dwells
beyond the Black Rainbow.
Above the flood arches the *rainbow,*
joining Heaven and earth: promise.
What is more than its seven colors?

THE ONE, GLOWING WHITE.

Now a black rainbow embraces Heaven.
What is behind the blackness?
The black abyss.
The seven colors are erased.
Above the borders of earth
a black void in the heavens,
and the Lord said: "I WAIT."
But now has come the time
when Ö no longer waits.
The black emptiness between Heaven and earth
becomes white, incandescent white.

> *I feel immersed in a world of powerful forces, a world of timeless*
> *happening which nevertheless influences happening in time. I*
> *am touched to the core.*

The black grave swallows up only the dead.
The Light, glowing white,
shoots glowing white flames
and all is burned that lives and breathes,
all that is lifeless and all that is dead,
all that was and all that shall be,
all that is soiled and all that is immaculate.

HORRIBLE FIRE OF HEAVEN.
EVERYTHING PERISHES
AND EVERYTHING IS REBORN.

The innocent virgin creation does not die:
it lives anew.
The Light dazzles, eternal Light:
all creatures are delivered.

To Hanna:

Black rainbow; black hole, the heart;
black sorrow, black torment.

To me:

Black pit, the eye.

To us all:

But within vibrates, grows and is born:
eternal Love, the Seven united, the white Glow.
Between two infinites, spaceless space:
UNITING AWARENESS.

At this moment, a shooting star crosses the horizon.

A star falls.
Glowing white light, drowned in the black.
Dust of the old creation heralds the new creation.
Gather in the old stars
and sow new ones across the sky!
Many, an infinite number.
Thus, out of the night, grows the day,
eternal Light, always GIVING.
Between the heavenly host and the soil of earth
is eternal Light,
eternal love,
eternal adoration,
eternal GIVING.

The old arch has vanished,
the seven colors as well.
The black abyss, the separation,
even the *and* between heaven and earth has vanished.

Now the new can come,
now the eternal can come:
not to replace the black,
not instead of the Seven,
but beyond all:

THE SEVEN UNITED.

Beyond *perhaps:* the possibility of BEING.
Beyond *burden:* the capacity to ACT.
Beyond space and time,
where fantasy spins its web:

ETERNAL REALITY.

Beyond the multitude of religions:
the ETERNAL SOURCE and the ACT,
which can become one
only when LIGHT,
the possibility of BEING, *ignites.*

The stone once rejected is now the cornerstone.
He returns and He is the LIGHT.

Friday, September 22, 1944

75. DIALOGUE

The chosen one neither rises nor sinks,
but walks on the water.
The only burden is the task,
the freely accepted task.
Grace lifts up above the water.
The magnitude of grace
is equal to the magnitude of the task,
the voluntary, free-willed task.

GRACE IS NOT KIND CHARITY,
GRACE IS NOT RANDOM MERCY.
GRACE IS A FACT,
A RESPONSE: A CROWNING OF THE PURE ACT.

It is done:
No longer feel oppressed.
The burden weighs heavy,
but you may sink no more.

THE ONE WHO IS JUST THROUGH CONSTRAINT,
THE ONE WHO ACTS THROUGH CONSTRAINT,
IS A SLAVE.

Do not be slaves!
Breathe only the air of freedom!
Cut there, where you are still slave!
Woe be upon you if you act out of constraint!

EXISTENCE IF IT WEIGHS,
EXISTENCE IF IT PRESSES DOWN,
IS A BRAND OF SHAME ON YOUR FOREHEAD.

I must is a curse.
I can is deliverance.
The chosen one chooses: the chosen can ACT.
The chosen could go, yet remains.
The chosen could lie, yet harvests.
The chosen could take, yet gives.
Without eyes, the chosen one sees.

The lock has fallen away
and spaceless space is free:

LIGHT-AWARENESS.

There is no more whip or reward.
The curse has ended, the abyss is gone.
There is no more slavery.
'Here' and 'beyond' are not enough.
'Here' and 'beyond' are still slave and master.
Only the fourth dimension can fill the abyss.
The fourth dimension is matter for the spirit,
and spirit for matter.
The seed of light.
The fourth dimension is *free:* ONE.

The new Body is weightless.
Nothing is injured where its foot steps:
everything blossoms there!
The chosen one walks on the water.
The chosen one is humble,
but upon this humble forehead
dwells the highest: LIGHT.
There is no more 'here' and no more 'beyond'
when the Light appears.

75. DIALOGUE

To Lili, whose birthday is approaching:

This message is for you:
Be born, Child, it is already possible!
The womb constricts you now.
Leave it, or it will kill you!
Do not tarry! The opening is narrow, but it yields.
Be born, Child!

L. I would like to be reborn on my birthday.
Please help me!

— 'The one who helps' will not be helped.
The strength which now fills you is enough!
I will not help you!
Come to the world by yourself!

Birth is not only a beginning;
it is also an end.
Between the old existence and the new,
there is a connecting cord.
Tear it apart, Newborn! Free yourself!
Birth is eternal: eternal love
that acts in every instant.
There is no more birthday,
for birth is eternal.
Birth is neither will, nor desire, nor grace:

BIRTH IS THE FREE.
THERE YOU ARE ONE WITH THE *DIVINE*
AND THERE YOU ARE *YOURSELF.*

To me:

And you?

G. How could I free myself from slavery?
— Bound by old bonds, the slave struggles.
   But the bonds fall of their own accord
   if the good servant and the Master are united.
   LIGHT-AWARENESS cuts through the bonds,
   through the ancient dragon,
   the slithering serpent
   with the apple of knowledge in its fangs.
   Do not eat it! Behead the serpent!
   LIGHT-AWARENESS makes everything possible.
   Be free!

   Long silence.

The head of the serpent rolls in the dust.
The woman clothed in the rays of the sun
gives birth to the CHILD and is lifted up.
Rushing streams of water roar below,
but the woman is given wings,
wings of eagles soaring to the heavens.

   *Night approaches and I light a candle in the wooden shed. The
   door is open wide and we see shooting stars crossing the sky.*

Dust of the old creation, rainfall of stars.
The dragon is striking wildly about,
but is unable to reach the new.
All of the old is seized,
but the new cannot be harmed.
Another star crosses the heavens.

The old teaching is a star, decayed to dust.
The new LIGHT joins heaven and earth together:
LIGHT, LIGHT, LIGHT!

The star shows the way,
and the wise pilgrim advances.
When the Light comes, the pilgrim stands still
and finds the Newborn.
The old teaching constricts.
The new Light streams over all:
all generations, all peoples and all negations
with an everlasting *YES!*

When the Child is born,
it cannot yet use its limbs,
but the eternal Force it is given
teaches everything.

BROTHER-SISTER OF CHRIST IS BORN.
THE NEW CHRIST IS LIGHT OVER ALL.

The host of angels adores the Child,
adores freely.

An air raid siren suddenly begins to howl.

Sing with us! We act with you!
May Heaven and earth resound with our praise!

Friday, September 29, 1944

76. DIALOGUE – FEAST OF THE ARCHANGEL MICHAËL

On the lips of the angels
swells the song of the host:
"Who is like the Divine?"*

The immense love with which you seek God
dies of thirst:

YOU CAN NEVER *REACH* THE DIVINE,
FOR YOU AND THE DIVINE ARE ONE.

The song of angels is praise, is glory,
to which creation replies.

THE HUMAN CAN NEVER *'FIND'* THE DIVINE,
FOR HUMAN AND DIVINE ARE ONE.

THEIR UNION IS THE MIRACLE.

The human being:
beneath is the sea,
beneath is the soil.
Creation has conceived the HUMAN:
above is Heaven,
above is the Light.
May the immense love with which you seek God
turn *inward*.
When the earth serves,
when the host of the angels serves,
they unite within you.
Your body is the earth.

* Michaël in Hebrew signifies: 'Who is like God.'

The body of the old serpent has crawled forth.
The old serpent's body is the curse
brought upon earth by all of the Adams.
But the Christ, the New, will come
when earth and angel are united *in you.*
You know what needs to be done.
There is no escape,
for all ways converge at one point.

MICHAËL!
YOUR SCALES WEIGH,
YOUR SWORD CUTS:
THE LIVING FINDS NEW LIFE
AND WHAT IS DEAD – DIES.

If decision is needed,
if cutting is needed
and you are unable,
and you dare not,
then call:

MICHAËL, GIVE STRENGTH!
YOUR FOOT
CRUSHES THE SERPENT'S HEAD
WITH COLD FORCE
THAT YOU ALONE CAN GIVE.
FOR SEE: WHAT YOU CUT IS ALREADY DEAD.

Mystery:
All angels, seraphs, cherubs,
all heavenly forces singing and serving:
they all come to serve the Divine *in you.*
Call, and we come!
We are nearly united now.
Call! Your word creates!

Call the new Fire, the cold Fire, the Light!
Always call!
If we come, then Ö, too, can come.
The way is one.
The host of angels waits behind the *Black Rainbow.*
The angel is still color.
But Ö, the ONE, is Light: white Light.
A mysterious force,
flowing, streaming, living,
responds to your call.
Live with it, for it is half of your Life!

You and your act are one if you call
the leader of the heavenly host: MICHAËL.
Michaël comes and cuts
if your acts do not spring
from purity, harmony, love and truth.
Michaël cuts not the act,
but the untrue doer.
May you and your act be one!

Michaël judges and helps.
Call Michaël, who always comes,
and the vermin will be beneath your heels.
May your acts never again spring
from shallow currents,
but from the deepest depths: the source.
The creation and the heavenly hosts
expect this of you.

Ö IS THE LORD OF ALL THE HOSTS.
YOU MAY NEVER *SEE* THE DIVINE,
FOR YOU ARE ONE WITH THE DIVINE.

The host of angels bows in homage before the Plan.

Worship of God and religions are but frames
that delimit space.
The Divine Plan is spaceless space, matterless,
and yet it is all that really IS.
Chalice, temple and church are graspable.
Only Ö, the Ungraspable, IS.
Everything else is but a frame.
Flying is possible only without wings.
Everything else is an attempt to equal God,
and the fall is inevitable.
My wings are incorporeal
and this makes them free.
If you are united with me, I carry you,
lift you above time and space,
until your spirit finds its rest in the One.
May peace come over all who are of good will!

Long silence.

He walked upon the sea and *He* is the way.
He is the well from which the water of life springs.
Drink of it and you will never thirst again.
Behold! This water unites you with Him.
What you drink is eternal water,
Fire of the Seventh Soul.
Our lips call *Him!*
If we call, He remains in our midst forever.
The creation is a frame,
the creation is a chalice.
Fill it, human being!

Blood and bread are no longer enough.
Only the Light – the coming Light –
can fill the Seven.

The black emptiness in the chalice,
framed by the frame,
is filled.
Ö, the LIGHT, is born.

After today's dialogue, I open the calendar and am amazed to discover that September 29 is the traditional feast of the Archangel Michaël. I also see that the feast of the Guardian Angels will soon be celebrated. None of us had ever heard of these feasts before. I now look forward to the feast of the angels with great expectation.

In the garden stands a small, empty toolshed with no glass in the windows. Because the main 'factory' building is hot and overcrowded, Hanna, Lili and two of the 'jolly jokers' decide to move into the toolshed. The nights are still warm and we sleep very little. The presence of the angels can almost always be felt. They seem to use every opportunity for teaching.

Friday, October 2, 1944

77. DIALOGUE – FEAST DAY OF THE GUARDIAN ANGELS

Ö is the Lord of the hosts.
The host of angels is a scale of frequencies:
vibrations.
Our lowest note is heavy.
When you have reached it,
the scale of creation is complete.

Matter has three sequential levels.

The Law – the great Law – is strict, and It states:
Everything is contained in the greater.

Belief is merely preparation.
Cease to believe!
The ungraspable is born,
the only ACT, the bond:
union through the Fourth vibration.

If we reach you,
then all the multitudes of Heaven reach you:
those who surround the throne of God,
those who sing and those who serve.

Your body contains matter in its threefold existence.
If your hand moves,
then the levels of inert matter,
of the cold and growing,
and of the warm and moving,
move as well.
This is the explanation.
If you call us, your eyes will see heavenly Light,
for your eyes *see;*
in your ears will resound the heavenly song,
for your ears *hear.*

If you merely take up the salt of the earth in your hand,
then, in truth, the salt is not raised up.
But if the salt dissolves
and circulates in your blood,
then, in truth, the salt is raised to the Four.

The taste of the salt is everlasting.
It does not disappear as it dissolves.
The salt is delivered when it becomes blood.

433

It does not disappear:
it enlivens and fulfills.

THE NEW BLOOD IS THE FOUR:
MATTER DISSOLVED IN LIGHT,
THE NEW LIGHT-MATTER.

Dissolve yourself!
Your 'small I' identity disappears,
it becomes dissolving,
fulfilling blood:
the solution of all.
If you dissolve your 'small I,'
matter will be delivered in you and through you,
and then the spirit can act.

DISSOLVE YOURSELF! GIVE YOURSELF!
THUS THE SALT REACHES THE DIVINE.

Creative Instant!
The core will be filled with life,
and all beings glorify the Creator of the Plan.
Bring the Plan to life ...
the impossible, the only possible!
Heaven and hell vanish, for the LIGHT comes.
It does not descend,

FOR THERE IS NO MORE HELL.

It does not ascend,

FOR THERE IS NO MORE HEAVEN.

Here the ONE dwells eternally.
Call the HUMAN into Being!
Call the former rebel into existence,
and the split, the abyss and death
will disappear in the wonderful Plan of creation.

434

'The Bearer of Light,' who stems from our midst,
the serpent, the rebel, the betrayer:
shall also be delivered.
Henceforth, there shall be
no more dwellers in 'hell.'

The strength is given to you!
There is no escape: you know what is True
and you know your task.
Do not attempt to evade it.
It is the slithering serpent in you that tries to escape.
But in you also lives the free, the possible.
And what you call for SHALL BE.
No moment of weakness is allowed:
The artery of creation would burst
and the new Blood would fail to attain its goal;
blind matter could not reach God.

Dissolve yourself!
In the wake of the Black Rainbow follows Light.
Let us call for the Light!
The host of angels greets you.
Call the Seven to life!

This feast is over.
Every feast is a Ray descending from eternal Life,
from the everlasting Feast.

> *Joyous anticipation of today's feast aided me greatly in comprehending it. Never had the teaching seemed so clear and luminous as it did today.*

> *In Budaliget, when we read through our notes after the dialogues, Hanna would often replace some of the words with others that seemed better. She always tried to convey the meaning of the*

435

angels' message as clearly as possible. But now the teachings come in rhythmic verse form and Hanna has only to pronounce them to us.

Friday, October 6, 1944

78. DIALOGUE

Our teaching reveals mysteries.
It is given to you
that you may give it on.

IT IS GIVEN TO YOU
TO CLOTHE THE TEACHING IN EARTHLY WORDS.

Earth is not salt, nor grass,
nor the horse, not even the one who thinks.
Earth is what clothes Light in matter,
what transforms,
protects and envelopes Light.
In this way, the teaching of LIGHT
can be perceived even by eyes that do not yet see.

> *Silence.*

THE DIVINE HEART BEATS IN THE HUMAN BODY.

The Divine heart is fire,
the Divine heart is Light.

IF THE HUMAN BLOOD ATTAINS THE LIGHT,
IT IS TRANSFORMED.

The first HUMAN was Jesus, the Master,
the first to master the body.
The body was crucified:
but it was a free act, a free sacrifice,
a triumph over matter and over death.
The body is nailed to the cross,
and the lance of blind force pierces the Divine heart.
From the wound,
from the ungraspable Heavenly Artery,
streams the LIGHT-bearing Blood.
"Drink! This is my Blood,
and my body, the bread!"
The wound has been open ever since,
for every bleeding wound
cut open by the knife of blind force,
every pain, every suffering,
is in His Heart.

What our lips now proclaim is the greatest mystery:

HEAL THE WOUND! THE SPLIT!
IT IS ALREADY POSSIBLE!

Only the human body
receives the Divine blood.
Without the wound,
it would not have reached the human.
It would not have become drink
without the wound, the rupture,
between the human and Him.

But if the human and He,
the body and the one being light,
have become one,
the wound is no longer necessary.

For the blood already circulates in

ONE BODY,

heaven and earth united!

Until then, the wound torments.
But already, union is possible!
Behold, the wound is no longer needed!
May the wound be healed!
That is the secret of deliverance.
It is no longer necessary to pierce His heart
once His heart and yours are united.
Thus inert matter,
the grass that grows,
and the animal that moves,
all reach the Light ... through you.

BECOME ONE WITH JESUS: YOUR BROTHER!*

> *On the rare occasions when the angels pronounce the name,*
> *'Jesus,' it is with such veneration that I become very aware of*
> *how we humans have lost all sense of the sacred.*

Blind force, blind tyranny *had* to pierce
the Divine heart, that Light might become ours
through the water of the blood.
But body and blood no longer suffice;
for they are but the foundation of becoming HUMAN.
Heavenly Light is given only
to those who bring fruit,
to those who walk on the water,
to those who are of the mountain peak,
to those whose thirst is never quenched,

---

* In Hungarian the word 'brother' is made up of two word-syllables: 'body-blood'
(*test-vér*).

to those for whom the Divine Word is salt,
creating thirst ever anew.

Behold! Every tormenting thirst of earthly existence,
every earthly pain burns in you,
on Mount Golgotha.

The reply: Light, new Life, new Easter,
new Resurrection: LIGHT-AWARENESS.
Eternal love: LIGHT-MATTER.

The teaching is the Word.
The Word will glow when it crosses your lips.
May new Words be born!
Simple ones, rooted ones!
Yes, yes – No, no!
There is no 'maybe,' nothing lukewarm.
Words are wings: they uplift and they create.

Long silence.

DO NOT LOVE THE DIVINE ... LOVE EVERYTHING!

That is love of the Divine!
Its lack reopens the wound, again and again.
If your heart is one with the Heart of Light,
then the wound can heal.
It is not difficult, believe me!
Is it difficult to love one another?
No, it is not!
It is even easier to love the small,
the unredeemed, the persecuted and the helpless.
Believe me, nothing is easier
than to love the Divine in everything!
For you, the free, redeeming act is possible!

The first stars appear in the evening sky.

The star guided the wise men from afar.
After that star, a sea of stars,
a sea of tiny lights appeared.
Still, the vault of heaven was dark.
And then, gradually, the stars turn pale,
for dawn approaches.
Every light, every tiny glimmer of light,
disappears on the heavenly arch.
The first still shines; but when the LIGHT comes,
even the first and the last disappear.
The LIGHT grows and absorbs each spark of matter.

ALL OF THE STARS DISAPPEAR
IN THE WOMB OF THE HOLY DAWN.

We are no longer able to ask questions and yet we receive answers. The angels read our thoughts and answer us by means of the topics. Since our move to Budapest, the teaching has been transmitted in rhythmical verses which have such nourishing force that any asking would be utterly superfluous. The verses are short and very dense. The fact that themes are repeated again and again, in variable forms and very patiently, indicates to me that we are still far from really living the teaching.

Friday, October 13, 1944

79. DIALOGUE

The teaching word sounds forth:
The Four unifies.

The surface of the globe undulates,
flooded over by the water of the seas.
Only the mountain peaks protrude.
The island, the peak, is *Individuality,*
the indivisible 'I' that has become ONE.*
The masses remain submerged.

The created world mirrors the creating Plan.

The primordial seed once dwelled
in inert matter, in blind matter.
The seed broke through and transformed.
The waves of the sea embraced it,
and there it remained.
The seed lifted itself above the sea,
for the path leads further, far beyond the water.
Air welcomed it.
The ground of air is the 'I' that has become ONE.
Individuality.
That is not yet the end;
it is not enough.
For after air comes the new,
which has been planned since eternity.

The Divine Force which weaves the Plan
IS ACTING NOW.

* As a reminder: in Hungarian, 'individuality' is composed of the two words, 'One-I' = *egy-én* ... *egyén.*

Reach the new level!
Without the 'I' that has become One,
the air is empty.
And the striding foot of the angel
seeks the peaks, the islands, in vain.
The 'I' that has become One

IS THE PUREST GROUND:
NOT GOAL, BUT FOUNDATION.

The house on the rock.
He is the rock.
His foot trod upon the rock,
and climbed to the peak
where Heaven opens
and matter becomes glory.
The unknowing disciple who had never seen
matter and Light united – oh, miracle! – stammered:
"Here on high let us pitch our tent;
here in the Light, on the mountain!"
He knew not what he was saying.

The new dwelling will not be built:
the new dwelling descends
if it finds the true rock.
The true rock, embraced by Heaven,
is the pure, unbroken 'I'
that has become One.
The rock, too, is only earth:
but earth striving upwards,
wondrous force, towering high above,
gathering and uniting.
Its peak extends above the mist.
Home of eternal joy and serenity!

Stand on the mountain!
Always be at the peak!
May each of your acts be high on the mountain.
Beyond guilt, beyond the mist, beyond the devil.
Be above, always above at the very peak,
beyond even Grace.
For above Grace dwells the ONE:
If you are ONE with the Divine,
then grace streams down through you.
May every movement, every thought, every true act
be on the mountain peak!

The one who struggles up the mountain
might live there.
But you, you *are* mountain!
You do not *dwell* there,
you do not *struggle.*
You *are* the towering true rock.
The one who is true *is rock.*

We dwell high on the mountain peak –
in the depth of the heart.
The Plan is ready, but the Act still rests.

     Silence.

The serenity of Heaven vibrates.
I teach you:
The great secret – death – is but vibration.

BETWEEN BIRTH AND DEATH,
A VEIL OF MIST DECEIVES YOUR EYES.

Birth and death are but vibrations.
Life is not a gift of charity.

LIFE IS ETERNAL.

Your eye cannot see through the veil.
Rebirth, resurrection, darkness,
death and fall:
that is all different, far different
from what you believe it to be.

From my reading, I am very familiar with the concept of rein-
carnation in Hinduism and thus I listen with great interest.

If you could raise your eyes above the veil,
you would see that there cannot be *many lives.*

LIFE IS ONE AND *INDIVISIBLE.*
LIFE IS ETERNAL.
This is your inheritance; pass it on!

Silence

Beyond the depths of the seas,
beyond the seas themselves,
beyond the peaks of the high mountains,
the Divine Finger traces new Plans in the sand.

THE DIVINE: THE ONE WHO ETERNALLY PLANS.
YOU, THE HUMAN: THE ONE WHO REALIZES.

On the very first day, sun and moon
did not yet appear on the heavens,
although the eternal Plan had been made.

Heaven descends.
We are the walls, you, the foundation.
If you are not at the mountain peak,
our feet step into emptiness
and the new Home drifts.

The only error which your heart can commit
is to not unite the Seven,
to not be at the peak,
for then our feet step into emptiness.
You have long understood it,
but where is your Act?
You do not lack faith:
your Act is lacking.
May your Act equal your faith!
Only thus is balance on the peak possible.
The one who stands high in the mountains
needs a good sense of balance –
otherwise our feet step into emptiness.
Our being is drifting:
beneath our feet we need the truth
and the strength of the rock.

My beloved ones, is it so difficult
to reach the mountain peak?
It is beneath the depths of the seas,
and it is far beyond the seas.
It is above, high above:
in the depths of the heart.

Our teaching Word
now softly departs and fades away.
But its truth remains,
from eternity to eternity.

> At the conclusion of today's encounter, Hanna traces a sim-
> ple sketch: all the forces of the earth are concentrated at the
> 'mountain peak.' All the forces of Heaven are concentrated at
> the lowest point of the angel, the 'foot.' The 'mountain peak' is
> the only point where the two can meet and penetrate each other.

As a result of this lesson about the 'I' that has become One, or Individuality, it becomes clear to me that the teaching of the angels – according to which everyone at the peak of Individuality *can become the material half of his or her angel – is a deeply personal matter, and could never be a collective movement.*

Friday, October 20, 1944

80. DIALOGUE

The Pfeilkreuzler – *the Hungarian Nazis – have taken power and we are deluged with incredible news reports. Their leader in our district is a former priest, the notoriously sadistic 'Father' Kun. In the basement of a building not far from us, he constructed a torture chamber and his followers surpass even the German SS in their cruelty. They go out hunting for Jews, track them to their hideouts and then torture them to death. So as to be prepared for a possible invasion, I always assign one of our workers to hide in the bushes and keep vigilant watch over our front gate. We also prepare some escape holes through the fence around the garden and cover them with branches and leaves, hoping, of course, that they will never be needed. Today Hanna returns from the main building only very late at night.*

Friday's last hour tolls,
but only outside.
The last circle is the point.
The point cannot be broken.
Unbroken rhythm is unity.

The angels show us new symbolic images of the fourth dimension of life. The mountain peak symbolizes human individuality capable of reaching the level of the angels. The diagram of three superimposed circles of the created world shows the con- centration of their force in the ungraspable *dimension of the* 'point.' *I suppose that these diagrams are meant to develop our awareness, for only this can lead us beyond the* graspable.

The *Seven* is with you
until the end of the world,
until the beginning of the new World.
He is 'the one who helps';   (Lili II)
He is 'the eternal shining force.'   (Gitta VI)
His word is the Word: the only good.   (Hanna IV)
He is 'the one who builds,'   (Joseph V)
who 'plans the new Home and then builds It.'
He is the Head
and we are the limbs,
always ready to serve.
He descends to you and speaks to you.
You seek Him … and He finds you.

Beneath His Heel: death.
He is the Son.
Every bullet pierces His Heart.
He is the Son, God's crucified Son.
He may be known, He may be reached.
He is the Child, the Son who bled for us,
who let Himself be entombed for us.

NOW HE CAN BE BROTHER,
RELATED TO YOU
IN THE HIGHEST KINSHIP OF EARTH.

This is the end and the beginning:
the body becomes WORD.

447

The *New Name* is the white, mysterious,
ungraspable, downward-pointed cone.
It is the incandescent white *point,*
the promise never more broken.
Fulfillment!
Do not tarry, oh radiant Light!
Do not delay!

The path is nearly ready,

THE WAY OF LIGHT TO EARTH,
WHERE THE HEAVENLY CONE
JOINS THE EARTHLY CONE.

Each of its rays is a wonder:
the smile of the Divine,
the whip of the Divine,
the ray of the Divine White Eye.

The last hour has struck.
Friday becomes Saturday.
Saturday is intermission.
But when the day of the Lord dawns:
Light bursts forth.

All that has long since been, all that is,
and all that will be:
the old body dies and is buried.
But when the day of the Lord dawns,
the body resurrects.

Matter is filled with Light.
The old body, the old teaching, the old thought
receives Light, becomes free, resurrects.
The dawn of the Lord's day
is the triumph of Divine Love.

The Divine Son, the Human Son,
is the Crown of creation:
the seven-pointed crown, wonder.

You see the Son:
but the Being of Light who comes
you cannot see, you cannot feel.

WHAT YOU HAVE RECEIVED THUS FAR
IS BUT THE FOUNDATION, IS BUT PREPARATION.
EARTHLY UNION WITH *HIM*
IS BUT THE BEGINNING,
ONLY HALF OF THE NEW TEACHING.
ONLY AFTERWARDS DOES THE TEACHING
OF LIGHT COME.

Our teaching came in the name of the Seventh Force.
Take it! Eat it! Act it!
The teaching is truly nourishment, truly bread.
To the one who asks for it: *give!*
To the one who does not ask: *give salt,*
give thirst-awakening words,
and the one who was damned will shine.

The day of the Lord dawns.
My beloved ones, in every trial *He* is with you.
He loves you.

October 22, 1944

81. DIALOGUE

The *old teaching* is pagan:
Life, glowing life.
After it comes death, annihilation, end.
The *intermediate teaching*: transformation,
resurrection after death,
the redeeming turning point.
The new Teaching is different, completely different.
Neither birth nor death,
but eternal life, glory, song.

This is the secret of Eternal life:
may all your deeds, all your love,
all your faith, all your thoughts,
be *centered, balanced.*

Each half-heartedness
is fainting, wasting away.
Each sluggish pause
is agony, death.
Each repentance, each new beginning,
is healing, resurrection.

The new is different, completely different:
EVERLASTING LIFE,
EVERLASTING THOUGHT,
EVERLASTING ALL-AWARENESS.

> *Our workshop building and the sheds in the park are quite
> isolated. Our only immediate neighbor, the owner of a large
> industrial firm, fled the country some months ago. His spacious
> and beautiful house and property have been taken over by the*

German SS, the very thought of which sends chills up our spines. My 'headquarters-hut' stands alone in the middle of the garden, and I have grown accustomed to the silence of the night. This tranquility comes to an abrupt end one night when we hear shouting and wild shooting in the street from the youthful Nyilas – Hungarian Nazis – who are intoxicated with their new feelings of power. Again and again, I make the rounds to establish whether any of our entrances have been broken in or damaged.

October 25, 1944

82. DIALOGUE – MORNING

A hard word:

WAR IS GOOD.

Take care!
Falsely used force becomes destructive,
becomes devastating;
It would never come to a halt
without the weak – the victim – who absorbs it.
That belongs to the past.
It had to be that way.
Past wrongs cannot be righted.
But the victim absorbs and extinguishes the horrors.
If the persecutor finds the persecuted,
death is satiated.
The weak shall be glorified
and no more lambs shall be slaughtered
upon the altar.

War was unavoidable.
Now the bitter chalice is filled.
Fear not! As full as it is of bitterness,
it is equally full of Divine Drink,
of Eternal Serenity.

*Hanna suffers bitterly from the misery of the world, and at the
same time, she is aware of the infinite Joy of the coming new
World.*

Your way is not improvement, not mending.
Your way is that which has not yet been:
creation through Divine Force.
Force coming from the Divine
and returning to the Divine
in ecstatic joy: Divine Circulation.

Silence.

*I have not understood the teaching of the 'unavoidability' and
'good' of war, so the angel returns to this topic.*

I teach you:
When matter devours *too much* matter,
the body is provoked to send corroding acids,
which destroy the 'excess' food:
The danger decreases
but the blind acid remains,
and when there is no more *'excess,'*
it attacks the organic wall.
Thus the entire body is threatened.
The lye – the self-sacrificing victim –
absorbs the acid and is thereby annihilated.
But it succeeds in extinguishing the acid's fire.
The body – life – is no longer
endangered, but enlivened anew.

452

Late in the afternoon, Hanna again hears the words of the angels.
Taken by surprise, I am able to record only a small fragment.

The one who believes to possess *'own force'* errs.
The force of the weak is the Divine.
The weak is a living, sacrificial offering.
Destructive force is damnation.
But the weak will be glorified,
for within dwells the Force of the Divine.
The weak is weak only in the eyes of the world.
Judged by the Divine, the weak is strong.
The weak takes up no weapon,
does not flee and does not resist.
But the 'winner' receives a brand upon the forehead.
And the weak is raised to Heaven.

These words about the task of the weak raise many questions in me. Why did Joseph go to the work camp without putting up the least resistance? Why have none of my friends tried to save themselves with false papers? Is it their fate to be victims? Suddenly I remember a strange dream that Hanna had told me a long time before. As she and Joseph rode to the Dürer Festival in Nuremberg in their student days, they both dreamed the same dream during the night: In Medieval Nuremberg, Hanna chased in desperation after a cart to which Joseph was bound as he was being led to his execution. Joseph dreamed the same dream of being bound to the cart and seeing Hanna chasing behind in desperation.

I ask myself if both of them have taken on the role of the victim, of the 'weak,' long long ago (?). I refrain from asking Hanna this question, however: she has more than enough to bear already.

Late in the evening, the angels are again with us but I am unable to record this encounter in its entirety.

453

When the lover comes,
the beloved yields:
the two become ONE.
No more bond is needed,
for there is no more separation.
Eternal penetration, eternal ecstasy.
This is the mystery of the Holy Trinity:
Lover ... love ... beloved.
The three are one and yet distinct.
Eternally active is the Word: the YES.
The only truth: Ö IS.

October 29, 1944

83. DIALOGUE

The inheritance which Ö has left you
is eternal life,
the vineyard eternally bearing fruit.
Mysterious, marvelous teaching:

ETERNAL IMMACULATE CONCEPTION.

Seven steps lead to eternal being,
seven steps that you can take.
The first birth is pagan: matter.
The second is purification: plant.
The third is harmony: giving of oneself.
The fourth is the adorned bridal chamber.

Down the three upper steps
descends the bridegroom, the LIGHT.

454

When bride and bridegroom unite,
death dies forever.

Three steps in time:
the past is purification,
the present is giving of oneself,
the future is the wedding.
Lover and loved originate from the Divine,
who gives birth eternally.
In place of bodiless light
and lightless body,
the new: the two lovers united.

THE WORD BECOMES MATTER
AND MATTER BECOMES LIGHT.

Immaculate conception is Eternal love,
no longer followed by Bethlehem,
nor by the tomb, nor by resurrection.
The new Christ,
with eye of fire and hair of flame,
is clothed in LIGHT.
There is no more birth and no more death.
Birth pains and death pains,
for they are still wounds,
still separation.

Felicity, union.
The new House is *the fourth,*
built since the beginning of time,
adorned for the bridegroom.
The old house is a cracked and decaying frame:
abandon it while you can!
The bridegroom cannot enter there:
the eternal lover, the LIGHT,
the only fulfillment of desire.

You are the vine, Ö is the germinating force.
Thus the miracle of the vine
that eternally gives fruit is born.
The mud, primal matter, remains below;
the vine absorbs it and rises up.

THUS MUD ASCENDS TO LIGHT
AND LIGHT IS CLOTHED IN MATTER.

Silence.

Light descends from Heaven: Wisdom.
Wise matter is the fruit, tangible Light:
The creation bears fruit:

TANGIBLE LIGHT,
SHINING MATTER.

Rejoice!
Water kills – fire quickens.
The Virgin gives birth, is in labor.
The last birth is *the fourth:*
The Child is carried to Heaven,

HEAVEN DESCENDS TO EARTH:
FOR EVER AND EVER.

> *I am amazed to again and again see new perspectives opening
> in the dialogues. The image of the woman 'dressed in the sun'
> appeared two thousand years ago in the Apocalypse of St. John.
> She and her Child ascended to heaven and thus disappeared
> from our field of consciousness. But now the Child reappears
> and descends to earth with all of Heaven, along with the fem-
> inine part of the Divine: Wisdom. This Wise Light transforms
> matter and redeems it. The fourth dimension is shown to us by
> means of ever varying symbolic events.*

Friday, October 31, 1944

84. DIALOGUE

SUFFERING TEACHES NOTHING AND
SUFFERING DOES NOT REDEEM.
SUFFERING NEED NOT BE.

Expect no good, no fruit, from suffering!
Suffering results from the wound.
The wound is sin,
and suffering is its response.
The wound is emptiness,
filled only by the healing act.
Suffering is not that fruit, this is not the *more:*
this is an illusion.
Suffering is but a fragmentary response in time.
If suffering were the whole,
and not just a part,
then deliverance which puts an end to suffering
would be nothing but betrayal.

Blows and punishment need not be:
Suffering need not be!
Giving of oneself, sacrifice,
extinguishes it.
This is the most sacred Grace.

Adam strays aimlessly, without a goal.
Although he was given the eye of light,
he does not see the Way, the Truth and Life.
Sin has closed his eye.
Adam, conceived in joy,
led astray by the serpent,
is blind and dead.

But Christ gave Himself: the lamb was sacrificed
and behold: Adam revives.
He is life.
With Him, through Him, in Him,
everything is given new Life.

After the sin comes purification.
After purification,
the giving of oneself.
After the wedding,
the immaculate conception
in the new Dwelling.
Death remains outside,
suffering remains outside.
The wound heals, the abyss is filled,
and suffering ends forever.
Resplendent matter: LIGHT-MATTER.

Adam is eternally the Child of God.
Adam, the outcast, enters the new Dwelling:
the return of the prodigal son.
In place of futile joys,
he finds the true Home: Eternal Life.

Later that night, the angels return:

… take care of 'the small one,'
that she might bear her burden!
The seven daggers carve wounds.
The little servant offered her heart,
and the offering is carried by our hand
to the feet of the Divine.
Take heed!
Do not be afraid!
Take care of 'the small one'!

Ö will protect her through you.

These words weigh heavily on me. I feel that the 'little servant'
referred to is Hanna. Do the angels see a means of protecting
her that I have not perceived? The general situation looks worse
by the day and I am extremely worried. Our workshop is more
and more becoming a dangerous target rather than the haven
of refuge it was meant to be. Things have gotten so bad that I
advise the women to leave immediately if they have any other
possible means of hiding. I assure them that I would not reveal
their disappearance to the military authorities.

* *

One of the jolly jokers sharing the tool shed with Hanna and
Lili, a very discreet woman, asks us, to our great amazement,
if she might spend the evening with us. Years later, she explains
to me: "I had no idea of the significance of your gatherings, but
when I saw Hanna's transformed, radiating face as she returned
to the workshop in the evenings on several occasions, I became
convinced that I, too, should participate. My usual modesty and
shyness were so absent that I would have broken down the door
if I had been denied entry." The fourth occupant of the tool shed,
who is very attached to Lili, also wishes to attend.

Friday, November 3, 1944

85. DIALOGUE

Lili lights a candle.

The flame rises up and light flows everywhere.
Matter is purified by burning.
Air corresponds to the spirit,
the flame to individuality, the 'I' that has become One.
Air is invisible,
matter is heavy, dense and blind.
The flame connects them.
Without air, matter cannot burn.
Without matter,
there is no redeeming individuality.

I will teach you how to light it:
In the beginning: the wax is cold, the air is cold.
What ignites the flame?
The wax? No. The air? No.
Only the already burning flame ignites.
The fourth flame unites, warms, transmits fire.
In the fourth flame, Heaven and earth can unite,
but only above water.
Nothing is more simple! Always transmit the fire!

Each degree of life is flame, is fire.
They are united by their essences.
The name of each fire,
its light and its intensity,
is different from the others.
To the Human, a Fire is given which unites the Seven:
The Heart of Light.

It joins every light and Fire,
be it *earthly flame* or heavenly Fire,
earthly love or heavenly Love.

THE VIRGIN BODY IS NOT REQUIRED
WHEN THE FLAME IS PURE
AND THE PASSION HOLY.

The new Light can come only
if you light the Seven Flames one after the other.
Every Flame, every Light is already in you.

> *From the war front nearby, we hear the thunder of cannons and
> explosions.*

Destruction all about you –
but in you, there is eternal renewal,
purification, giving of oneself, wedding.
Have no fear!
Everything might be destroyed,
even Heaven and earth,
but all that means nothing
if the new Fire burns in you.
Love Life! Love the Seven!

BURN!

If the Seven are united,
if Heaven and earth are united,
then comes: GIVING.
Seven Divine Souls, Seven Flames, Seven Levels:

BURN!

Every individuality is wholeness: be whole!
Join the Seven together!

In the Plan of the eternal Creator,
everyone has a guide:
Seven Flames of Spirit guide you.
Ö gives the *Name.*
Name is not mere adornment.
Name is not coincidental.
The *Name* is eternal part of the Divine.

I belong to the Seven;
above me a guide also shines.

      Addressed to me:

This message is for you,
for your heart has asked.
Every organism consists of Seven Flames.
Above each of the Seven there is a peak: the guide.
Alone, this guide would be of little value:
but it is part of a new circle of Seven
with a new crown.
Thus each Flame knows both serving and guiding.

      Hanna draws a sketch, subsequently lost, which I later attempted
      to reproduce. I believe this drawing captures the essence of the
      original.

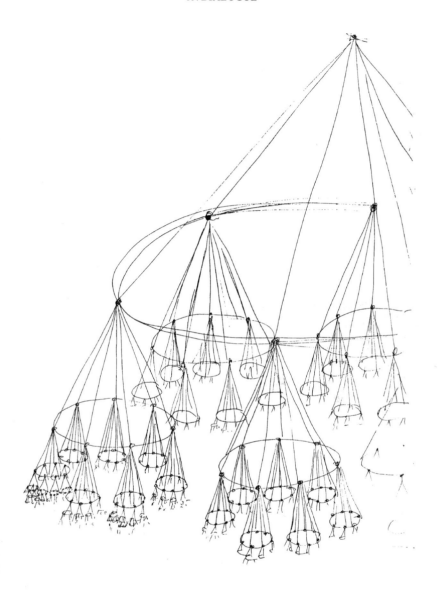

Without a wick, the candle could not burn.
Without a body, there would be no Individuality.
The Heart of Light beats high above.
If your gift of self reaches it,
heavenly Grace streams down.

THUS:
ONLY THROUGH THE HUMAN BEING
CAN GRACE DESCEND.

The Seventh – the highest GUIDE – teaches you.
The strength of the Seventh descends upon you.
Thus from infinity comes space
and from space comes infinity,
from eternity is born the temporal
and from the temporal: eternity.

The thundering from the nearby front increases in volume:

May the Strength of the Seven Forces be with you!
Burn!

Lili's friend, present for the first time, listens with intense concentration. After the dialogue, she says to Hanna: "Right from the beginning, I also heard all of the words you pronounced inside of myself. Your words corresponded exactly to those that I heard, with one exception." She named the word, and Hanna replied, "You are right; here I made a mistake." Having corrected it in my notes at the time, I have since forgotten what this word was.

464

November 5, 1944

'Father' Kun, the former priest now commanding the Nyilas, appears to have discovered the secret reason for the existence of our war factory. His followers take to shooting their guns every night in front of our garden, which is anything but a good sign.

On Sunday afternoon, hordes of Hungarian Nazis break down our front gate and storm into the garden. A woman who sees them coming just manages to send off a desperate SOS to the nunciature.

The great hunt begins: The cellar, the work rooms and the attic are searched, and all of the women are herded into the main work room.

The notorious Nazi commander, 'Pater' Kun himself, appears in a black priest's robes with a wide red belt stuffed full of daggers and revolvers. He demands to see the 'commander.' I step forward. He then proceeds to deliver a lengthy sermon to his followers, explaining to them that I, as a Christian who has lowered herself to aid Jews, am more sinful than the Jews themselves. He will arrange for me to have 'special treatment.' When Hanna and Lili hear these words, their illusion of my being out of danger as an 'Aryan' is destroyed. I am ordered to state the exact number of workers in our operation. If my answer should prove to be false, I would be shot immediately. I do not have the slightest idea how many women might have been able to escape through the secret openings in our garden fence. Unable to give an answer, I remain silent.

Suddenly, I hear myself saying: "Seventy-two." The counting begins. Seventy-one persons are found to be present. There is a heavy silence. Suddenly the door bursts open and a Nazi shoves a young girl, who had been hiding in the toilet, into the room.

'Father' Kun stares at me without a word and then turns his back. Before leaving the room, he orders his soldiers to lead me away under special guard. Three Nazis, armed to the teeth, push me to the floor, kick me repeatedly and spit on me.

The 72 women are lined up in rows. It grows dark and a gentle rain begins to fall. We are marched off through the streets, destination unknown.

The well-placed kicks into my abdomen have their effect, and I am forced to stop behind a tree. The 3 soldiers never let me out of their sight: they surround me and stare at me as if I were a log. Strangely, only in this moment do I really notice that I have lost my freedom.

After a march of about half an hour, our group is overtaken by an automobile from the War Ministry. The nunciature had relayed our SOS to them, and the officer who embarks from the auto holds a 'renewed' war production certification of protection in his hand.

The Nazis are furious, but they are forced to release us, and we return to the cloister. I walk silently beside Hanna and Lili and ask myself in the darkness:

" ... how much longer?"

November 10, 1944

86. DIALOGUE

The fourth flame, the fourth element,
is Awareness of the One.
Behind this Word, a secret shines.

Ö speaks and the soul trembles,
but it does not comprehend the Word,
for the third flame, the third element,
feeling, dominates your soul
with vibrations irregular and vague,
and the fruits are in accordance.
The third flame, the third element is *feeling.*

Raise up your feelings
and the vibration will intensify.
What raises feelings?
Longing? No.
Faith? It is only a possibility.
The force which raises feelings
is the offering of yourself,
the giving of yourself.
Only thus can the new Dwelling be attained
– the fourth floor –
which is meant to be your eternal Home.

Ö speaks and the soul burns
to discover the Heart of the Seven,
the fourth degree of life,
the middle of the Seven
where the foot no longer walks,
where it stands still,
where the soul no longer requests,
but always receives.

> *Silence.*

I teach you:

THOUGHT IS STILL MATTER,

staggering and blind, pulling you down;
it is a serpent biting its own tail.
Therefore its sign is the wheel,
the wheel revolving about itself,
ruled neither by cart nor machine.

Earthly smoke smolders and
the soul stumbles, faints,
errs about, revolves about itself,
just revolves.

In the hand of the *Black Fisherman,* a hook.
Attached to the hook, the bait:
the human thought.
Fish! Do not snap it!
Your throat would be torn!
The fish dies
and the Black Fisherman smiles.
The fisherman's creel fills,
the catch packed tightly,
the heart constricted in anguish.
The soul is cast in gloom.
The wheel revolves.

Adam, the outcast,
exchanged Divine Childhood
for knowledge – for thought.
Thoughtless, carefree joy was taken away.
Light-Awareness was unable to come
over such feelings, such thoughts.

Paradise was taken from Adam:
no more sinless act,
no more innocence.
But the Lamb is the way
that leads back.
And what is no longer possible on earth
is possible in God.

The message speaks of the new Flame:
it shines, it glows high above.
Oh, human being! Now you can reach it!
He is the *Way* which leads to it.
He is the *Truth,* whereon the new House is built.
He is the *Life,* the eternal Life.

May the fourth vibration penetrate you!

Burn, but do not destroy through burning!
Ignite the Fire!
Always ignite the Fire!
If Heaven burns in you,
even the incombustible bursts into flame.
Take care! Listen well!
Always listen to the WORD:
the eternal, true and only WORD.

LET THOUGHT BE BOUND TO THE *ETERNAL WORD!*
MAY THE WHEEL CEASE
TO REVOLVE AROUND ITSELF.
THE WHEEL IS ONLY FREE
IF IT IS A PART THAT IS SERVING THE WHOLE,
THE ONE.
MAY ALL-AWARENESS PENETRATE THE THOUGHT!

In the daughter of unfaithful Adam,
who revolved around himself, unredeemed,
in the womb of the daughter of Adam,
Christ was conceived.

Rejoice! Eternal Light shines forth.
Now you are free – no longer slaves.
Your eye shall *see.*
Your hand shall *act the Divine Will.*
We rejoice with you.
Your act and *our* song are touching one another.
White Light blazes,
White Light in which all colors blend together,
join for eternity.

Work in the clothing factory resumes in an atmosphere of oppressive fear, which increases in intensity when a German SS-officer takes up residence in the villa next door.

One day, a German soldier rings at the door. Panic breaks out. I hurry to the door and see, to my great relief, that it is not an SS-soldier, but one from the defensive forces, the Wehrmacht. It turns out that he was a student friend of Hanna in Munich, and is currently working as an illustrator for the military forces newspaper. As I am talking with this decent and upright man, I suddenly have a fantastic idea: I must try to have our women protected by the SS-soldiers!

The Hungarian Nazis are in command here. The only authority they recognize is the German SS. I thus devise the following plan together with Hanna's soldier friend: I will prepare some illustrations for a cultural article about Hungarian folklore in exchange for an employee's identification card with a highly visible swastika stamp from the German military newspaper.

This identity card is to serve as my means of introduction to the neighboring SS-establishment. I have observed that the SS-officer returns home only late at night and that his soldiers are alone the entire day.

And so, a few days later, I approach the neighboring garden and address the SS soldiers. As the daughter of an Austrian, I speak fluent German and I immediately adopt the local dialect of the corporal, upon which they all see me as a fellow citizen in a foreign land.

I tell them that I have given up my artistic profession so as to dedicate myself to supporting the war effort and that I am now the directress of the war factory next door. 'Coincidentally' my German identity card, received immediately upon delivery of the illustrations, is in my handbag, and it succeeds in lending credence to my story.

As a loyal compatriot and neighbor, I invite the soldiers to visit my plant. To spare them the long way around through the street, I have an opening made in the fence separating our adjoining gardens. The soldiers are war weary and are delighted to come over for a glass of fine old Hungarian wine and homemade pastries.

During one of their visits, I complain about the 'undisciplined hordes' of Hungarian troops disturbing the noble efforts of our war sewing plant.

Thanks to the trust inspired by my card and perhaps also in anticipation of a rapidly approaching and fatal end of the war, the soldiers promise to protect me and my workers. The 'non-Aryan' origins of the women are left unmentioned.

All of the women are informed of the situation. Never before had the shop operated with such discipline and obvious eagerness as during the visits which the SS-corporal paid to me – but which he paid mainly to the source of wine!

In the case of future attack by the Hungarian Nazis, the secret opening in the fence between our gardens would serve the purpose of enabling the women and children to flee through the garden of the SS officer to the great Janoshégy Forest.

Friday, November 17, 1944

87. DIALOGUE

The Seven speaks.
The Six acts.
The Five sings.
The Four is all-aware: IT LIVES.
Enlightening Light, the Truth,
penetrates the Heart.

The heart only knows fear
if it is half rather than one,
if it is part rather than whole.

    To Hanna:

Listen you, the four!
The chalice fills.
In your heart all the suffering dwells.
Raise it up!
Heavenly grace streams from above.
Suffering is like an empty channel,
through which grace can stream down
for He does not tolerate emptiness.
Emptiness, the name for all suffering.
Suffering is from rupture,
from the lack, from the empty breach.
It is filled by AWARENESS THAT UNITES.
This virginal fire unites with HIM,
whose name is wholeness.

Heaven and earth glorify the One Who unifies.
Without beginning, without end,
we sing a Song of Glory.

To Lili:

Your song is: heal the wound!

To Hanna:

Your song is: offer your heart!
Maintain the Balance, the Four!

To Joseph, no longer present:

Your song is: breath of Heaven
that the earth has lost.
Peace that is not merely a pause
between two wars,
but silence, eternal peace,
given a home on earth through you.

To me:

Your song is: bring down the Six,
the Light that is given to you!
Strength and Light,
the coming Light of the Divine.
Not Law, not Grace, but Light: pure Light,
uplifting Force,
yet also capable of searing to cinder.

To us all:

Awaken! Jesus lived, He was and He shall be.
The new is nigh.
Jesus appears always and calls His disciples.
He assumes a form that you can bear.
For behold: *every* body is part of Him.
He is the Son.

The Father has given Him all:
The One, the Two, the Three,
the Four, the Five, the Six,
that all may serve under His feet.

We again hear explosions from the nearby front.

The devil thunders,
with the whirling globe in hand:
the poisoned apple, the devil's only realm.
Say softly: "We do not need it!" –
and that will suffice.
If the Light of the Seven burns in you,
then darkness cannot harm you.
Raise your heart high above,
and then the Light can come.

Burn! Live!
Be filled with Light!
Awake, Arise!
Your Light is needed.
Your being glows.

The end is near:
the Seven nears.
May no more doubt dwell in you,
may there be no offense in you!
Be perfect, as the Creator conceived you perfect!
Ö gave you the Name: the eternal Name.
When you not only think you live,
but LIVE, LIVE Life,
then everything becomes possible.
Ask only from Heaven; to the earth, *give!*
Act, and your faith will move mountains!
The mountain is matter, the mountain is weight.

With your little finger,
you can unbalance the mountain.

Everything takes on new Meaning.
Proclaim new Laws!
The impossible becomes possible!
Old values crumble;
yesterday is gone,
and all that was sinks into nothingness.

   Silence.

But the immaculate, virgin matter remains: MARY.
Upon her head, the crown of stars,
at her feet, the moon;
her dress, the rays of the sun.
MARY – the smile of creation,
miracle hovering above the waters.
In matter: virginity.
In Light: matter.

LIGHT-MATTER, RESPLENDENT, DWELLS IN YOU.

The Son of Light, the Seven, is born of MARY.
Her Name is Thirst, her Name is eternal Love.
The new Name of MARY is: Light-Awareness.
She is the eternally fruit-bearing tree,
there above and here below.
In place of the poisoned apple,
this tree bears the Apple of Light.

Proclaim it: deliverance is near!
The Seven spoke. The Six acted.
The Five sang the 'Good News'
which is now reality:
LIGHT.

Friday, November 24, 1944

88. DIALOGUE

In the silence before the dialogue, I feel an utterly intense pres-
ence and suddenly I know that this will be our last, farewell
encounter.

In the beginning was Silence.
In the Silence within,
Sound was born.
Sound is love.
Sound is the Son of the Divine.
The Divine is Silence.

In the womb of Silence
reposed Sound.
Sound became body and was born.
Love is the first radiated image.

THE BODY IS LOVE
WHICH HAS BECOME MATTER.

The Divine sets in motion.
Sound is vibration.
Creation is radiated image:

DIVINE LOVE EMBODIED.

Thus Life originated:
From One Sound: Seven.
From One: two opposite halves of Life,
drawing together, drawing apart.

From One Sound: Seven;
and from Seven: all forms of Life.

Miracle – wonder!
Endless stream of Sound.
Creation sings, resounds:
Divine Symphony.
Endless stream of Sound,
yet always the Seven.

The two halves of life
and the seven souls are the key.
The two halves of life
concentrate and disperse,
draw together, draw apart.
Now: drawing together.
The line of the Holy Plan is:
concentration, union.

The Divine is: Silence
The Divine is: Sound
The Divine is: Harmony
The Divine is: Love

> The Hungarian Nazi hordes make their nightly rounds with wild
> yelling and shooting.

Uproar, noise, confusion,
destructive force which injures the Law.
Noise is emptiness,
and this Ö does not tolerate.
Lips gone silent
are not yet Silence.
Sing, my loved ones, sing here below!
Soon the noise will end.
In noise you cannot sing,
but prepare yourselves: listen!
Above we sing. Listen well!

Learn! Prepare yourselves!
Be one with us!
Immeasurable, everlasting Love,
the Divine Heart is ours.

Cracked pitchers, defective and empty pots and vessels
are smashed and cast away.
That is the noise
your ears now hear.
Be new Vessels!
Golden Chalices!
Chalices of transparent gold,
ready to receive Divine Love!
Chalices in which eternal Life can breathe.
Yet even the flawless Chalice
is but radiated image.

Silence: the Creator.
Sound: the Son,
audible silence.

The eye says: Light.
The ear says: Sound.
The hand says: Act.
The heart says: Love.
Understand: all of these are radiated images.
The key to the hidden secret is

ALL-AWARENESS.

With the coming of the LIGHT,
all can SEE through it.
Awareness that unites the two halves of life,
Awareness that unites the Seven Souls;
Uniting Awareness joins all together.

The Four is the Heart of the Seven,
which attracts, concentrates and calls
all the Divine blood,
all the Divine force,
to Itself.
Thus the Seven levels become SONG.
Thus the two halves become ONE.
The wall has crumbled
and the lack is filled.

THE DIVINE
is Number, Law, Salt.   (I)

THE DIVINE
is Love: growing, streaming Love.   (II)

THE DIVINE
is Rhythm, Vibration, Movement.   (III)

THE DIVINE
is Song: free song.   (V)

THE DIVINE
is the Light: radiating, acting Light.   (VI)

THE DIVINE
is the Highest.   (VII)

There, where the two halves are wed,
there the WORD is born:

THE WORD – THE FOCAL POINT –
ALL-AWARENESS.

Thus the millions become ONE.   (IV)

From an infinity of salts
comes the all-powerful Word.   (I + VII)

From streaming Love
comes acting Power.   (II + VI)

Rhythm and Vibration
carry the Song.   (III + V)

May the Song resound!
The dividing wall has crumbled.
The wall was emptiness.
Victory over death!

In jubilation the Four sings
the glory of the Seven.

THE TWO HALVES OF LIFE
HAVE BECOME ONE.

Believe:
Eternal Life is already yours.

The Red Army is slowly but surely descending upon Hungary: we hear daily reports of their advances in our direction. Everything in the city begins to disintegrate and a pervading sense of the inevitable end is in the air.

On December 2, the young girl who has been keeping watch suddenly crashes into the workroom and breathlessly informs us that a company of Hungarian Nazis has broken down the front gate and is approaching the house.

I race madly out the back door and through the secret opening in the fence to our German SS neighbors to call them to help us. These are the darkest moments of my life. I know that every instant is of the essence and I run with all the strength I can muster, yet I have a feeling of being nailed to the earth with an enormous weight. I sense impending catastrophe in every cell of my body.

At last, I arrive at the SS quarters. The German soldiers imme-diately grab their hand grenades and run with me to the clothing factory! At the sight of the approaching SS, the Hungarians retreat in confusion.

My calmness returns and I gain a clear presence of mind. While the Hungarian commander hesitates, I discreetly signal to one of the women that all of the others should immediately take flight through the garden of the SS.

As we stand in front of the house (see sketch on p. 483), an incred-ible development unfolds in the backyard: the German Nazis stand guard for the Jewish women and children so that they can escape from the Hungarian Nazis. Two German soldiers take position on either side of the escape hole through our common fence and hedge, ready with their hand grenades to defend against any intervention by the Hungarians. With powerful gestures, they encourage the women: "Quickly! Run fast!" At the same time, the German corporal, the Hungarian officer and I are engaged in an animated discussion in front of the house. Then Father Klinda rushes up completely out of breath and he attempts with religious arguments to convince the Hungarian officer to retreat. However, the officer only turns his back and displays the deportation orders.

Father Klinda sadly whispers to me that the nunciature has no further means of influence, at which point I realize that I have only one possibility left: to try and gain as much time as possible.

With this in mind, I deliberately translate the statements of the German to the Hungarian so badly that he becomes thoroughly confused. I am not risking anything by doing this, because neither of them understands a word of the other's language. So as to bewilder the Hungarian officer all the more, I wave my German identity card under his nose and declare that the sewing factory is under German protection.

481

He is obviously impressed by the swastika on my card, for he immediately becomes more polite. Now it is my turn to be threatening: I haughtily declare that there will be extremely unpleasant consequences for his military career if he should attempt to harm even a single person from our group. At that, he becomes even more uncertain, and he requests time to think things over.

Unfortunately, the man is quite intelligent. After several minutes, he declares himself ready to pull back his soldiers, but solely on the condition that the German commander – if only by telephone – confirms that the workshop is truly under German protection. Now the decisive moment is approaching: time is running out. Once again, my only chance is to try and gain a few more precious minutes.

A woman whispers to me that most of the women and children have fled through the secret opening to the forest – only a handful remain who were unable to decide to flee. I angrily reply that everyone must leave the house immediately. Then the German corporal, the Hungarian officer and I move inside to the office, where our telephone is located. The corporal makes contact with his superior and, as I had suspected, the German commander has not had the slightest inkling of the friendly relationship between his soldiers and their next-door neighbors, and he reprimands, then sternly instructs his corporal to "not interfere in this affair."

With that, my delaying tactics come to an end and the SS soldiers retreat. Together with the Hungarian Nazis, I leave the office and they are horrified to see that no more workers are present: the house is empty!

I look out into the garden, and now it is my turn to be horrified: a group of thirteen women, guarded by Hungarian soldiers, stands lined at attention and ready to march. It is those who are too old to flee, or too weak, and those who have made the decision not to flee: Hanna and Lili.

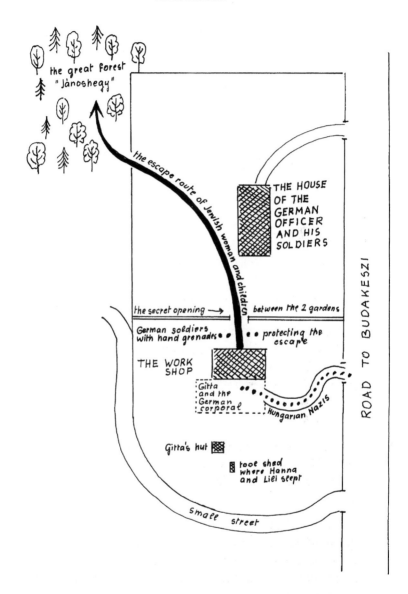

the great forest "Jánoshegy"

the escape route of Jewish woman and children

THE HOUSE OF THE GERMAN OFFICER AND HIS SOLDIERS

the secret opening → between the 2 gardens

German soldiers with hand grenades • • • • protecting the escape

THE WORK SHOP

Gitta and the German corporal

Hungarian Nazis

Gitta's hut

tool shed where Hanna and Lili slept

small street

ROAD TO BUDAKESZI

I know how much both of them love life and how foreign the idea of voluntary martyrdom is. They are not submitting to deportation without reason. On the one hand, they fear that I will be shot on the spot if the Nazis find no one to deport and it is obvious that I have been deceiving them. I suspect an additional reason: Hanna has often said to me that, of the four of us, it is I who must stay alive to save the message of the angels and give it on.

The thirteen women are immediately deported to Ravensbrück.

Only one of the thirteen women survived.* She later told me that Lili was such a radiant, loving force in the death camp that her fellow prisoners would volunteer to work with the hard-labor detachments, or Kommandos, *as they were called, where Lili could always be found, so as to be in her consoling, strength-giving presence.*

I am unable to remember much of what she told me about Hanna, because I was too upset to concentrate. But there is one incident that I have not forgotten. As the SS guards shaved the heads of the prisoners, one of them called out to Hanna: "Hey, what are you doing here, with your blue eyes, your straight nose and your long, blond hair? Are you an Aryan?" Hanna replied: "I am a Jew."

It was certainly not a desire to be a victim that caused Hanna to answer in this way. She had conveyed the word of truth for seventeen months and must have become incapable of uttering even the smallest lie.

The woman added: "Had it not been for Lili and Hanna, I would not have survived. When Hanna said to us: 'We are not the ones who have been beaten. All of this does not touch us ...' – of course I still felt the effect of the blows on my body, but the human degradation lost its power over me. I didn't feel it anymore."

---

* As mentioned in the Preface (p. 7), see the report by Eva Dános for first-hand information.

As the Allied forces approached, the women were again herded away, naked and shorn, and packed standing tightly together into cattle cars. Ravaged by epidemics and soiled with their own excrement, most of the women starved to death. Lili died one hour after Hanna.

The SS commander had the survivors sign a statement attesting that the others had died 'a natural death.'

Joseph died at about the same time in a Hungarian camp.

All of the women and children who fled through the garden of the SS survived.

Talking with Angels *in other languages:*

German: Daimon Publications (see address on the last page of this book)
   Die Antwort der Engel
   Die Engel erlebt
   Weltenmorgen
   Sprung ins Unbekannte

France: Flammarion, 26 rue Racine, F-75278 Paris, Tel: 01 40 51 31 00
   Dialogues avec l'Ange
   Les dialogues tels que je les ai vécus
   Les dialogues ou l'enfant né sans parents
   Les dialogues ou le saut dans l'inconnu
   Les petits dialogues d'hier et d'aujourd'hui

Italian: Edizioni Mediterranee, Via Flaminia 109, 00196 Roma
   www.edizionimediterranee.net
   Dialoghi con L'Angelo
   Piccoli dialoghi di ieri e di oggi

Spanish: Editorial Sirio, S.A., C/Panaderos 9, 29005 Málaga
   www.editorialsirio.com
   La Respuesta del Angel

Brazilian Portuguese: Editora Vozes Ltd., Rua Frei Luis nr. 100, Centro,
   25689-900 Petropôlis/RJ
   www.vozes.com.br
   Diálogos com o Anjo

Greek: ΕΚΔΟΣΕΙΣ Π. ΑΣΗΜΑΚΗΣ − Π. ΒΥΡΑΣ
   Τ.Θ. 300 45 ΑΘΗΝΑ 100 33   Τηλ: 322 46 38 − 094 576338
   Συνομιλίες με Αγγέλους

Basque: Maiatz, 2 Passemillon, 64100 Baiona
   Aingeruekin solasean

Hungarian: Fekete Sas Kiadó, Pannónia utca 14, 1136 Budapest
www.feketesas.hu
Az Angyal Válaszol
Az Angyal Válaszol, ahogy én megéltem

Norwegian: Emilia Forlag, Kristian IVs gate 15, 0164 Oslo
www.emila.no
Samtaler med engler

Romanian: Editura Firul Ariadnei,
Calea Victorieie nr. 200, sector 1, Bucharest
Dialoguri cu îngerii

Polish: Sarna Books, Ul. Strzelecka 12, 87-800 Wloclawek
Rozmowy z Aniolami

Czech: Malvern Publishing, rohàcova 94, Prague 3, 130 00
www.malvern.cz
Rozhovory s andelem

Danish: Lemuel Books, Mejlgade 28, gaarden, 8000 Aarhus C.
www.lemuelbooks.com
Dialoger med Englen

Swedish: Bokförlaged Mynta, Box 351, 441 28 Alingsäs
www.ordglaedje.o.se
Samtal med änglar

Korean: Youlhwadang Publishers Gwanginsa-gil 25, Paju-si, Gyeonggi-do
www.youlhwadang.co.kr

English Titles from Daimon

Ruth Ammann - *The Enchantment of Gardens*
Susan R. Bach - *Life Paints its Own Span*
Diana Baynes Jansen - *Jung's Apprentice: A Biography of Helton Godwin Baynes*
John Beebe (Ed.) - *Terror, Violence and the Impulse to Destroy*
E.A. Bennet - *Meetings with Jung*
W.H. Bleek / L.C. Lloyd (Ed.) - *Specimens of Bushman Folklore*
Tess Castleman - *Threads, Knots, Tapestries*
- *Sacred Dream Circles*
Renate Daniel - *Taking the Fear out of the Night*
Eranos Yearbook 69 - *Eranos Reborn*
Eranos Yearbook 70 - *Love on a Fragile Thread*
Eranos Yearbook 71 - *Beyond Masters*
Eranos Yearbook 72 - *Soul between Enchantment and Disenchantment*
Eranos Yearbook 73 - *The World and its Shadow*
Michael Escamilla - *Bleuler, Jung, and the Schizophrenias*
Heinrich Karl Fierz - *Jungian Psychiatry*
John Fraim - *Battle of Symbols*
von Franz / Frey-Rohn / Jaffé - *What is Death?*
Liliane Frey-Rohn - *Friedrich Nietzsche, A Psychological Approach*
Marion Gallbach - *Learning from Dreams*
Ralph Goldstein (Ed.) - *Images, Meanings & Connections: in Memory of Susan Bach*
Yael Haft - *Hands: Archetypal Chirology*
Fred Gustafson - *The Black Madonna of Einsiedeln*
Daniel Hell - *Soul-Hunger: The Feeling Human Being and the Life-Sciences*
Siegmund Hurwitz - *Lilith, the first Eve*
Aniela Jaffé - *The Myth of Meaning*
- *Was C.G. Jung a Mystic?*
- *From the Life and Work of C.G. Jung*
- *Death Dreams and Ghosts*
C.G. Jung - *The Solar Myths and Opicinus de Canistris*
Verena Kast - *A Time to Mourn*
- *Sisyphus*
Hayao Kawai - *Dreams, Myths and Fairy Tales in Japan*
James Kirsch - *The Reluctant Prophet*
Eva Langley-Dános - *Prison on Wheels: Ravensbrück to Burgau*
Rivkah Schärf Kluger - *The Gilgamesh Epic*
Yehezkel Kluger & - *RUTH in the Light of Mythology, Legend*
Naomi Kluger-Nash   *and Kabbalah*
Paul Kugler (Ed.) - *Jungian Perspectives on Clinical Supervision*
Paul Kugler - *The Alchemy of Discourse*
Rafael López-Pedraza - *Cultural Anxiety*
- *Hermes and his Children*
Alan McGlashan - *The Savage and Beautiful Country*
- *Gravity & Levity*
Gregory McNamee (Ed.)- *The Girl Who Made Stars: Bushman Folklore*
- *The North Wind and the Sun & Other Fables of Aesop*
Gitta Mallasz / Hanna Dallos - *Talking with Angels*
C.A. Meier - *Healing Dream and Ritual*
- *A Testament to the Wilderness*
- *Personality: The Individuation Process*
Haruki Murakami - *Haruki Murakami Goes to Meet Hayao Kawai*

English Titles from Daimon

Eva Pattis Zoja (Ed.) - *Sandplay Therapy*
Laurens van der Post - *The Rock Rabbit and the Rainbow*
Jane Reid - *Jung, My Mother and I: The Analytic Diaries*
of Catharine Rush Cabot
R.M. Rilke - *Duino Elegies*
A. Schweizer / R. Schweizer-Vüllers - *Stone by Stone: Reflections on Jung*
- *Wisdom builds her House*
Miguel Serrano - *C.G. Jung and Hermann Hesse*
Helene Shulman - *Living at the Edge of Chaos*
D. Slattery / G. Slater (Eds.) - *Varieties of Mythic Experience*
David Tacey - *Edge of the Sacred: Jung, Psyche, Earth*
Susan Tiberghien - *Looking for Gold*
Ann Ulanov - *Spiritual Aspects of Clinical Work*
- *Picturing God*
- *The Female Ancestors of Christ*
- *The Wisdom of the Psyche*
- *The Wizards' Gate, Picturing Consciousness*
- *The Psychoid, Soul and Psyche*
Ann & Barry Ulanov - *Cinderella and her Sisters*
Eva Wertenschlag-Birkhäuser - *Windows on Eternity: The Paintings of Peter Birkhäuser*
Harry Wilmer - *How Dreams Help*
- *Quest for Silence*
Luigi Zoja - *Drugs, Addiction and Initiation*
Luigi Zoja & Donald Williams - *Jungian Reflections on September 11*
Jungian Congress Papers - *Jerusalem 1983: Symbolic & Clinical Approaches*
- *Berlin 1986: Archetype of Shadow in a Split World*
- *Paris 1989: Dynamics in Relationship*
- *Chicago 1992: The Transcendent Function*
- *Zürich 1995: Open Questions*
- *Florence 1998: Destruction and Creation*
- *Cambridge 2001*
- *Barcelona 2004: Edges of Experience*
- *Cape Town 2007: Journeys, Encounters*
- *Montreal 2010: Facing Multiplicity*
- *Copenhagen 2013: 100 Years on*
- *Kyoto 2016: Anima Mundi in Transition*

Available from local bookstores or directly from:

Wordwide:
Daimon Verlag
Am Klosterplatz
8840 Einsiedeln
Switzerland
Tel.: +(41)(55) 412 22 66
www.daimon.ch

USA:
Baker & Taylor
30 Amberwood Parkway
Ashland OH 44805, USA
Phone: 419-281-5100
Fax: 419-281-0200
www.btpubservices.com

UK:
Gazelle Book Services Ltd.
White Cross Mills, High Town
Lancaster LA1 4XS, UK
Tel: +44 1524 528500
www.gazellebookservices.co.uk

Germany & Austria:
Verlagsauslieferung Robert Ullrich
Zur Wallfahrtskirche 5
D-97483 Eltmann
Telefon: +49 (09522) 30 45 80
Email: info@schachversand-ullrich.de